PROPHETIC REALISM AND THE GOSPEL

Books by
JOHN WICK BOWMAN
Published by The Westminster Press

Prophetic Realism and the Gospel
The Intention of Jesus

PROPHETIC REALISM *and the* GOSPEL

A PREFACE TO BIBLICAL THEOLOGY

JOHN WICK BOWMAN

Philadelphia

THE WESTMINSTER PRESS

230
B68p

33,499
Mar., 1956

Dedication

To the Senatus Academicus of St. Andrew's University
and to the Faculty and Students of St. Mary's College
in grateful appreciation of the honorary degree of
Doctor of Divinity
Of the oldest university in Scotland
and of their graciousness in receiving
into their halls and hearts a visitor who
with his wife achieved an affection for the
" university of the scarlet gown " which time
will never efface

Contents

Part III

THE CONTENT OF SCRIPTURE'S PROPHETIC REALISM

A. The Gospel of Jesus Christ

B. The Gospel of God

C. The Gospel of the Kingdom

D. The Gospel of Our Salvation

The James Sprunt Lectures

M R. JAMES SPRUNT, of Wilmington, North Carolina, in 1911 established a perpetual lectureship at Union Theological Seminary in Virginia, which would enable this institution to secure from time to time the services of distinguished ministers and authoritative scholars as special lecturers on subjects connected with various departments of Christian thought and Christian work. The lecturers are chosen by the Faculty of the Seminary and a Committee of the Board of Trustees, and the lectures are published after their delivery in accordance with a contract between the lecturer and these representatives of the institution.

The series of lectures on this foundation for the year 1951 is presented in this volume.

B. R. LACY, JR.
President

Union Theological Seminary
Richmond, Virginia

Preface

T HIS BOOK is an essay in the field of Biblical theology. Its *aim* is to recover a point of view. This relates to the right way of viewing Scripture and its teaching as a whole. The *thesis* of the book is that this right way is to be seen in what the author terms the " prophetic realism " of Scripture, a point of view that has been largely displaced by the humanistic and apocalyptic views current in our time.

The book is little more than an outline or preface indicative of the direction which in the author's judgment the study of Biblical theology should take. It is written with theological students and their needs more especially in mind. But if it should happen that the parish minister found here " grist for the mill," this too would be welcome.

The substance of the volume was first delivered in the form of lectures on the James E. Sprunt Foundation at Union Theological Seminary, Richmond, Virginia, though the whole has been thoroughly revised for the purpose of the present publication. In the names of both my wife and myself, I should like to express our united gratitude for the innumerable kindnesses shown us while in Richmond, first by President Ben R. Lacy and Professor and Mrs. B. H. Kelly — our hosts — and then by all the faculty and student body of the Seminary, as well as by the like personnel in the General Assembly's Training School for Christian Workers. I am particularly grateful to the trustees of the Seminary for the stimulus afforded me to work over the materials found in the volume.

For the Scriptural quotations I have in large part followed the R.S.V. — and these quotations as well as those from other standard English versions are always in double marks. Where single marks occur, these represent translations or paraphrases of my own.

It remains to express my most hearty thanks to my former student, Professor Roland Wesley Tapp, M.A., B.D., of Centre College, Danville, Kentucky, for the painstaking work which he has expended upon the making of the indexes (both Author-Subject and Scripture Quotations). He has made this laborious service a real " labor of love " and it exemplifies the sort of disinterested co-operation that one has learned to expect of him.

Introduction

THE TITLE of this volume calls for a word of explanation. The phrase " prophetic realism " is used here in an inclusive sense and as a rough equivalent for what on the Continent today in theological circles goes by the name of *Heilsgeschichte*. Both terms stand for a theological position which may be styled *evangelicalism brought down to date*. Theology, if it is to be relevant, dare not remain static: it must interpret life and revelation to every new generation in terms intelligible to it. Evangelical theology in the twentieth century can ill afford to endeavor to interpret the gospel for which it stands sponsor in the terms of the fifth or even of the sixteenth century. The theology of prophetic realism, accordingly, is evangelicalism speaking the terminology of the present day and in the context of modern thought.

It has long been the author's conviction that to restrict the adjective " prophetic " to the Old Testament and the phrase " prophetic literature " to a single portion of the book is to employ these terms in a manner out of accord with the practice of the Scriptures themselves. If it is intended thereby that some portions of the Old Testament were written by prophets or their disciples, then it is to be noted that this is true of the entire book. The word " prophet " indicates a man to whom a revelation has come from God and with the message therein contained a commission to proclaim it, and it was to enshrine the teachings

13

of such men that the Old Testament was formed. The Hebrew prophets or their protégés wrote history, laws, hymns, sermons, and a philosophy (or theology) of history around the single theme of a religious message which constitutes the content of the entire book. It is a mistake, therefore, to isolate a portion of the Old Testament Scriptures and to ascribe to that portion the title of " prophetic literature." The whole of these Scriptures is prophetic literature in the best sense of the term and the Synagogue has been nearer the facts in speaking of the historical books as " former prophets " and the so-called prophetic literature as " latter prophets " than the Christian Church in restricting the adjective " prophetic " to the latter series of writings.

Moreover, the terms " prophet " and " prophetic " stand rather for the spirit of the Old Testament than for its format. Philosophers of history, " sweet singers of Israel," writers of the Wisdom of God, *theo*logians in the sense of teachers of God's theology as revealed to them rather than of pioneer thinkers in their own right, preachers of righteousness — the Hebrew prophets are all these things. But even thus the Scriptural connotations of the term " prophet " are by no means exhausted. The Hebrew prophets are merely the norm of what is to be labeled " prophetic " and the Old Testament Scriptures do not limit the category to the norm. " Which way went the Spirit of God from us to you? " — in these Scriptures this arrogant question is the mark of the false prophet. Anyone at any time and any literature anywhere sharing the charism of God's Spirit and deriving from his redemptive message for mankind is *ipso facto* prophetic: such is the intent of the Old Testament writings themselves and such is the proper use of the term therefore.

By " prophetic realism," accordingly, is intended revelational theology, God's theology so to speak, wheresoever, by whomsoever, and in whatsoever cultural milieu it may be found. Prophetic realism is the theology of the Spirit and its content is determined by the Spirit. Man may not impose upon it any of his cherished limiting categories, such as those of time and space, of race or class, or even of creed in the historic sense of that word. Man constructs such hedges about his little world of thought with a view to attaining a certain sense of security through finding all his little theological blocks in place. But the Spirit has not exhibited an interest in these hedges.

In the Scriptural sense of the word, indeed, the New Testament is equally " prophetic " with the Old; " apostles and prophets " are not two separate and distinct categories, but one; hence the very order of the words in Eph. 2:20. We rather too glibly assume that the prophets spoken of in New Testament times are to be dismissed as far below the standard set by the group so called in the Old Testament. The very names of many of the Old Testament prophets have not been preserved for us, and in the New Testament the term " prophet " tends to be overshadowed by that of " apostle," though probably these two words are intended to give expression merely to two different aspects of the one Hebrew term *nabhî*, " prophet " to this figure's message, " apostle " to his mission.[1] And, further, the living Scriptures composed of the Church of Christ — that Church of which it may be fairly held that Moses' prayer (" Would that all the Lord's people were prophets! ") has found in it fulfillment — these Scriptures also are prophetic!

The title of this volume equally is intended to voice the conviction that the term " gospel " as employed in Scripture stands for the entire content of the prophetic revelation. Thus the quotation, " The gospel of God . . . promised . . . through his prophets." That is to say, the phrase, " And the gospel," in the book's title is descriptive: it states the subject with which the theology of prophetic realism deals. The ground for this claim is stated in Part II below. That this gospel content is never diverted from its concern with the whole of man and his needs, and with the inclusive character of the salvation which is afforded him along material, physical, intellectual, social, moral, and spiritual lines, is an insight, indeed *the* insight at the heart of Scripture's prophetic teaching. This idea represents also one of the major emphases of this book. To exhibit the differences

[1] Cf. the treatment of this subject in *The Religion of Maturity*, pp. 20 ff., and T. W. Manson's illuminating study in *The Church's Ministry*, pp. 35 ff.

in the modes of expression, terminology, and even concepts employed by the several writers of Scripture as these present various facets of its gospel message is a task worthy of the best efforts of Biblical scholarship. But to discover the unity of " the mind of the Spirit " in the midst of this diversity is also a meritorious endeavor. It is this latter with which we shall be concerned in the present book.[2]

In modern times two methods of approach to the study of Biblical theology have been proposed, namely, the dogmatic and the historical. By the dogmatic method is meant that sort of superimposing of a theological point of view upon the Biblical text which characterized much of the theological controversy of the nineteenth century, when in scholarly as in popular circles it was the custom to adopt a position and then to search for proof texts to support it. By the historical method, on the other hand, is intended that approach to the problems involved in the interpretation of the Scriptures which freely employs the tools and seeks to work in the spirit of " scientific and historical criticism."

One has no hesitancy in subscribing to the second of these two approaches. But the position of the Biblical theologian is not so simple as this choice between two opposite methods would suggest. For he soon discovers that his scientific endeavor to come to grips with the Biblical data puts him in contact with a group of men — the Hebrew prophets — who care not a fig for " pure history " (if there be such a thing) , and who have written the Biblical narratives from a very decided bias of their own. In fact, these prophetic historians give us, not an unbiased chronicle of events set down as by men recognizing the limitations of their own perspectives and hedged in by the horizons of a world of relativities, but rather a theology of history (*Geschichtstheologie*) such as only men conscious of insights granted them by the God of history could claim to apprehend. As Professor Baab has recently written of them, " history, as

---

[2] It is this latter also with which C. H. Dodd is concerned in his *According to the Scriptures*. Charles Scribner's Sons, 1953. Quotations used by permission.

organized human experience, derives its meaning and organization for the Hebrew writers from the purpose of the living God, who controls the process according to his will and nature." [3]

For the Biblical theologian, then, the presence of this prophetic theology of history which he finds in the Biblical materials that constitute his field of inquiry is a datum of major proportions and one that for him must be a matter of the greatest concern. The presence of this datum, indeed, may ultimately determine the course on which he will set the sails of his exposition of the Biblical data as a whole. Even though he be an unbeliever, he can scarcely fail in all fairness to note the presence of such a theology of history in the several books of Scripture. If he be a believer, it may appear to him that all the Biblical data rightly fall into place only when this theology of history is recognized and made the norm for an appreciation of these data. Such has been the author's own experience and he has no hesitation, therefore, in equating the prophetic theology of history with true Biblical theology and the reverse. That is to say, the Bible contains a theology of its own — a theology here termed " prophetic realism " — which it is the function of the Biblical theologian to expound. No doubt the Bible contains much else besides — matters of archaeological, cultural, even popular religious interest. But for the Biblical theologian these matters are of concern only in so far as they contribute to his understanding of the prophetic realism of the Scriptures. These statements, moreover, are equally true for both Testaments.

The present volume was largely written before Paul Tillich's recently published *Systematic Theology,* Vol. i, came into my hands. He uses the term " kerygmatic theology " approximately in the sense here intended by prophetic realism. One prefers the latter because it serves to throw into relief the unity of Scripture and because one believes it to be the more inclusive term. Ethel-

[3] Cf. Otto J. Baab, *The Theology of the Old Testament* (1949), pp. 15 ff. and p. 27. For an instructive discussion of the problems involved, cf. also Floyd V. Filson, art. on " Method in Studying Biblical History," JBL, March, 1950, pp. 1 ff., and Robt. H. Pfeiffer, art. on " Facts and Faith in Biblical History," JBL, March, 1951, pp. 1 ff.

bert Stauffer's *Die Theologie des Neuen Testaments* (1941),
while differing at one major point from the thesis of this book
— viz., in adhering to the apocalyptic strand of New Testament
teaching as determinative in large measure for its viewpoint —
is at one with me in finding a *Geschichtstheologie* which runs
like a golden thread throughout Scripture and interprets the
meaning of its redemptive events.

I should like, however, to express my general agreement with
Tillich's approach to the problem of theology and particularly
as regards the endeavor " to avoid the shortcomings of fundamentalism by subjecting every theology, including orthodoxy,
to the criterion of the Christian message." " This message," as
Tillich continues, " is contained in the Bible, but it is not
identical with the Bible. It is expressed in the classical tradition
of Christian theology, but it is not identical with any special
form of that tradition " (p. 4). The message of the Bible first
and last is the gospel (or alternatively, the prophetic theology
of history), and it is this which it is the prerogative and responsibility of theology to expound. At any rate, this I conceive to be the function of the Biblical theologian, and such I
shall endeavor in brief compass to do in the pages that follow.

THE THREE CURRENT POSITIONS
IN BIBLICAL THEOLOGY

'If one will
His will to do,
knowledge will be his . . .'
— GOSPEL OF JOHN 7:17.

The Three Current Positions
in Biblical Theology

SYNOPSIS

*I*N THE *Christian Church at the present day there is observable a* tension *over matters pertaining to Biblical theology.
This tension is the product of a* maladjustment *to the series of
new facts and ideas presented by a scientific age. On examination it is discovered that there exist among Biblical students differing schools of thought which approach the problem in quite
diverse ways and with opposing postulates.*

*Various endeavors to solve the problems with which man is
concerned are discussed and the conversational or dialectical
method is proposed as covering all man's efforts in this direction. Several examples of the use of the method are then presented.*

*In the three short chapters which succeed the opening one
in this section the three current uses of the discussion method
in the field of Biblical theology are briefly discussed, namely:*
(1) Humanistic Optimism or The Monologue of Reason,
(2) Apocalyptic Pessimism or Conversing with God at Long
Range, *and* (3) Prophetic Realism or The Dialogue of Revelation. *Part I closes with the contention that what is fundamental
to man's knowledge of God is in the end to be attributed to the
functioning of the prophetic dialogue between God and man.
This, at all events, is the view of the prophetic Scriptures of
Old and New Testaments alike.*

1. *Progress in Thought by Discussion*

IN A RECENT volume entitled *The Einstein Theory of Rela-
tivity* (1949), two British mathematicians, H. G. and L. R.
Lieber, have much to say about what they term the " tension "
produced in the fields of physics, thermodynamics, and astron-
omy by the natural phenomena with which these subjects deal.
This tension, of course, existed in the minds of those concerned
with these subjects, not in the natural phenomena involved.
But as these writers remark, it almost seemed as though there
was " a ' conspiracy ' on the part of nature against man's efforts
to obtain knowledge of the physical world "! The data, indeed,
appeared to argue for opposite conclusions at the same time,
with the natural result that scientists ranged themselves on the
two opposing sides indicated. The net product of this situation
has been what we now know as the Einsteinian revolution in
this area of human thought.

In analyzing the event these writers conclude that, " When a
' revolution ' takes place in any domain, it is always preceded
by some maladjustment producing a tension, which ultimately
causes a break, followed by a greater stability — at least for the
time being." That is to say, the " tension " and " break " observed in this case are by no means to be thought exceptional.
They represent, rather, the kind of thing that usually happens
when there is real advance in human discovery or thought.

These observations by the two Liebers are made in the course
of their careful and discriminating analysis of what happened

21

a scant quarter century ago in the fields of scientific inquiry of
interest to them. Because their statement of the situation so
clearly parallels that which one finds to exist at the moment
in our Biblical studies, it will merit somewhat lengthy quotation.

" As Einstein regarded the situation," these writers observe, " the
negative results of the Michelson-Morley experiments, as well as of
other experiments which seemed to indicate a ' conspiracy' on the
part of nature against man's efforts to obtain knowledge of the
physical world . . . these negative results, according to Einstein,
did not merely demand explanation of a certain number of isolated
difficulties, but the situation was so serious that a complete examination of fundamental ideas was necessary. In other words, he felt that
there was something fundamentally wrong in physics, rather than a
mere superficial difficulty." [1]

It may perhaps be not unfairly remarked that just such a situation now exists in the general field of Biblical theology. Here
too the data involved appear to argue for opposing conclusions
and it almost seems that Scripture has conspired to hide away
that knowledge which man longs to acquire in the spiritual and
moral realms. Possibly, then, those Biblical scholars have a fair
a priori case in their favor who are beginning to tell us that
" there is something fundamentally wrong . . . rather than a
mere superficial difficulty " in the realm of the Christian faith.

Let us look for a few moments at the situation as it now presents itself to students in the Biblical field. It is now nearly a
hundred years since Darwin published his *Origin of Species*
(1859) and three quarters of a century since *The Descent of
Man* appeared (1871). During the intervening period there has
occurred in theological circles a " maladjustment " to the new
ideas, and this maladjustment has given rise to a " tension "
referred to on all hands as " the conflict between science and
religion." This tension, however much we should like to think
otherwise, has produced a " break " in our world of studies and

[1] The quotations all occur on page 20 of the book. The Michelson-
Morley experiments concerned the theory that all space is filled with a
substance called " ether " — a view now abandoned as a result of the labors
of these scientists.

this break has not as yet been healed.

In popular religious circles it is easy to discern the cleavage referred to in every thoughtful group that assembles to discuss problems that are germane to our faith at its deeper levels. And when we examine the works of the theologians we find that the situation is no better. The books which issue with such rapidity from our religious presses are found on examination to be poles apart, so much so that anyone untrained in Christian thought and coming to such works for the first time would find it difficult to recognize any common ground between the extremes on either side of the discussion. Moreover, these extremes are fully aware of the differences that exist between them, and each is not averse to branding the other, at the worst as unchristian or heretical and at best as illogical, irrelevant, antiquated.

But one gains the impression that matters are even worse than is generally supposed. The religious, theological, and ethical differences that show on the surface of the controversy have their roots deeply embedded in the soil of Biblical studies. They are the product of the acceptance or otherwise of certain critical techniques which are of comparatively recent origin, of contrary views regarding subjects like revelation, inspiration, and right ways of interpreting the Scriptures, as well as of opposing judgments on the authority of these Scriptures in the whole field of human living. Certain individuals, schools of thought, and even Churches have accepted without serious " growing pains " the newer scientific methodology and have applied it unhesitatingly in the fields of the study of the Christian Scriptures, theology, and religion, even in the realm of ethics. Other individuals, groups, and Churches have strenuously resisted the encroachment of this methodology and have drawn back for the greater safety of the faith as they conceive it, taking refuge in the traditional or orthodox beliefs and attitudes.

There exists, then, at the present day a kind of stalemate in Biblical and theological studies. It seems quite clear that this stalemate has resulted from a parallelogram of forces called into play since the incursion into the field of the scientific methodology. Differences of temperament and of emotional framework, the presence of a multitude of complexes, the fact of varying religious background and of differing intellectual equipment, the not inconsiderable factor of diversity of I.Q., variety in the matter of social and cultural environment — all these and doubtless others must be reckoned as elements in the situation. The assignment of adequate causes and the attempt to prescribe proper remedies are problems for the religious psychologists and for those expert in counseling. I have no wish, as I have also neither the ability nor the aptitude, to enter into these matters. My one concern here is to state the nature of the problem as far as it is of vital interest for the Biblical theologian — who along with everyone else is enmeshed in it — and to suggest something of the contribution that Biblical theology is qualified to make toward a solution for it.

The Discussion Method

Thoughtful minds have long accepted the idea that intellectual advance may be achieved by means of some sort of discussion or conversation. The "round-table" or panel type of discussion, the student "bull session," the seminar method of instruction — these and the like are popular examples of the method. And it may be fairly argued that the present stalemate in Biblical circles, as well as that in scientific ones which Einstein discovered, merely represents a stage in the discussion process.

The value of the stalemate is that it succeeds in clarifying the issues involved, and if all parties to it prove sincere seekers after the truth it may mark a step in advance. For until affirmation and negation, until the "yes" and the "no," have been made and spoken, there can be no problem at all — none, at all events, that is clearly present to the minds of those concerned. Within reasonable limits it ought to be recognized that, with advance in knowledge and the consequent necessity of turning away from traditional views to new and unexplored ones, it will always be inevitable that such a stalemate shall occur. When it does occur, the ensuing conversation which is directed toward its resolution is usually termed in philosophical and theological circles a " dialectic."

Thus far, one may hope, there is general agreement. It is when the attempt is made to analyze the ensuing conversation or dialectic that we find great diversity of opinion as to the right way to proceed and, indeed, as to how in the history of thought and culture men have proceeded. A few examples of this diversity will suffice to illustrate the divergence of opinion on the subject. The so-called " Socratic method " is a sort of dialectic for which the claim is made that all advance in human learning should follow the rational laws of thought which govern our conversations with one another, and, further, that this method may be carried through in an unemotional manner in the classroom between teacher and student. Provided one observe the laws involved, so this method claims, any human problem should be found capable of eventual solution. Pascal is credited with holding that such a dialectic in fact proceeds at all times within the soul of every man, and that no human mind is ever free from it. Some modern psychologists would add that this sort of monologue goes on even while the mind is asleep!

The *rishis* of Hindu India, one imagines, are nearer to Pascal at this point than to Socrates (or to Plato if the Socratic method be attributed to him). For they are, by definition of the Sanskrit word for " seers," those who look into Reality, meditate upon the same, and return to the world of multiplicity to tell of the Unity which they have seen. The prophets of Israel, on the contrary, signalized themselves by making the claim that they had carried on a conversation with the Almighty One himself. After each trip to the mountain peak of such intimacy with the divine Being, they returned to the plain of human activities aglow with new insights into the ways of God and his purpose relative to mankind. The first of these methods of dialectic, that of Socrates and the prophets, rather obviously takes the form of a *dialogue,* while the second, sponsored by Pascal and the *rishis,* is equally a *monologue.*

In modern times a host of new types of dialectic has appeared. Perhaps one should say rather that numerous new applications of the one dialectic methodology have been made. These include its application to the processes of *thinking and metaphysics* by Kant, Fichte, Hegel, and Feuerbach, to *history* by Hegel, F. C. Baur, and the Tübingen school, to *economics* by Karl Marx and Lenin, to *theology* by Kierkegaard, Lenin, and Karl Barth, to *politics* by Lenin, Adolf Hitler, and Stalin.

Among the earliest on record to discover a dialectic movement — or swing of the pendulum back and forth after the fashion of the give-and-take of ordinary conversation — in the nature of events themselves rather than in man's discussion about these events were the ancient Greeks Heraclitus (500 B.C.) and Parmenides (525 B.C.). Heraclitus explained the existence of everything by means of a double movement which he termed the *hodos anō katō* (i.e., the way up and the way down): everything, he taught, was in flux and flow and so going in either one direction or its opposite. In our modern terminology — derived to be sure from the Greeks — this might be termed *a method of creation by metabolism,* the two sides of which (anabolism and catabolism) are continually in operation. Parmenides, who has been called the only metaphysician before Socrates, similarly offered a division of all things into two categories, respectively called by him *to on* (being) and *to mē on* (not-being). These two divisions corresponded roughly to those of Heraclitus, and like his were intended to offer a solution to the process of becoming along dialectical lines. Philosophers from the day of these two Greek thinkers to that of Emmanuel Kant developed their insights into the nature of Reality along dialectical lines of one sort and another.

It remained, however, for Georg Wilhelm Hegel to apply the method to history and to man's cultural advance. He held, that just as in ordinary human conversation there is the interplay of *thesis,* or original proposition, and *antithesis,* or opposing reply, followed usually by some sort of compromise or *synthesis,* so the history of man's cultural advance proceeds. Arnold Toynbee's more recent theory of " challenge and response " represents an application of the method in the same field and along much the same lines as those laid down by Hegel. In view of the current popularity of Toynbee's views it will be worth our while, one imagines, to glance at a single sentence in his *A Study of History* in which he rather marvelously describes the dialectic method as applied to the history of man. He is speaking of the way that growth is actually achieved in human affairs, if at all, and he remarks, " To convert the movement into a repetitive, recurrent rhythm, there must be an *élan vital* (to use Bergson's term) which carries the challenged party through *equilibrium* into an *overbalance* which exposes him to a *fresh challenge* and thereby inspires him to make a *fresh response* in the form of a *further equilibrium* ending in a *further overbalance,* and so on in a *progression* which is potentially infinite." [2] If the reader will observe the italicized words (which are mine) and equate the following — *progression* with dialectic, *challenge* with thesis, *response* with antithesis, and *equilibrium* with synthesis, he will have a beautiful picture of the dialectical method applied in the realm of history. Karl Marx transferred this dialectic, which Hegel and Toynbee observed within history, to the clash between economic classes and his system known as " dialectical materialism " was born. The Danish philosopher and theologian, Sören Kierkegaard, and the Swiss theologian, Karl Barth, have applied the method in the field of theological inquiry without significant change.[3]

Turning now to the problem with which we are immediately concerned in the field of Biblical theology, it is to be noted that we are confronted here with the dialectical method in two senses. There is, first, a dialectic clash observable in the situation itself wherein opposing views are ranged on opposite sides against each other. Again, the forces that line themselves up on

[2] Cf. *A Study of History,* by Arnold Toynbee, p. 187 (1947, First Amer. Edition).

[3] A fresh discussion of the dialectical systems referred to will be found in Edwin A. Aubrey's *Present Theological Tendencies* (1936). There is a good chapter too on " The Dialectical Method " in Birch Hoyle's *The Teaching of Karl Barth* (1930). Cf. also Paul Tillich's *Systematic Theology,* Vol. i, pp. 56 f. (1951).

either side claim to be in possession of religious truth which
has been arrived at through one or other type of dialectic
process. Throughout this book the reader will at all times be
conscious of dialectic in the former of these two senses; so that
nothing further need here be said about this phase of the matter
by way of explanation or of emphasis. The several claims made
by one and another of the disputants in the field to having in his
possession the right sort of dialectic for solving our problem,
however, must now engage our attention. Our current theological dilemma, indeed, may be said to pose for us the question,
Which of the several modes of dialectic proposed is calculated
to put us in contact with the truth about God?

It is a major part of the thesis of this book that this problem
is among the most important confronting the Christian Church
today. It is no secret that the old ecclesiastical lines are no
longer of significance when theological considerations are to
the fore. Theological thinkers of every shade of opinion are to
be found in all the leading denominations. There are Baptist,
Methodist, and, until very recently at any rate, even Unitarian
Calvinists; and there are *Arminian* Anglicans, Presbyterians,
and Congregationalists; as well as *Pelagians* in every communion and in none.

The like curious intermingling and crossing of the old lines
holds also for the newer schools of thought, such as fundamentalism, liberalism, orthodoxy of every sort, and modernism.
Almost every Church in Christendom contains adherents of all
these schools. Schools of thought, accordingly, are more significant today than denominational cleavages, for the very good
reason that they cut across the lines set by the latter. But more
significant still than these schools of thought are the various
dialectical systems about to be mentioned. For the three types
that we shall look at are found in all the Churches and — more
important still — in all the schools of thought as well.

The problem — Which dialectic? — therefore transcends all
other present-day theological problems in importance and is
relatively more creative as a criterion for analyzing theological
differences than any other that has been suggested. Accordingly,

it is now proposed in the three chapters that follow to explore the main tenets of the three types of dialectic that are currently striving for the mastery in Biblical and theological circles.

2. *Humanistic Optimism — The Monologue of Reason*

THUS FAR we have been considering the very popular endeavor of man to attain knowledge in every field of interest by the discussion method. We turn now to the various applications of this method that have been made in the realm of Biblical theology. And we shall look first at its use by those who believe the human reason to be an adequate instrument for securing all the knowledge man requires.

Here is to be placed every sort of dialectic that resolves itself into a monologue carried on within the breast of man himself, whether this be man the individual or man the group. This monologue employs the best techniques of research and experimentation, as well as inductive-deductive logic, hypothesis, and every other methodology known to human investigation. All the philosophies and sciences are to be included under this first kind of discussion method for the reason that in the end they subscribe to the maxim that " man is the measure of all things."

It is not to be thought unfair to speak of this dialectical system as a monologue carried on by man's unaided reason. Those who accept it as a valid methodology are the first to assert as much — herein they discover its chief glory to reside.

In the Biblical area this monologic or rationalistic type of approach to the problems of religion has its background particularly in the philosophical dialectic of Fichte and Hegel. These thinkers — as we have already observed the discussion or dialectic method generally to do — proposed that advance in religious thought proceeds through a synthesizing of opposite propositions. A *thesis*, they held, is first proposed and defended. Its opposite or *antithesis* is then asserted. Finally, through a

process of sublimation or compromise, the one passes over into
the other and both are fused into a *synthesis*. This last then becomes a new thesis for the process to start all over again: this
goes on endlessly as the human race advances stage by stage to
ever greater heights of knowledge.

F. C. Baur and the Tübingen School in Germany applied this
Hegelian dialectic to the problem of the history of doctrine in
the Christian Church. These Biblical scholars concerned themselves especially with the interplay of thought and teaching in
the Church's earliest period as recorded in The Acts, the Pauline Epistles, and the writings of Peter and James. According to
their analysis of this interplay, the original theological thesis
about which discussion revolved was the doctrine of works under the law as taught by the Judaizers within the Church. The
antithesis, then, which countered the former teaching was
Paul's doctrine of freedom and justification by grace through
faith. Finally, the synthesis or compromise which eventuated
was the legalistic orthodoxy of the Catholic Church of the second century.

This example of the method might, of course, be multiplied
again and again for the history of the Christian Church according to these thinkers and its significance for the development of
doctrine — if true — is apparent. The Church would require
no revelation beyond that provided by its own fertile reasoning
to arrive at a theology adequate to all of its needs.

The scientific relativism of Ritschl, Adolf Harnack, Wilhelm
Hermann, Ernst Troeltsch, and their modern disciples also belongs under the present heading. It is this system that has given
rise to what is popularly termed " liberalism " or " modernism." Historically it has been the first within theological circles
to embrace the principle of evolution, with its dialectic struggle
for existence and the survival of the fittest, and to apply the
same to the history of religions, including the Christian faith.
Like Hegel, Baur, and the Tübingens, Ritschl and his successors have accepted the basic principle that the reason of man
must be allowed the honored post of final arbiter of what he is
or is not to believe. Essentially, therefore, liberalism in all its

forms indulges in a monologue by means of which man hopes to arrive at ultimate truth.

It is worth observing at this point that we are not endeavoring here to " catalogue " persons or even groups with regard to the thought-content of the system they hold. The motive in referring to these individuals and schools of thought is merely, by way of a series of well-known illustrations, to characterize the various types of dialectical method employed in Biblical study circles. When looked at from the standpoint of their thought-content rather than that of methodology, these individuals and schools succeed in breaking through the categories that we are using and straddling over into one another's parishes in a rather startling manner. The very fact that theologians are constantly under the necessity of speaking of a *right-* and *left-* wing of every school of thought is the final proof of this contention. To suggest, for example, that all liberals or modernists subscribe to the tenets of humanism considered as a system of thought, rather than as a discussion method as we are doing here, would be entirely unwarranted. It is correct to say, however, that Ritschlianism — or to adopt the popular term, liberalism — in view of its emphasis on the creative powers of the human reason, finds its natural placement under the label of the humanistic dialectic.

At the same time, however, a method of arriving at truth cannot be entirely divorced from the results that it achieves. And there is a correlation between method and eventual doctrine accepted within any system of thought that appears significant. Thus, the dialectic of humanism lends itself naturally to all studies of a historical, psychological, and social nature — indeed, in the direction of any and all subjects that deal with man the individual and man the group. This is because its monologic nature *ipso facto* suggests its usefulness in these directions. In accepting the principle of evolution as indigenous to the dialectic monologue in nature, the adherents of this system naturally place man at the pinnacle of the process and take him as the rightful subject of their major interest. On the right, then, some who employ this humanistic method of discussion sit close to the Biblical tradition and speak of man as the "child of God"; on the left there are others who nearly (if they do not quite) equate God with man and think of man's evolution as one with God's own. H. G. Wells with his god who grows up as man grows morally is a good example of the leftest element here.

From the moment that this dialectic method became acceptable on the part of some within the Christian fold — that is to say, from the early decades of the last century with F. C. Baur and the Tübingens — its adherents have shown an interest in all literary studies pertaining to the canon of the Scriptures. The Graf-Wellhausen theory of the formation of the Hebrew Old Testament and the two- and four-documentary hypotheses suggested in explanation of the "Synoptic problem," together with certain attempted solutions for the Johannine problem, have been products of the work of scholars adhering to this form of dialectic.

The "social gospel," which for over a generation has been such a prominent feature of the Christian program at home and abroad, was elaborated by those who adopted this monologic methodology and is one of its chief grounds for praise within Christian circles. Accepting wholeheartedly the doctrine of evolution as relates to man's historical development and believing in the inevitability of human "progress" ever onward and upward, the devotees of the social gospel identified the progressive amelioration of man's lot along social, intellectual, moral, even economic and political lines, with the Biblical concept of the Kingdom of God. It was held that the latter was seen to come in a horizontal progression through the efforts of men who could be referred to as "building the Kingdom." Moreover, this Kingdom was identified with a social order to be set up within history.

Deeply influenced by the newly discovered views on evolution, theologians of the Ritschlian school saw man as inherently and normally good, and left no place in their theology for a genuine doctrine of sin in the sense of moral contamination of man's entire personality. Nor could they find any place for a

" fall " of man. Man's progress from the time of his emergence
from the subhuman, animal level had always been one directed
toward and gradually achieving emotional and intellectual maturity, never the reverse. It is this significant factor in the monologue that man's unaided reason carries through in this type of
dialectic, finding, as it claims to find, its counterpart in man's
historic evolution from lower to higher, that justifies the adjective " optimistic " usually attached to it.

This upward progress man has achieved by his unaided powers and growth in knowledge, this latter by no means through a
divine revelation but rather by accumulating what was termed
" religious experience." This experience, be it noted, was not,
or at any rate not necessarily, experience of God. Indeed, no
such metaphysical problem as that of the existence and nature
of God was ever raised by many who held to the humanistic
type of dialectic. One might very well share in the humanistic
discussion and believe in God or otherwise as he pleased. All
that was required was — to adopt William James's phrase applied in another direction — that one observe that religious experience " goes on," let its metaphysical origin and nature be
what it may. Accordingly, the most inclusive definition was allowed for such experience; it became, so to speak, a catchall for
every kind of awareness of a relationship with a higher power
of sorts!

Introduced into the realm of Biblical theology, it soon became evident, adherence to the humanistic dialectic made it
possible to eliminate, not only the thought of a personal God,
but as a natural corollary the doctrines of a Mediator between
a now nonexistent deity and man and of a redemptive community (the Church), inasmuch as man required no redemption
that he could not well enough provide himself in the course of
his unabated advance. In place of the redemptive community, it
was proposed that social amelioration involving man's existent
groups was quite enough to further the coming of God's
Kingdom (conceived in the most general sense) on earth. As
for the doctrine of a divine-human Mediator, it was suggested
that the seamless robe of the person of Jesus Christ must be

torn in two, leaving the disrelated " Jesus-of-history " and the
" Christ-of-faith." One or other of these was to be accepted as
one's final judgment regarding this person, never both at once.
If one chose the " Jesus-of-history " for one's allegiance, then
one was clearly on the side of history and was espousing the dialectic of the human reason, for the " Christ-of-faith " had never
had any existence outside the dogma of the Christian Church.

3. *Apocalyptic Pessimism — Conversing with God at*
Long Range

IF HUMANISM makes of dialectic a monologue within man's
own heart and quite without any need of God, apocalypticism at best converts it into a long-distance conversation between God and man. " God is in heaven, and you upon earth "
— this oft-quoted saying which Kierkegaard drew from Eccl.
5:2 seems to sum up in few words the essential teaching of the
apocalyptic dialectic. For wherever it is met — whether in the
Jewish extracanonical writings, among Christian millenarians,
or in the Kierkegaard-Barthian tradition, this point of view is
characterized above all else with the thought of the " wholly-
otherness " of God as compared with man. Man is in time, God
in eternity; man is of the earth earthy, God is transcendent and
his throne is above the universe.

It is opportune to speak of this sort of conversational method
immediately after reference has been made to humanism because in modern times it has characteristically arisen as a reaction to the latter. This is true of all three types of the apocalyptic dialectic that follow. Thus, (a) *the Kierkegaardian dialectic*
represented a determined stand on the part of the " gloomy
Dane " against the Hegelian system, both Hegel and Kierkegaard accepting the same conversation pattern in arriving at
their conclusions and presenting their views, but with quite opposed results as to the content of their teachings. For, like all

apocalyptists, Kierkegaard believed in a true — albeit a veiled and so incomplete — revelation of God to man, a long-range conversation with a God whom he conceived as the " Wholly Other," above and beyond man and quite incomprehensible to the latter. Such a dialectic, though in form similar to the mono-logic variety to which Hegel subscribed, inasmuch as both followed the conversation pattern, obviously was nonetheless poles apart from the latter in its fundamental postulates and its final results.

(b) *The Barthian movement* — together with its American child, Neo-orthodoxy — likewise represents a reaction against the scientific liberalism of Ritschl and his school. Barth and his colleagues followed the older Kierkegaardian pattern as to motivation and postulates, adopted much of the same terminology as their predecessor, and on the whole arrived at the same results.

(c) *The consistant eschatology* of Johannes Weiss and Albert Schweitzer also in some degree represents a reaction against Ritschlianism. This third representative of the apocalyptic type of dialectic, however, is not quite on all fours with the other two that have gone before. It is true that, like Barth, Weiss and Schweitzer reacted violently against Ritschl's teaching and found it equally repugnant; but their concern was chiefly with an elucidation of the teaching of Jesus in terms of apocalypticism rather than of the social gospel. And Schweitzer, at any rate, in his personal views is to be grouped with those who adopt the prophetic realism to be discussed below. For the substance of his teaching is that Jesus is not a safe guide in the latter's " consistent eschatology "; indeed, Jesus has really nothing to teach us save that from his example we may learn to follow in the way in which the will of God appears to be directing our paths. Jesus' example in following out what he (mistakenly) conceived to be God's will for him is better far than his precept and is alone to be emulated. It is this curious paradox that explains Schweitzer's tumultuous and otherwise inexplicable career.

Both Barth and Schweitzer opened their broadsides against

the Ritschlianism in which they had been trained with an attack upon its acceptance of the scientific (particularly, the psychological and sociological) approach to the content and history of the Christian faith. Barth spoke of these as peripheral matters of little moment to the substance of the Christian message. Schweitzer's opposition concerned particularly the endeavor to adopt the techniques of modern psychology in a study of the person of Jesus [1] and those of sociology in estimating the social implications of the Christian message in terms of community.[2] Both scholars have since modified their former antiscientific attitudes to some extent, or at any rate Barth has done so. Schweitzer rather inconsistently attempted himself to " psychologize " Jesus at the very time and in the very work in which he attacked the Ritschlians for doing so.[3]

This antiscientific bias of modern apocalypticism has left its stamp on Continental theology and its American prototype, Neo-orthodoxy. Essentially it is an expression of something that is indigenous to the apocalyptic point of view and is certain, therefore, often to emerge at one point or another. The repugnance which is felt toward the " psychologizing " of Jesus' person arises in fact out of a fundamentally Docetic attitude toward the latter which we shall examine presently, while that relating to a " sociologizing " of the Christian gospel springs from the thought that the Kingdom of God is altogether an eternal entity which can find no temporal counterpart in history. For the apocalyptists the person of Jesus Christ is of interest exclusively as he is the transcendent and eternal Word of God and the Church only as it shall appear in the *Endzeit* (eschatological period) or in the " beyond-history " as the New Jerusalem and the Bride of Christ.

To these modern examples of the apocalyptic dialectic school should be added, of course, those other more ancient ones found within the ranks of orthodox and Pharisaic Judaism, as

[1] Cf. *The Quest of the Historical Jesus: A Critical Study of Its Progress from Reimarus to Wrede* (1931 and 1948) , p. 360.
[2] *Ibid.,* pp. 402 f.
[3] *Ibid.,* p. 386.

well as inside the primitive Christian Church, and also modern fundamentalism. In this matter of apocalypticism, indeed, we find today a curious *rapprochement* between extreme liberals and fundamentalists: both accept the thought of a dialogue between the transcendent God in heaven and the lowly man on earth, the apocalyptic separation of history from eternity, and the final, cataclysmic coming of the Kingdom of God by direct divine fiat as the *only* coming of the same. Save for these three major points, however, the two differ markedly, particularly as to whether Jesus himself believed in and taught the near approach of the Parousia. Modern Continental apocalyptists have experienced no difficulty in admitting this on the basis of such passages as Mark 9:1; 13:30; and 14:62. But such an interpretation is quite inadmissible to American fundamentalism as it makes Jesus out as mistaken in predicting the time of the end.

The rise of many apocalyptic groups at the present time is not difficult to explain. It has often been remarked that apocalypticism breeds on tragedy and world disorder; accordingly, every war such as the two last produces a crop of those who find in the current tribulations " signs " of the near approach of the *Endzeit*. Despairing of the establishment of God's Reign on the plane of history and pessimistic of man's ability to do anything about it in any case, the apocalyptist looks to the " beyond-history " for the vindication or salvation of God's people.[4]

Speaking rather generally — and I am now thinking of the entire range of the movement from pre-Christian times down to the latest American fundamentalist aberration — it is characteristic of apocalypticism that God never quite succeeds in revealing himself to man. This is because of the premise (implicit in the transcendentalism accepted by all branches of this movement) that God is the " Wholly Other " over against and above man, and in consequence he is unable to come into real contact

---

[4] In view of this undoubted situation or *Sitz im Leben* out of which apocalypticism usually takes its rise, it is far more likely that it was the primitive Church of the post-Neronian period, rather than our Lord, that first adopted this form of dialectic. Though, to be sure, the Jewish Apocalyptic literature had been read in Galilee from the days of the Maccabean uprising in the early part of the second century B.C.

with his creature. Upon this point all apocalyptists insist in one way or another as rigidly as the Gnostics of the second century, though they do so at times quite inconsistently in view of their acceptance of certain of the cardinal doctrines of Scripture (such, for example, as that of the historic incarnation). Their motto is that expressed in the phrase, "*Non capax infiniti finitum*" — the finite (here, of course, man) cannot comprehend the Infinite. Hence, in the long-distance conversation between God and man there can be no conclusion arrived at on the plane of history. Man is doomed to wrestle with God as Jacob wrestled with the angel and to no real avail. There are *thesis* and *antithesis,* but there can be no *synthesis,* here below. This last must await eternity. And so man is left in a constant state of frustration and even of despair; hence, the adjective "pessimistic" constantly applied (and rightly, one believes, in this sense only) to this form of dialectic.

By way of illustration of the way in which this apocalyptic sort of dialectic, with its attachment to a metaphysical gulf between God and man, affects the cardinal teachings of the Christian faith for those who adhere to it, let us glance at three of the acknowledged implications of its central thesis. The first of these concerns the person of Jesus Christ. In line with apocalypticism's thesis of the ineffable nature of God it becomes clear that his incarnate Son must walk among men as the "great Incognito," to employ Sören Kierkegaard's expressive phrase. The Man of Nazareth, the Jesus-of-history, *cannot reveal God* — he can only succeed in "veiling" him. Human personality can never really be the vehicle of the divine revelation nor the "*imago Dei*"; not even the Jesus-of-history can be that because of the great gulf separating the transcendent God from lowly man, because God is the "Wholly Other."

It is clear, accordingly, why the Ritschlian dichotomizing of the person of Jesus Christ into the "Jesus-of-history" and the "Christ-of-faith" is so congenial to the apocalyptist. The only difference between the two views at this point is that, whereas the Ritschlians accept the Jesus-of-history because they can fit him into their evolutionary *historicism,* the apocalyptists choose the Christ-of-faith as the center and circumference of their Christological thought. They can find no place for the Jesus who walked among men save as one who was by no means what he seemed to be, a hopeless riddle, a shadowlike enigma. This looks very much like Docetism brought down to date, a sort of Christian doctrine of *maya* (illusion) centering in the person of the central Figure of the faith. If pressed — as this view gives us every right to do — such teaching results in a new " Christ myth," a Christ quite divorced from historical associations and with only the most tenuous relations with the historical person known to his contemporaries as Jesus of Nazareth.[5] In the end this position makes history of little, if any, value and transforms Christianity from being a historical faith such as it has always claimed to be into a mere ideology — a philosophical system instead of a historically grounded revelation.

The second implication of the viewpoint of apocalypticism, which some, at least, of its devotees are not averse to acknowledging, is man's inability on the plane of history to arrive at the *synthesis* which this dialectic sets forth. This must await the " beyond-history," or at least the eschatological epoch within time. This is due to the fact that man — even Christian man — is hopelessly enmeshed in the sin of the race as a whole, so that he can neither know nor knowing accomplish the divine will. The apocalyptist, accordingly, does not hesitate to ally himself with the solution of the problem presented in Rom. 7:7–25 which acknowledges the continued existence of " two minds," " two wills," and consequent complete frustration, within the Christian life and spirit.

A. Roy Eckhardt, in his volume entitled *Christianity and the Children of Israel* (1948), calling upon the witness of the " depth psychology," suggests as a " hypothesis " that this ambiv-

---

[5] So also Donald Baillie in *God Was in Christ* (1948), pp. 48 f., who has coined the term " logotheism " for the crisis theology's doctrine of the person of Christ; cf. Willard L. Sperry's instructive chapter on " The Fact of Christ," pp. 17 ff. in his *Jesus Then and Now* (1949).

alence in the soul of the Christian man may help us to un-
cover the motivation behind *Judenhass* or anti-Semitism. The
argument runs, *" We reject the Jews in order to reject Jesus as
the Christ.* Hatred of the Jews is the result of our hatred of
Christ.

" The process may be elaborated somewhat as follows: Whenever we think of Jesus as the Christ, we must think of the Jews.
Jesus was a Jew and Christianity is a Jewish religion. As sinful
men, we have an ambivalent attitude towards Christ. The gulf
that ' runs through the very center of our personality ' makes
us hate and love the same object at the same time. We must have
tangible means of showing our hatred of Christ. We find this
means in the Jews " (p. 55) . All of this, be it noted, is being
said from the standpoint of American Neo-orthodoxy about
Christians and the so-called " Christian rejection of Christ "
(p. 58) .

Much more might be quoted of the same sort. One does not
suggest that all crisis theologians would subscribe to this particular sort of frustration in the soul of the Christian; in point of
fact, they very certainly do not do so. I merely wish to point out
that such a deduction as Eckhardt makes from within the movement itself is a quite logical one, considering the premise with
which he has to work — namely, that man cannot arrive at the
synthesis of his dialectical situation within history. It seems to
this writer that he has merely followed out with commendable
frankness and courage one of the obvious implications of the
dialectic to which he stands committed.

The third implication of the dialectic of apocalypticism is
one that has seized the imagination of the more extreme elements of the movement from time to time and borne fruit in
the realm of practical Christian living. This is the essential
bypassing — if not the actual denial — of the work of the Spirit
in calling forth and sanctifying His Church on earth. Indeed,
through its denial of any sort of vital identification between the
Kingdom of God and the historic community of believers, apocalypticism has not only failed in general to exhibit a genuine interest in the Church Universal, but has even led to schism in

the existent Church of Christ, to sectarianism, and to scandalous treatment of Christian brethren.

It is not difficult to see how the logic of apocalyptic can lead to such antinomian practices. If the final *synthesis* of man's dialectical position cannot be arrived at on earth, then it may be not unfairly argued that not even the Spirit of God can alter matters at this point. In consequence, no mere man, not even the Christian man, is to be thought of as sanctified in any real sense. And the earthly community of believers by the same token is not the real Church of Christ; for that we await the " beyond-history," the eternal order. Accordingly, the Christian's allegiance must be, not to the Church on earth, but only to the Church in heaven — a very comforting doctrine to be sure, seeing that it is so much easier to love a departed saint than those sinful saints who sit with one in the same pews! Again, I should be the first to deny that all apocalyptists carry their teaching to this extreme. It does seem, however, that the logic of this sort of dialectic tends in this direction, and accordingly it is not surprising that there are those who follow it through relentlessly to such a conclusion.

4. *Prophetic Realism — The Dialogue of Revelation*

WE TURN NOW to the third type of conversational methodology which claims to put man in touch with the truth of God. This is to be identified with the movement known on the Continent as *Heilsgeschichte,* one which we shall here term " prophetic realism." [1] It is a major thesis of this volume to demonstrate that this dialectic is found throughout the Scriptures in all their parts. The most significant distinguishing feature of this method is the claim that it consists of a dialogue be-

[1] This term was first suggested to me by my former student and present colleague, Professor Surjit Singh, Ph.D. It represents an advance, one imagines, on Hendrick Kraemer's phrase " Biblical realism," avoiding the possibility of any sort of bibliolatry such as is implicit in the latter phrase.

tween God and man — a dialogue of such an intimate nature
that man within history really comes to know God and to purpose to do his will.

That such fellowship between God and man is normative,
is assumed from the earliest pages of the Hebrew Scriptures —
pages written by men of prophetic insight, as Old Testament
critical scholarship has long recognized. However one chooses
to interpret the early chapters of Genesis — whether as strict
history or allegorically or in some other fashion — they are
certainly intended to teach that from their first dealings with
one another God and man have possessed a *garden spot* wherein
they may have fellowship together with a view to God's communicating his will to man. Genesis, ch. 3, however, suggests that
there has come about a rift in this fellowship — a rift so serious that man is driven away from constant companionship with
his Maker. This is *realism* at its best: men have known for centuries that they have lost the secret of direct and constant communion with God, and across those centuries and across the
world they have been found endeavoring to renew the broken
contact. This is the reason that the pagan world is full of religions whose chief concern seems to consist in the devising of
techniques for pursuing the so-called " search after God."

In the Hebrew-Christian tradition the literature containing
this prophetic story of man's intimate conversation with God is
chronologically prior to that of apocalypticism, as is generally
recognized. It also, of course, antedates the modern humanistic
dialectic of which we have spoken. The Genesis story of the
" Garden of Eden " not only contains a hint of the chronological priority of the intimate type of prophetic dialogue between
God and man, but also appears desirous of establishing a sort
of necessary logic in favor of such priority as inherent in the nature of man's relation to God.

Thus, in Gen., ch. 3, the prophetic author assumes that a
series of conversations have been carried on between God and
man previous to the " fall " (ch. 3:1, 3, 5, and cf. chs. 1:28 ff.
and 2:16 f.) . In these conversations it is suggested that God instructed man regarding his will for man's life and activity and

promised him abundance of " good living " as well as authority over all his creatures on condition of man's implicit obedience. These conversations, then, will constitute the rapport which the *prophetic realism* assumes as normal for man's relationship with God.

But it is equally evident that, in addition to the divine-human encounter which is conceived as basic, there is another sort of dialogue — represented in the story as that between the serpent and man (ch. 3:1–7), in which God disclaims having any share (v. 11). Whether we think of this as a dialogue as represented in the story, or as a monologue proceeding within the spirit of man himself, in either case it is to be identified with the *dialectic of humanism* — that dialectic which unblushingly leaves God out of the conversation entirely!

Then, as for the *apocalyptic dialectic,* whose most distinguishing feature we have seen to be the assumption of a great gulf separating man from God so that any conversation between the two must be of the nature of a long-distance communication, at first blush there appears to be room for this also in the closing episode of the story. For man is driven from the garden of fellowship after the entrance of sin into the picture (vs. 22–24). And it might be supposed that the suggestion would be made that henceforth man and God would communicate with one another at long range. However, the prophetic Scripture itself does not make this apocalyptic deduction. Rather it assumes that the break is final and complete: henceforth, man as man never again is to hear God's voice speaking to him — not even from a great distance.

If man is to hear God speaking at all, this will be because God searches him out as an individual, communicates to him his will, and gives him a mission to go forth and proclaim it to his fellows. This surely is the meaning, not alone of the immediately succeeding narratives beginning with Cain (ch. 4:6 ff.), Enoch (ch. 5:24), and Noah (ch. 6:13 ff.), but of the entire teaching of the rest of Scripture as well. Such individuals as God searches out in this way are called " prophets " in both Old and New Testaments alike, and to them he speaks on terms of the

greatest intimacy " as a man speaks to his friend " (Ex. 33:11).
The apocalyptic dialectic, accordingly, has laid hold of a
valid idea in suggesting that at present a great gulf exists between God and man. But it is wrong in assuming that this condition is normative for their God-appointed relationship and
it is wrong in suggesting that God, so to speak, shouts at man
across an unbridgeable chasm that exists between the two. On
the contrary, the prophetic Scriptures rather insist that God is
prepared at all times to bridge the gulf, and that he does so in
the case of those " chosen vessels " through whom he communicates his redemptive purpose and in the end with utter abandon
in the person of his Son, the " prophet greater than Moses " and
so greater than all those prophets who came before him.

Fundamental to the prophetic or intimate revelational type
of conversation between God and man are certain characteristics which it shares with both humanism and apocalypticism,
according as the one or other draws from it or crosses its path.
It is important, however, to note that in all such cases it is the
prophetic type of encounter that is primary and the others derived from it. Accordingly, to claim any of these characteristics
as typical of either of the other two types of dialectic as though
their possession of it served to signalize the dialectic in question
is entirely beside the point. It is worth-while to remark this fact
since it has so constantly been overlooked in Biblical and theological circles.

The characteristics distinguishing the prophetic dialectic in
the sense that they belong in origin to it are these — first, it
testifies to the fact that *God speaks to man for his well-being and
that the latter may learn God's will for him* — such is its *thesis*
or the first third of the God-man conversation which the prophetic dialectic affirms. That this is the prophetic claim appears
in the oft-recurring phrase employed by the Hebrew prophets,
" Thus says the Lord," or, " Oracle of Yahweh " (Isa. 22:15;
50:1; Jer. 1:4; 14:1; Hos. 1:1; Amos 1:3, etc.) ; from the numerous Old Testament theophanies (Gen. 12:1; 18:1 ff.; 32:30;
Ex. 33:17 ff.; Num. 12:7 ff.; Judg. 6:12; etc.) ; and from the
New Testament representation of the nature of the incarnation

(Matt. 1:23; John 1:14–18; II Cor. 3:18; 4:6; Heb. 1:1–5; I John 1:1–4). At this point the apocalyptic dialectic makes a large draft upon the prophetic type in modern times, as, for example, in the so-called " dialectic theology," though the like could not be said for the ancient Jewish and Christian apocalypses.[2] The Barthian emphasis upon the " speaking God " (*Deus dicens*) — an emphasis which it is here contended derives from the prophetic type of dialectical method — represents a Continental swing of the pendulum away from the humanistic claim that man's advance in religious knowledge comes through his unaided reason.

Secondly, the prophetic dialectic testifies to the fact that *man hears God speaking to him,* that is to say, such men as God addresses, men of prophetic stature whom he raises up to hear his voice — such is its *antithesis* or the second third of the God-man conversation as conceived by the prophets of all times. This affirmation assumes that man is capable of hearing God's voice when he is addressed. It is made in line with the prophetic belief that God has made man " in his image after his likeness " (Gen. 1:26 ff.) — an image and likeness that man never loses however great his sin may be. For the effect of man's sin is, not the loss of God's image, but rather banishment from God's presence and fellowship (ch. 3:22–24).

At the very least to possess God's image means, as the Genesis narrative affirms, to be capable of hearing and seeing God and it is nowhere stated that man is robbed of these fundamental potentialities. The trouble with man is, not that he *can*not hear and see, but that he *will* not. Sin has stopped his ears and blinded his eyes. The ears are still present and the eyes are present — man is whole and intact. Only, since the incursion of sin into his experience, man *chooses* to listen to other voices than God's (vs. 9–11). Man's entire being, including his spiritual eyes and ears, is dominated by the sin-principle which now rules over his whole person (Rom. 6:12–14) and of which he

---

[2] Relative to the lack of stress in these apocalypses upon the fact of God's speaking to man, reference may be made to my book on *The Religion of Maturity* (1948), pp. 203–207.

is the willing slave (vs. 19 f.). It is this lack of the will to hear and see — essentially, that is to say, *rebellion against God's will maintained continuously throughout man's history* — that according to the prophetic Scriptures has destroyed the divine-human fellowship and maintains the rift between God and man.

Thirdly, the prophetic dialectic declares that man acts with resolution to fulfill God's will once he has been brought to listen to what it is — such is the *synthesis* or the final resolution of the God-man dialogue as conceived by the Hebrew prophets. It is to be noted as of the greatest importance that this can and does transpire on the plane of history. This synthesis is demanded by the nature of the prophetic thesis that begins the dialogue. For this always consists of a "call" on God's part to the man of prophetic stature to go forth and fulfill a mission, proclaiming the message committed to him with the call.[3] Abraham is a splendid example of the true prophet (Gen. 20:7) who responds in the divinely appointed way. For he "went out, not knowing where he was to go" (Heb. 11:8) — in his case to become an example of those who are to proclaim God's message more by his life than by his words, though he also handed on the message to his posterity (Gen. 24:1–9). Jonah is the stock illustration of the prophet who, at first refusing to obey God, eventually turns about and obeys (Jonah 1:1–3; 3:1 ff.). Albert Schweitzer in our own times is also a case in point here. For he rejects what he conceives to have been Jesus' position of "consistent eschatology" (that is, thoroughgoing apocalypticism) and, accepting rather the position here described as "prophetic realism," fulfills what he has come to believe God's will for him as a medical missionary to Africa. This is as good a modern illustration of "consistent prophetic realism" as one could wish!

It will be our endeavor in the present volume to attempt something like a sketchy demonstration of the thought that the Old and New Testament Scriptures represent a continuum or-

---

[3] *Cf.* William F. Albright's definition of the "prophet" in his *From the Stone Age to Christianity* (1940), pp. 231 f.

ganized throughout on the framework provided by the prophetic type of dialogue. This is not, of course, to affirm that the
other types of dialectic do not make an occasional appearance
here and there. But it does mean that *what is fundamental to
man's knowledge about God is in the end to be attributed to the
functioning of this form of dialogue between God and man.*
Wherever the monologic type of dialectic occurs (as in Job),
or that of the apocalyptic variety (as in Daniel and Revelation),
it will be found, one is led to believe, that nothing new in principle relative to the divine purpose and working appears. These
dialectics represent, not methods for the communication of new
truth from God to man, but merely *forms of literary technique*
adopted by certain writers of Scripture for the presentation of
such truths as they wish to set forth — truths already known to
the prophets and communicated to them through the intimacy
of the revelational dialogue experienced by them. These techniques are in every way comparable to other literary forms, such
as the parable, the prophetic sermon, the psalm, the historical
narrative, and the like. The Revelation of John, for example, is
in the writer's judgment a marvelous illustration of the use of
dramatic artistry to present the gospel message: it is a drama
pure and simple, whose theme is the prophetic theology of history, and it is charged from beginning to end with the powerful
message at the heart of the prophetic realism. But it would be
difficult to discover anything *new* in the book, and certainly its
author does not claim that its apocalyptic scaffolding contributes anything save an interesting stage effect against which to
portray the gospel drama.

THE THEME OF SCRIPTURE'S PROPHETIC REALISM

A. The Gospel

' And since the Scripture foresaw
that it was by faith God would
justify the Gentiles, it preached
the gospel beforehand to Abraham . . .'
— GALATIANS 3:8.

The Theme of Scripture's Prophetic Realism

A. The Gospel

SYNOPSIS

*C*ONTINUING THE TOPIC *suggested at the close of the previous section that Old and New Testaments constitute a continuum, it is here proposed that the theme of Scripture's prophetic realism is the gospel. A study of the New Testament passages in which the terms " gospel," " to preach," " promise," and their cognates are found leads to the observation that there are here three strands of tradition regarding the matter: first,* that of Paul *to the effect that the promise to Abraham was the gospel in essence and that we have accordingly from Abraham to Christ a historical " gospel-span " to serve as a norm for a theology of history and of God's dealings with men for their salvation; secondly,* that of the Synoptic sources *which, taking their clue from Second Isaiah, place the Herald of the New Age at the center of the gospel, it being through his labors that the gospel finds fulfillment; thirdly,* that of Stephen and Hebrews, *who jointly hold that the promise to Abraham, which was repeated by Joshua and David to the chosen people, eventually is the same as the gospel preached in the Christian centuries and fulfilled in Jesus.*

This gospel-span, it is shown, inasmuch as it finds the support indicated above in the Old as well as in the New Testament, represents the proper prophetic attitude toward the theme of the Scriptures as a whole. It was the Pharisees who, through their interpretation of the divine instruction (Torah) in terms of " commandments and ordinances," gave rise to the mistaken idea that the Old Testament should be understood in terms of law.

5. *Paul's Theology of History*

WE TURN NOW from the dialectical methods of prophetic realism to a consideration of its product. The unity of the Old and New Testaments, to which reference was made at the close of the last chapter, first exhibits itself in their common theme. That theme is the gospel — the good news of God's redemptive activity on behalf of man.

This statement is made in conscious opposition to the current popular view that Old and New Testaments are opposed to one another at this point, the theme of the Old being the law and only that of the New the gospel. Such a view in our judgment cannot be vindicated from a study of the Old Testament itself. It represents the acceptance on the part of Christian students (though no doubt in most cases quite unconsciously) of the Pharisaic interpretation of the Old Testament in terms of a code of laws.

But such an interpretation gives the one who accepts it a wrong slant on the Bible's entire message at the very start, and quite naturally leads to a second step, namely, to interpreting the New Testament as well along the same lines. This is actually what happened in the case of the Judaizers, with whom Paul had to battle at the beginning of the Christian movement. And the like mistake has recurred many times throughout the history of the Christian Church on the part of those making the initial blunder of postulating two themes, rather than one, for the whole of Scripture.

Moreover the Pharisaic interpretation of the message of the Old Testament in terms of a legal code does not do justice to the thought of the Hebrew prophets who by and large were its authors. For those prophets the God of the Old Testament was as deeply concerned with man's salvation as is the Father of our Lord Jesus Christ in the New Testament. That salvation was, indeed, his *first* concern. And in consequence theirs was to write down the gospel message of how God through a series of saving acts was accomplishing his purpose relative to man.

The Message of the Hebrew Prophets

The reason for the Pharisees' misinterpretation of the Old Testament is not our present concern. The ready acceptance of that misinterpretation on the part of many Biblical students at the present day, however, is quite understandable. It is due in large part, at least, to the fact that so many of the Biblical terms meant to Hebrew ears something quite other than the words by which they are commonly translated into other languages. Thus, *sedeq* and *sᵉdāqāh*, usually translated "righteousness," might in many cases better be rendered into English by "saving purpose" or even by "salvation" (or "saving acts" when used in the plural). The R.S.V. has actually rendered it "deliverance" in such passages as Isa. 51:6 and 8, where it is clearly to be equated with "salvation," as the latter occurs synonymously with it in these verses.

Later we shall have something more to say on the subject of God's righteousness as the prophets of Israel conceived it. For the moment it will be sufficient to note that with them the term stood for the impact of all his moral person upon his world in a series of redemptive acts. Too long it has been assumed that terms like *righteousness, justice, judgment* as applied to God in the Scriptures stand for the negative, condemning side of his nature. Nothing could be farther from the truth. *Righteousness* refers rather to the totality of God's activity with reference to man — an activity motivated particularly with man's redemption in view. Into every one of his righteous acts — as the Hebrew prophets conceived the matter — God pours *all* that he is and not simply a part of himself, the aggressively saving side of his nature generally, as well as its negative, condemning side! And the same is to be said for God's *justice* and *judgment,* as the prophets of all time have understood these terms. Justice would, indeed, be worse than blind if its sword had but one side (that of condemnation) and not two (to include vindication or acquittal — justification in Biblical terminology) !

The series of redemptive acts referred to collectively as God's righteousness formed the subject of meditation on the part of the Hebrew prophets from the ninth century B.C. forward, and perhaps long before that date. This was also the major theme of the earliest writers of the Pentateuch and of other parts of the Old Testament Scriptures. God's saving work in calling forth Abram from Ur and bestowing on him and his descendants the Land of Canaan, as well as the like calling of the Israelites out of Egypt and settling them in that Promised Land, are early examples of God's righteous activity as viewed by the prophetic historians who worked over these narratives. The later prophets and psalmists never tired of dwelling on these and the like incidents in the history of the chosen people.

This fact must be recognized as basic if the writings of these prophets are to be seen in proper perspective. The so-called "crisis theologies" are in grave danger of missing this right perspective if in their overweening desire to stress the judgment (Greek, *krisis*) of God, they forget the twofold aspect of that judgment — its saving as well as its condemning side. There is no gospel involved in the declaration that God " puts a man on the spot," so to speak, with a view to his testing and eventual refinement as gold is tempered by the fire of purging. The gospel enters the picture only when we are told that *God himself comes down onto this same spot to deliver man out of it.* This he does in the Old Testament theophanies, in the messages of the prophets, above all in the incarnation of our Lord, His Son. And of the fact that God does, indeed, come onto the spot in which man finds himself to redeem man there and then — of this fact the prophets never lose sight at any time. The Hebrew prophets, it is true, are " preachers of righteousness," as has often been remarked. But it is of this *total* righteousness on God's part — his saving as well as his condemning activity — that they speak and are convicted.

Against this background, then, we may allow for an Amos, with his proclamation of God's judgment on the sins of Israel (Amos 2:6–8; 3:1 to 6:14) and Judah (ch. 2:4 f.) ; a Micah, with his " doom songs " directed against the same people of God (Micah, chs. 1 to 3) ; and a Jeremiah, with his " jeremiads " of complaint mingled with anguish of soul at the sins and consequent punishment of both Israel (Jer. 3:6–13, 19–25) and Judah (ch. 2) . But one may never lose sight of the fact that this righteous indignation of the prophets, directed as it is against the sins of God's " chosen people," has point and can be justified only against the background of a common knowledge of God's redemptive purpose and activity on their behalf.

The argument of the prophets runs, ' You have been specially privileged above other men, therefore of you will the more be required ' (Luke 12:47 f.) . Amos, recalling that Yahweh had brought Israel out of the land of Egypt, concludes, " You only have I known of all the families of the earth: therefore will I visit upon you all your iniquities " (Amos 3:2, A.S.V.) . Micah in like manner makes the false prophets and other leaders of the people say: " Is not the Lord in the midst of us? No evil shall come upon us " — a sure sign that Micah and his contemporaries recognized what God had done for Israel and Judah. But the prophet replies to this false logic, " Therefore because of you Zion shall be plowed as a field " (Micah 3:12) . As is the privilege of God's people, so shall their responsibility be: such is the universal teaching of the Hebrew prophets.

This recurring theme of privilege and matching responsibility is sounded by these prophets within the purview of the universal redemptive purpose of God and of this they never lose sight. The logical sequence of ideas in their writings, as may often be very clearly traced, is: God's universal purpose to save all the " families of the earth," choice of a particular " family " (that of Abram) , fashioning of this same into a redemptive group (the Israel of God) , mutuality of blessing and responsibility in this group's experiences, salvation of all mankind through the missionary activity of this chosen people. This logical sequence unfortunately did not become wholly realized because of the failure of the chosen people to measure up to the demands placed upon them. But there can be no doubt that the great prophets of Israel and Judah were aware of the series of ideas involved here and that the theme of their messages first and last concerned this series. Roughly, it is this sequence that we have termed the gospel and that constitutes the theme of the prophetic realism throughout Scripture.[1]

It is indigenous to the nature of this prophetic realism that it requires considerable perspective — perspective derived from wide experience of God's dealings with men — for the prophet to see God's purposes with a degree of wholeness. Such perspective, while enjoyed to an extent by the Hebrew prophets as just indicated, is naturally to be expected with somewhat more assurance among those who in New Testament times enjoyed the far greater privilege of contact with the incarnate Word, either directly or through those " who from the beginning were eyewitnesses." The New Testament appears, accordingly, to contain three separate strands of tradition — those of Paul, the Synoptic Gospels, and Stephen with Hebrews — which in as many distinct ways bear witness to the possession of such prophetic insight within the Christian Church.

The apostle Paul was fortunate above most of the Hebrew prophets in that he had their insights at his disposal, and at the same time possessed a good knowledge of the history of the Hebrew people. He knew both how God had wrought for that people's redemption (his redemptive acts) and also how God's prophets had interpreted that working (his redemptive words). Moreover, Paul came on the scene of God's saving activity just in time to see its consummation to a degree in the person and work of Jesus Christ and he was himself drawn right into the

[1] Cf. Gen. 12:1–9; 26:23–25; 28:10–22; Ex. 3:15–17; Deut. 5:6; I Kings 19:9–18; I Chron. 17:1–27; Hos. 6:1–11; Micah 4:2 f.; Isa. 2:3 f. with Ps. 86:8–10. Father A. G. Hebert's *The Throne of David* (1941) is most instructive in this connection. Cf. particularly pp. 25–32 and chapter iii on " Israel's Universal Mission," pp. 73–96.

vortex of the maelstrom stirred up by the necessity laid upon the Church of bringing to pass God's universal redemptive purpose.

It was in this context, in the storm and stress of fashioning doctrine to fit the needs of man's salvation and God's purpose to save, that Paul fastened upon the age-old prophetic teaching of God's righteousness or redemptive activity as central to the gospel message. It would be unjust to the prophetic tradition to suggest that the doctrine of justification by grace through faith which emerged in this crisis was something wholly new with Paul. This is sometimes said to be the case and quite wrongly so.[2] Certainly the elements of the doctrine are as old as the recorded dealings of God with man. In both the Hebrew and the Greek the same words (or at any rate, words from the same stems) are employed alike for righteousness and justification. It is quite likely, indeed, that Paul derived his forensic teaching of justification through faith from the Second Isaiah and the latter's fellow prophets and psalmists. It is true, however, that Paul's was the prophetic voice that proclaimed the doctrine most clearly as of the essence of the gospel and attached it to the work of the historic figure of Jesus Christ.

This Paul did first in his Epistle to the Galatians, as it was in Galatia that the maelstrom above referred to took on cyclonic proportions. It is in the third chapter of this epistle that we find Paul's theology of history and his keenest insight into the true nature of the gospel. He is here developing his favorite theme that " it is men of faith who are the sons of Abraham " (v. 7). And in the course of the argument he points out that the promise to Abraham (v. 16), as in the case of a man's last will or testament (v. 15), cannot rightly be annulled but must remain over for his offspring to receive (v. 16). This offspring,

___

[2] As Father Hebert remarks, " the unity of the two Testaments is stated by Saint Paul in words that may well make the modern theologian rub his eyes "; he then quotes Gal. 3:8, 9, 16, after which he proceeds: " Justification by Faith is, then, no new doctrine; it was ' foreseen ' in the Scriptures from the beginning that this, the only true righteousness in God's sight, was to be not for Abraham's seed only, but for all the world " — *ibid.*, pp. 73 f. Cf. also J. Skinner's *Commentary on Isaiah* (1898), Vol. ii, pp. 238 ff.

Paul argues, in the present instance is " Christ " (v. 16) .

This use of the term " Christ " requires some notice. For in connection with it the apostle injects a somewhat difficult reference to the fact that at Gen. 12:7 which he is quoting, the collective singular (progeny, offspring, or seed) occurs rather than the plural of the noun. From the argument that follows it becomes clear that Paul is speaking here, not of Jesus Christ the individual, but rather of the corporate community which, as he often remarks, forms his " body." His words are, " For in Christ Jesus you are all sons of God, through faith. For as many of you as were baptized into Christ have put on Christ . . . you are all one in Christ Jesus. And if you are Christ's, then you are Abraham's offspring, heirs according to promise " (Gal. 3:26–29) .

The import of the passage, then, is clear. It may be expressed somewhat as follows: to Abraham and his spiritual progeny, says the apostle, the promise was given, the sole condition of its fulfillment and reception in particular cases being faith on the part of the recipient. This promise received its historical embodiment in the work of Jesus Christ and accordingly it is toward him that the faith required is to be directed. Therefore, they who are members of the corporate Christ, who are " in Christ " (to use Paul's phrase) in the sense that by faith they have established for them a unique fellowship with him — these are that " progeny " of Abraham to which the promise was originally given. Thus, the spiritual principle of *faith responding to promise* (or alternatively, to gospel) makes " Abraham's offspring " and those who are " sons of God . . . in Christ Jesus " spiritually one.[3]

For our present purpose it is important to observe that Paul brackets this normative stretch of history from Abraham to Christ under the aegis of the gospel. As he remarks, " the scrip-

[3] This exegesis is essentially that of C. A. Anderson Scott in his *Christianity According to St. Paul*, p. 155. Cambridge University Press, 1927. Scott there remarks that " believers in Christ are in fact the stock who were contemplated in the promise to Abraham. So in v. 16, Paul wrote ' Christ ' not of the individual, but of the corporate personality of which He was the Head."

ture . . . preached the gospel beforehand to Abraham " (v. 8) .
This phrase, " Preached the gospel beforehand," in the Greek
is represented by the single rare verb *proevangelizesthai,* a form
found elsewhere only in Philo and Sophocles before Paul's
time.[4] It is quite likely, therefore, that it represents here a spontaneous creation of the apostle for the purpose in hand, for he
never uses it again in his extant writings and it is doubtful if
he knew the works of either author referred to above. Paul's
meaning, then, will be that the Christian Church has no claim
to originality in its use of the terms " gospel " and " to preach
the gospel," or at any rate in employing the concept they represent. For the Scripture itself in Gen. 12:7 already had the
essence of the matter in the promise to Abraham and his offspring. It is indigenous to Paul's thought here that the content
of an idea or concept is of more importance than the word (s)
with which it is clothed and that, if it can be shown that the
content is identical in two given cases, then the words used to
describe it can be interchanged. Hence, here " promise " and
" gospel " become one and the same thing and *the principle
emerges that the great word which brackets God's dealings with
men from Abraham to Jesus Christ is promise or gospel.*

The following diagram will serve to illustrate Paul's theology
of history as thus outlined:

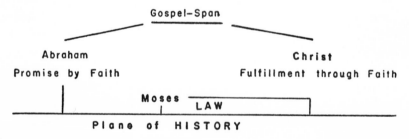

Reference to Moses and the law is made in the above diagram
because Paul conceives it necessary to answer an objection which
he has had leveled at his doctrine of the gospel-span. He had

---

[4] Cf. Liddell and Scott's *A Greek-English Lexicon* (Ninth Edition,
1940) .

been trained in the Pharisaic school, as had also his opponents, the Judaizers, and that school taught that the great word in the Old Testament was " law." This was law understood, not in its original sense of *instruction* (Hebrew, *torah*), but rather of a collection of " commandments and ordinances " (Eph. 2:15). If, then, not law (as the Pharisees held) but rather promise or gospel is the word that is all-inclusive of God's overarching purpose for man and his salvation from Abraham onward, the question must arise, " Why then the law? " (Gal. 3:19) and, " Is the law then against the promises of God? " (v. 21).

These questions are quite valid from the standpoint of the Pharisees and of the Judaizers representing their position within the Christian Church. They are important in fact for any sincere desire to understand the relation between the Old and New Testaments. But Paul has no difficulty with them. The law was added, he suggests, " because of transgressions " on man's part (v. 19) and to assume the role of the *paidagogos,* the Greek slave whose task it was each day to lead the child to school and so to the teacher (v. 24, R.S.V., translates the word " custodian "). Sin necessitated man's being thus kept under restraint (v. 23), until such time as Christ should come (v. 24), or better, until man should acquire the requisite faith in the Great Teacher through contact with him and so should no longer require to be " under a custodian " (v. 25).

In other words, Pharisaism had missed the point in its interpretation of the divine instruction (torah) whereby this was resolved into a series of commands to be observed each in its own right as a separate unit of the divine will. The history of God's dealings with his people indicated that before Moses and the law came Abraham, and that to Abraham the gospel had been preached in the form of promise. Accordingly the law must be subsumed under God's inclusive purpose as contained in the promise and interpreted in this light. In other words, " gospel " or " promise " is an Old Testament word before it is a New Testament one, and the stretch of history from Abraham to Jesus Christ becomes a convenient yardstick whereby to measure all God's dealings with men.

The argument of the fourth chapter of Romans with reference to the faith principle in the case of justification as exhibited, first in the case of Abraham, and then in that of all those who are of the faith of Abraham, is to the same effect as that just outlined. Though here the word " gospel " does not occur in relation to Abraham or his descendants, Paul's argument is that the method of salvation at the heart of the gospel message has clearly been at work in Abraham's case. Accordingly here as in the Galatians passage Paul's point is that to be found adequate our theology of history must posit the gospel and God's saving purpose through it as the criterion for understanding all of his dealings with men.[5]

It would be difficult to overestimate the importance of these passages for an earnest endeavor to state the inclusive theme of Scripture's theology of prophetic realism. It is scarcely too much to say that Paul's argument has placed in our hands the key by means of which the divine purpose throughout Scripture may be explored. That purpose is the making of sons of God who are one in Jesus Christ — one despite the differences which are recognized by man, though not by God, " heirs according to promise " of the gift of life (Gal. 3:27–29) .[6]

[5] The kernel of the argument is also found in Rom. 1:1 ff., 17; 3:21 ff., as well as in abridged form at I Cor. 15:3 f.

[6] Schniewind and Friedrich object to Paul's equation of " promise " and " gospel " as above elaborated, so far as these when equated seem to posit " the conception of a unified history-under-divine-control, the like of which is unknown to the Old Testament under the idea of an awaited promise." Cf. Kittel's *Wörterbuch*, II, p. 575, lines 21–25. They point out that Luther translated certain passages by *verheisen* (to promise) where the Hebrew has merely common verbs meaning " to say " and the like. The objection overlooks the fact that the idea of the promise is present in such passages regardless of the verb employed. Accordingly, in such passages the translation of *The Holy Scriptures according to the Massoretic Text,* published by the Jewish Publication Society of America in 1917, reads *to promise* (e.g., Ex. 12:25; Num. 14:40; Deut. 1:11; 19:8; 27:3; and numerous other passages) .

6. *The 'Herald' in the Synoptic Gospels*

W E HAVE BEEN DEALING in the previous chapter with Paul's contribution to the gospel theme which runs like a golden thread throughout Scripture's prophetic realistic teaching in both Testaments. A second line of tradition in the primitive Christian community — that found in the sources lying behind the Synoptic Gospels — also bears testimony to this theme.

In order to exhibit the witness of these Gospels it will be necessary for us to examine the use made by them or their sources of certain terms that lie at the heart of the tradition which they follow. By far the best modern statement of the meaning and usage of the terms in question is to be found in certain exhaustive articles contributed by Gerhard Friedrich and Julius Schniewind to Kittel's *Theologisches Wörterbuch zum Neuen Testament* (1933–   ). Unfortunately there is nothing in English remotely approaching the adequate treatment given in this German work. In the following discussion, accordingly, we shall in large part follow the lines laid down there.[1]

To begin with, as these writers point out, it is to be noted that the familiar terms " gospel," " to preach," and " to preach the gospel " — so common on the pages of the New Testament — have a long history behind them extending far back into the pages of the Old Testament and the contemporary Jewish and Hellenistic literatures. Behind the Greek equivalents of the above English terms, for example, stand the Hebrew verb *bisser* and its noun *besorah*, respectively for *evangelizesthai* (to preach the gospel) and *evangelion* (gospel). Hitherto Old Testament scholars rather generally have held that these Hebrew words mean simply " to proclaim," or publish " news," or " tidings " respectively, irrespective of whether the news in ques-

---

[1] Students who have access to this work should consult the articles *evangelizesthai* and *kērussein* and their cognates for a complete statement of the evidence upon which we are drawing in the above discussion.

tion be good or bad.[2] Friedrich, departing from this older view, now asserts that the etymological meanings are clearly " to proclaim *good* news " and " *good* news," or tidings. That is to say, he finds the idea of goodness inherent in the root meaning of the word itself (both verb and noun). The older view in this author's opinion arose from the fact that the adjectives " good " (*tobhah*) and " bad " (*ra'ah*) were at times added to the noun, apparently by way of definition of the nature of the news in question. But as he shows, comparison with such languages as Accadian, Ethiopic, and Arabic, which belong to the same linguistic family as Hebrew, clearly indicates that the idea of goodness is indigenous to the roots of these words themselves. It is only, therefore, he contends with a view to greater clarity that the adjectives mentioned are added at times and a sort of redundancy produced.[3]

So much for the meanings of the words in themselves. Friedrich next proceeds to show that the transition from what one might term the *secular* usage to the *religious* meaning of the words occurs in a passage like I Sam. 31:9. Here the news of the battle on Mount Gilboa with its good result — good, that is, from the standpoint of the Philistines and their gods — is heralded across the land to the people, even " to their idols," in the manner of a religious celebration. This heralding of the good tidings has now become " a cultic act."

From this pagan cultic signification of the word it is but one step to the point where it is used of the good news which the true and living God places in the mouths of those who are to proclaim it on his behalf to men (Ps. 68:11). This act on God's part — his transmitting the good news to his messengers (the prophets) — makes it a prophetic or revelational Word. Again,

[2] Cf. G. Dalman's *The Words of Jesus* (1902), pp. 102 f.; Millar Burrows' article on " The Origin of the Word ' Gospel,' " JBL, vol. xliv, 1925, p. 25; and Ludwig Koehler in *Lexicon in Veteris Testamenti Libros* (1948 –).

[3] The O.T. has little to contribute to our knowledge of the use of *kērussein;* it translates a number of Hebrew words and this very variety of usage shows that of itself it does not stand for any particular sort of announcement. The N.T. use of the word is not derived from the O.T.

another step is taken when this prophetic word becomes "a new song" as in Ps. 40:3, A.S.V., a "glad tidings of righteousness" or salvation (v. 9), to be proclaimed to the "great assembly" of God's people, that is, to his Church.

The final Old Testament development of the words with which we are dealing appears in Isa. 52:7:

> "How beautiful upon the mountains are the feet of him
>   who brings good tidings [*mᵉbhasser*],
>   who publishes peace [*mashmia'*],
>   who brings good tidings of good [*mᵉbhasser*],
>   who publishes salvation [*mashmia'*],
>   who says to Zion, 'Your God reigns.'"

In this passage it is clear that Yahweh's victory over the world, the coming of a new era (the eschatological period), and the gospel of peace and salvation which will be found in it, are being proclaimed. These great tidings are good news par excellence, so much so that their announcement requires the appointment of a special herald by God.

At this point Friedrich's work serves to substantiate conclusions already arrived at by Biblical scholars relative to the origin of the word "gospel" in its New Testament usage. George Milligan and Millar Burrows, for example, had quite independently suggested that in "the Second Isaiah is to be found the main source for the Christian use of the term." [4] The passage usually adduced for evidence in this connection is Luke 4:16 ff., wherein Jesus applies to himself the work of the gospel herald whose words are read from Isa. 61:1 ff., at the synagogue service. For our purposes here the point of outstanding importance is that in Second Isaiah the emphasis is upon the person and work of the Herald who brings the gospel message. He is termed both *mᵉbhasser* (the one who brings the good news, or gospel) and *mashmia'* (the one who causes the hearing of the same) in the Hebrew — words which without doubt stand behind the New Testament usage of the terms *evangelion* (gospel or good news)

---

[4] Cf. Burrows' article above cited; also "*St. Paul's Epistles to the Thessalonians*" (1908) by George Milligan, Appendix E on "The History of *evangelion, evangelizesthai.*"

and *akoe* (hearing) as applied to its distinctive message.[5] " The
*m*ᵉ*bhasser*," to quote Friedrich — and he might equally well
have employed here the other term (*mashmia*ʻ) — " is God's
' messenger ' who proclaims God's sovereignty and with his truly
powerful Word itself brings in the eschatological time."

We turn now to the New Testament evidence for the use of
these words. A complete list of the passages involved will be
found in note 6 for those who wish to pursue the subject in detail. To begin with, it is to say the least striking that none of the
words for " gospel," " message," " to preach the gospel," and " to
preach," or " proclaim," in Lists A and B occur in the Johannine writings and that they are almost absent from the Catholic
Epistles and from The Revelation of John. The case is, however,
quite otherwise with the Synoptic-Acts and Pauline traditions.
Here the words for " gospel " and " to preach the gospel " are
found in profusion and in a variety of usage on the part of the
individual authors. Paul, for example, uses all the terms involved but shows a decided preference for the noun (*evangelion*), employing the two verbs about equally. Luke-Acts, on
the other hand, follows the Septuagint in the almost exclusive
use of the verbs rather than the nouns. Of the other Synoptic
sources, Mark and Matthew's special source (designated " M ")
employ only " to proclaim " (*kērussein*) and " gospel " (*evangelion*), while the source common to both Luke and Matthew
(designated " Q ") uses both verbs and " message " (*kērygma*).
These facts argue for a certain freedom of choice on the part
of the writers of these sources and particularly for the independence of Luke-Acts as over against Paul.[6]

[5] Cf. John 12:38; Rom. 10:17; Gal. 3:2, 5; I Thess. 2:13; Heb. 4:2.

[6] The materials under discussion in this section are as follows: *List A —
evangelion, evangelizesthai, evangelistes:* (1) The verb is found: In Q at
Luke 7:22; Matt. 11:5. In L at Luke 1:19; 2:10; 3:18; 4:18, 43; 8:1; 9:6;
16:16; 20:1. In Ac at Acts 5:42; 8:4, 12, 25, 35, 40; 10:36; 11:20; 13:32;
14:7, 15, 21; 15:35; 16:10; 17:18. In Paul at Rom. 1:15; 10:15; 15:20; I Cor.
1:17; 9:16 (bis), 18; 15:1, 2; II Cor. 10:16; 11:7; Gal. 1:8, 9, 11, 16, 23;
4:13; Eph. 2:17; 3:8; I Thess. 3:6. In Heb. 4:2, 6. In I Peter 1:12, 25; 4:6.
In Rev. 10:7; 14:6. (2) The noun *evangelion* is found: In Mark at Mark
1:1, 14, 15; 8:35; 10:29; 13:10; 14:9 (cf. ch. 16:15). In M at Matt. 4:23;
9:35. In Ac at Acts 15:7; 20:24. In Paul at Rom. 1:1, 9, 16; 2:16; 10:16;

It is clear from the mass of evidence here, however, that the idea of the herald for the one who proclaims the gospel and the near approach of the eschatological time, which we have seen to be a contribution of the Second Isaiah to the concept of the Messiah, has deeply influenced particularly the Synoptic tradition. This appears, *first* from the use of the two verbs meaning "to proclaim" and "to preach the gospel," which are synonymous for all practical purposes here, in the context of the proclamation of the gospel message. Thus, Matthew's and Luke's common source (Q) in Luke 7:22 (Matt. 11:5) represents our Lord as adopting the language of Isa. 61:1 (with perhaps also ch. 35:5) in reply to the disciples of the Baptist, a passage in which the preaching of the gospel to the "poor" is represented as one of the functions of the Herald of the New Age. Here the

---

11:28; 15:16, 19; 16:25; I Cor. 4:15; 9:12, 14, 18 (bis), 23; 15:1; II Cor. 2:12; 4:3, 4; 8:18; 9:13; 10:14; 11:4, 7; Gal. 1:6, 7, 11; 2:2, 5, 7, 14; Eph. 1:13; 3:6; 6:15, 19; Phil. 1:5, 7, 12, 16, 27 (bis); 2:22; 4:3, 15; Col. 1:5, 23; I Thess. 1:5; 2:2, 4, 8, 9; 3:2; II Thess. 1:8; 2:14; I Tim. 1:11; II Tim. 1:8, 10; 2:8; Philemon 13. In I Peter 4:17. In Rev. 14:6. (3) The noun *evangelistēs* is found: In Ac at Acts 21:8. In Paul at Eph. 4:11; II Tim. 4:5.

   List B — kērygma, kērussein, kērux: (1) The verb is found: In Mark 1:4, 7, 14, 38, 39, 45; 3:14; 5:20; 6:12; 7:36; 13:10; 14:9 (cf. ch. 16:15, 20). In Q at Luke 9:2 (Matt. 10:7); Luke 12:3 (Matt. 10:27). In L at Luke 3:3; 4:18, 19; 8:1; 24:47. In M at Matt. 4:17, 23; 9:35; 11:1; 24:14. In Ac at Acts 8:5; 9:20; 10:37, 42; 15:21; 19:13; 20:25; 28:31. In Paul at Rom. 2:21; 10:8, 14, 15; I Cor. 1:23; 9:27; 15:11, 12; II Cor. 1:19; 4:5; 11:4; Gal. 2:2; 5:11; Phil. 1:15; Col. 1:23; I Thess. 2:9; I Tim. 3:16; II Tim. 4:2. In I Peter 3:19. In Rev. 5:2. (2) The noun *kērygma* is found in Q at Luke 11:32 (Matt. 12:41). In Paul at Rom. 16:25; I Cor. 1:21; 2:4; 15:14; II Tim. 4:17; Titus 1:3. (3) The noun *kērux* is found in Paul at I Tim. 2:7; II Tim. 1:11. In II Peter 2:5. *List C — epangelia, epangellesthai, epangelma, proepangellesthai:* (1) The verb *epangellesthai* is found: In Mark 14:11. In Ac at Acts 7:5. In Paul at Rom. 4:21; Gal. 3:19; I Tim. 2:10; 6:21; Titus 1:2. In Heb. 6:13; 10:23; 11:11; 12:26. In James 1:12; 2:5. In II Peter 2:19. In John at I John 2:25. (2) The noun *epangelia* is found in L at Luke 24:49. In Ac at Acts 1:4; 2:33, 39; 7:17; 13:23, 32; 23:21; 26:6. In Paul at Rom. 4:13, 14, 16, 20; 9:4, 8, 9; 15:8; II Cor. 1:20; 7:1; Gal. 3:14, 16, 17, 18 (bis), 21, 22, 29; 4:23, 28; Eph. 1:13; 2:12; 3:6; 6:2; I Tim. 4:8; II Tim. 1:1. In Heb. 4:1; 6:12, 15, 17; 7:6; 8:6; 9:15; 10:36; 11:9 (bis), 13, 17, 33, 39. In II Peter 3:4, 9. In John at I John 2:25. (3) The noun *epangelma* is found in II Peter 1:4; 3:13. (4) The verb *proepangellesthai* is found in Paul at Rom. 1:12; II Cor. 9:5.

verb used is *evangelizesthai*.[7] Q also compares Jonah's preaching (*kērygma*) with that of Jesus at a critical period in God's dealings with men (Luke 11:32; Matt. 12:41), and represents Jesus as sending out his disciples to preach (*kērussein*) the Kingdom of God and to heal after his own manner, *word* and *work* thus supplementing each other in the proclamation of the new day (Luke 9:2; Matt. 10:7 and Luke 12:3; Matt. 10:27). Mark is equally decisive in his representation of Jesus as the one who heralds (*kērussein*) the dawn of the new age with the message, " The time is fulfilled, and the kingdom of God is at hand; repent, and believe in the gospel " (Mark 1:14 f.), and who announces that such preaching (*kērussein*) is his major function (ch. 1:38). Luke's special source (L) takes pains from the beginning of Jesus' ministry to indicate him as the Herald of the new day and the preacher of its gospel (Luke 4:18 ff.), employing in this connection both verbs (*evangelizesthai* and *kērussein*).[8] Matthew's special source (M) likewise introduces our Lord's ministry with the announcement that he went about in Galilee " preaching the gospel of the kingdom " (Matt. 4:23) in its synagogues.

Secondly, the use of the noun *evangelion* (gospel) also indicates the influence of the Second Isaiah upon the Synoptic tradition, though admittedly we have here more of a problem than that pertaining to the use of the verbs. Mark alone of the sources of the Synoptic Gospels uses this noun as on the lips of Jesus. Moreover, in three of the five cases involved, the other Gospels

[7] C. J. Cadoux (*The Historical Mission of Jesus*) rejected the clause, " The poor have the good tidings preached to them," in Matt. 11:5 because it is not found in k syr[sin] and Clem. But see T. W. Manson's *The Teaching of Jesus* (1935, Second Edition), p. 67, and C. F. Burney's *The Poetry of Our Lord* (1925), p. 117, both of whom argue that the passage is poetry reminiscent of Isa. 26:19; 29:18 f.; 35:5 f.; 61:1, and requires the clause to fill out the meter. Martin Dibelius also accepts its genuineness. Cf. his *The Message of Jesus Christ* (1939), pp. 25, 140, 143. He remarks, " The reply to the Baptist . . . shows . . . that for Jesus himself his healings were signs of the coming of the Kingdom of God " (p. 143), and suggests that of the entire saying we may be certain of " verbal accuracy " here (p. 140).

[8] L also employs *evangelizesthai* at Luke 8:1; 9:6, and *kērussein* at ch. 8:1 regarding the work of Jesus or of his disciples.

fail to place the noun on Jesus' lips. Mark on his own account in Mark 1:1,14 and Matthew's special source (M) in ch. 4:23; 9:35, also employ the noun in descriptive passages. It is found as well in Mark 16:15 in a spurious portion of the Gospel.

Friedrich dismisses the three passages in Mark (chs. 1:15; 8:35; 10:29) which fail to appear in the parallel Gospels as unauthentic, on the ground that they will not have been in Ur-Markus (the theoretical first draft of Mark's Gospel, now lost, to which some scholars subscribe), else they would have been found in one or other of Mark's colleagues of the Synoptic tradition. As for the other two passages in Mark in which the noun is found on Jesus' lips, Friedrich, following Bultmann here, objects to ch. 13:10 on the ground that it contains a reference to the Gentile mission of the Church. Similarly, he thinks ch. 14:9 to be suspect because vs. 8 and 9 in this passage do not present a unified thought when taken in conjunction with the preceding verses (vs. 3 ff.).

I am by no means convinced by Friedrich's arguments relative to these five Marcan sections. One had hoped that it was agreed that Canon B. H. Streeter had forever " laid the ghost " of the " phantom UrMarkus " by the patient and discriminating labor expended by him upon the relevant passages in his *Four Gospels* (1930, Fourth Edition).[9] His conclusion from this study has always appeared to me justified, viz., " If, therefore, the coincident agreements of Matthew and Luke can only be explained on the theory that they used a different edition of Mark from the one we have, then it is the earlier of the two editions, the UrMarkus in fact, that has survived "! (p. 305).

Again, it appears to me that the Marcan tradition as exhibited in these five passages is more likely than not to be authentic and so from our Lord's own lips, if for no other reason than that *they appear to reflect an early period when the gospel was still something that Jesus heralded rather than something that he was himself.* It is admitted on all hands that in the later Church the latter meaning attached to the word " gospel " and it seems inconceivable, therefore, that the five passages in Mark which

[9] Cf. chapter xi, pp. 293–331.

represent Jesus as merely the gospel's Herald, rather than its embodiment, should be the creation of that later Church.

The examination of the two verbs as used in the Synoptic tradition has pointed in the same direction, as we have already seen. It would appear, accordingly, that the Synoptic sources — through their use of both verbs and nouns — point to Jesus as having been the Herald of the Second Isaiah who through his preaching ushers in the new age. This identification has *Messianic* implications in the broad sense of that term. Whether Jesus himself ever saw this is a moot question at present. It is one which in the end cannot be overlooked and it does seem difficult to accept this Synoptic tradition, while at the same time rejecting its implications for Jesus' awareness of his function relative to the Kingdom of God.[10]

Be this as it may, we conclude from the foregoing evidence that in the sources lying behind the Synoptic tradition there is clear evidence for the recognition of the term " gospel " as an Old Testament one with a New Testament reference — that is, as referring to the coming of the new day which the Gospel writers and their contemporary friends recognized as having been fulfilled in their own experience. A diagram to illustrate the relationship of these sources with Second Isaiah would appear somewhat as follows:

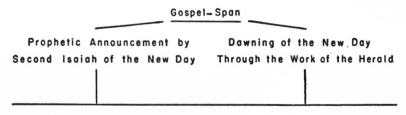

Gospel - Span

Prophetic Announcement by   Dawning of the New Day
Second Isaiah of the New Day   Through the Work of the Herald

[10] Cf. T. W. Manson's illuminating chapter on " The Messianic Herald " in his *The Servant-Messiah* (1953).

7. The 'Gospel' in the Stephen-Hebrews Tradition

WE TURN NOW to a consideration of the terms which we have been discussing as they are employed in The Epistle to the Hebrews. Of these terms this author uses the verb " to preach the gospel " (*evangelizesthai*) only, and that in but the two verses at ch. 4:2, 6 f., as follows:

'For *the gospel came to us* as it came to them; but the message heard by them did not profit them, for they were not united by faith with those who heard it.'

'Since therefore it remains that some are to enter it, and those who previously *received the gospel* (*were evangelized*) failed to enter because of disobedience, again he appoints a day, "Today," saying in David after so long a time, as already said, Today, if you hear his voice, harden not your hearts.'

The author takes his start here from Ps. 95:7–11, in which the admonition about Today occurs. The psalmist had spoken of God's unwillingness to put up with a " hardhearted " and " disbelieving " people (vs. 6 ff.; cf. Heb. 3:18 f.). Such would never enter into his " rest." That meant — as every Jew and every Christian conversant with the Septuagint would know — that no one lacking in faith would receive God's salvation (Greek *katapausis*, rest, ch. 3:11, and *Sabbatismos*, the equivalent of the Hebrew *shabbath* and also standing for rest, ch. 4:9). The occasion to which the psalm refers is that of the Exodus and the subsequent rebellion of Israel in the wilderness when they lacked sustenance (Heb. 4:8).

Appealing at once to this incident and the psalm above cited, The Epistle to the Hebrews suggests that *the gospel has been preached three times at least throughout Israel's history* — viz., at the Exodus (Heb. 4:2, 8); in the psalm itself (Heb. 4:6 f.); and in the early Christian period contemporary with its readers (vs. 2, 11). The argument proceeds on the assumption that, once a promise is given by God to his people, it cannot be withdrawn. God, by virtue of his nature as God, is bound to fulfill his promises. If, therefore, the immediate group or person to which a promise is uttered does not accept it or fails to measure up to the conditions required for its fulfillment, then it is left over, so to speak, for succeeding generations to accept (v. 6). Hence the second preaching of the gospel in the psalm, because it was not received by faith at the early preaching under Joshua (Heb. 3:12–19; 4:7 f.). Hence, also, the third preaching of that gospel in the early days of the Christian movement (ch. 4:2, 9–11).

There are those who object to this argument on the ground that the good news preached on these three occasions are not the same. But it is to be observed that such an objection arises out of the viewpoint of the twentieth century Christian or unbeliever. It overlooks the fact that Scripture does not so compartmentalize experience as we tend to do in the Occident today. To the mind of the prophetic realist of the Hebrew ethos, essentially the same saving purpose of God was revealed in God's promise to give his people a land flowing with milk and honey, to bless the " remnant " who through the preaching of the prophets should return to him, and to grant the redemption offered in Jesus Christ.[1] In principle these preachings of the gospel do, indeed, amount to the same thing, provided we consider life as one and God's redeeming purpose as embracing the whole of life and experience. When God saves, he saves man in every part of his being, therefore, and it is the part of the gospel to say as much. Such is the point of view of Scripture and such is the thesis of the theology of prophetic realism.

The treatment of his theme on the part of the author of Hebrews, accordingly, suggests the following diagram as illustrative of his treatment of the gospel and its threefold proclamation:

---

[1] Cf. the article on *epangello* in Kittel's Wörterbuch, II, p. 581, note 67. Here Schniewind and Friedrich cite H. Windisch and E. Riggenbach as holding that for The Epistle to the Hebrews " the Jews like the Christians have received a gospel. For the Jews the promises which now in Christ have come to fulfillment constitute a gospel, and the gospel of the N.T. is nothing save a resumption of the old promises. Both expressions have the same sense."

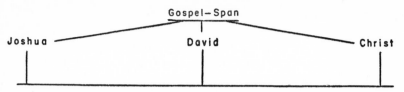

This theme of the giving of the promise and its remaining open for future generations to claim lies at the very heart of the teaching of Hebrews throughout. It recurs in and undergirds the argument of the great eleventh chapter as is specifically stated in vs. 39 f.:

"And all these, though well attested by their faith, did not receive what was promised, since God had foreseen something better for us, that apart from us they should not be made perfect."

The same idea is found as well in vs. 9, 13, 17, 33. Moreover, the necessity of one's maintaining one's original faith or commitment at a high level that the promises of God might be fulfilled in the case of any given generation (an obviously complementary thought to the former one), occurs like a refrain throughout the epistle (cf. chs. 6:12, 15; 10:36).

We have, then, in Hebrews, as in Paul, a sort of *gospel-span* forming for us a norm for a theology of history. The point in both writers is that God's ways with men may be observed in the period covered by this gospel yardstick and thereby we may discover how he will always deal with them for their salvation. And out of this discovery we may safely construct our theology of history, including therein God's purpose for history and the means whereby he accomplishes that purpose. The elements common to Hebrews and Paul in such a theology are: first, the promise given and the gospel fulfillment; [2] secondly, the stress upon faith as the *sine qua non* for receiving the promise in its gospel-fulfilled form; [3] thirdly, the suggestion that a promise once given by God remains open for future generations to receive.[4] It is instructive too to note that Paul employs the inci-

[2] For Paul, cf. Gal. 3:14, 16–18, 21 f., 29.

[3] For Paul, cf. Gal. 3:2, 7–9, 12, 14, 23–25, and for Heb., chs. 3:18 f., 4:2; 6:12; 10:22, 36, 39, with ch. 11 throughout.

[4] For Paul, cf. Rom. 3:3 f., with chs. 9 to 11 throughout.

dent of the wilderness wandering in I Cor. 10:1 ff. to point up his thesis of the danger of spiritual arrogance (*hybris*), as Hebrews also does in the passage before us. But, unlike the latter, Paul takes the sacraments of the cloud and the manna, rather than the preaching of the gospel, as the point of comparison between the old and the new experiences.[5]

The problem of the interdependence of Paul and Hebrews relative to this thesis of promise and gospel is somewhat obscure. Both are able to take in the entire sweep of the prophetic revelation as embracing the " gospel of God " as its message. But the two, nonetheless, go much their own ways as regards choice of a personnel from among the prophets to whom they apply the promise-gospel thesis. Indeed, the only persons whom they mention in common in this connection are: Abraham (Rom. 4:13 ff.; Gal. 3:8 ff.; Heb. 6:13; 11:8); Isaac (Rom. 9:7; Gal. 4:28; Heb. 11:18); Jacob (Rom. 9:13; Heb. 11:9, 20 f.); and Sarah (Rom. 9:9; Heb. 11:11). These form one group, of course, that is, the descendants of Abraham.

On the other hand, as a study of the above references in List C indicates, there is a far closer and more striking coordination to be observed between Stephen's speech in Acts, ch. 7, and Hebrews in this matter than between Paul and the latter. William Manson has recently pointed out the close approximation between the message of Stephen and the teaching of Hebrews as a whole, and on the basis of his examination of the two he comes to the striking conclusions that the writer of Hebrews was " an Alexandrian Jew who had received his institution in Christianity from the followers of Stephen " (p. 167), that this will explain the similarity in eschatological outlook and emphasis upon the world-mission of Christianity (pp. 36 ff.), and that Hebrews must be dated rather earlier than is usually supposed — viz., about A.D. 60 (pp. 162–167).[6]

Adopting these views of Manson as a working hypothesis, it is instructive to observe that in his speech in Acts, ch. 7, Stephen

---

[5] Cf. William Manson's *The Epistle to the Hebrews* (1951), p. 58.
[6] *Ibid.*, p. 36.

not only brings Abraham (vs. 2, 16 f.), Isaac (v. 8), and Jacob (vs. 8, 12, 14 f., 46) into the picture as recipients of the " promise " (v. 17), but also records the fact that Joshua and afterward David had a significant part to play in the matter of maintaining or finding a " habitation " or a " place " for God's " rest " (vs. 45 f.).[7]

It is true that there is a formal contrast between the themes of Stephen and Hebrews. Stephen speaks of God as one who can find no " rest " and who needs none, while for Hebrews God has acquired a " rest " from the Creation onward, a rest into which he would lead his people. But the underlying harmony between the two is no less certain. For, though Hebrews speaks of God's rest as a desirable thing for his people, it is to be won at a price — that, namely, of " going out " and following wherever God leads away from the old life. This is a sort of trumpet call in Hebrews " which Stephen's ear detected everywhere in the Old Testament record, and which for him was the keynote of God's whole calling of his people Israel," as Manson observes.[8] This trumpet call appears in Hebrews particularly in chs. 11 and 12, and in its author's call to God's people to " go . . . outside the camp " with Jesus (ch. 13:10–14).[9]

This same thought of the " divine call to the people of God being a call to ' go out ' " is expressed in Stephen's speech both in his suggestion that the time of the promise which God witnessed to Abraham was drawing nigh to fulfillment at the Exodus (Acts 7:17), and also by his emphasis on the tent or tabernacle rather than upon the Temple — that is, upon an impermanent and transitory abode as against a stable one (vs. 44–50). Again to quote Manson, " In its mobile character — so we may here fill out the interstices of the argument — the tent was a type or figure of God's never-ceasing, never-halted appointments for his people's salvation." [10] According to both great Christian leaders (Stephen and the author of Hebrews), therefore, God calls his people to follow in the way he leads for their

----

[7] *Ibid.*, p. 36.
[8] *Ibid.*, pp. 73 f.

[9] *Ibid.*, pp. 149–156.
[10] *Ibid.*, pp. 33 f.

salvation — a way that leads out from among the peoples of the world and into the deserts where God alone may supply the sustenance they require.

It is equally clear that for both the rest that God enjoys and to which he calls is one where " the Most High does not dwell in houses made with hands " (Acts 7:48), but rather above the heavens which are his throne and the earth which is his footstool (v. 49; Isa. 66:1 f.; cf. also Heb. 1:8–13). The same thought underlies the entire discussion of Hebrews about God's rest; for this is conceived first and last as from " the foundation of the world " (ch. 4:3) and apart from the six days consumed in creation and so " on the seventh day " (v. 4); here too the impermanent tabernacle is always in view, never the Temple (chs. 8:5; 9:1 ff.).

There is a further striking similarity between Stephen and Hebrews which Paul does not share. Unlike Paul, both the others make Egypt stand for every sort of worldly splendor that draws men away from God and both suggest that Moses was peculiarly tempted to succumb to that enticement. Stephen suggests as much in stressing Moses' becoming " instructed in all the wisdom of the Egyptians " (Acts 7:22). Moreover, in his recital of the singular rebuff which Moses received from his brethren when he endeavored to interpose on their behalf (vs. 23–35), and in their turning to Egypt in their hearts as indicated by Aaron's making the golden calf at their request (vs. 39–43), Stephen suggests that the secular glories of Egypt were always an enticement for God's people.

Hebrews has the same motif at chs. 3:16 ff.; 8:9, and particularly at 11:26 f., on which Manson remarks: " When Moses forsook the court of Egypt to cast his lot with his Hebrew brethren, the writer declares that he thereby chose the reproach of ' the Christ ' (vs. 25, 26), and this . . . not in a merely analogical but in a real sense. The Christ, the preincarnate Son of God, was actually, though invisibly, an agent and participant in the redemption effected for Israel at the Exodus, and Moses by his decision of faith was sharing in the Saviour's passion." [11]

[11] *Ibid.*, pp. 184 f.

It is quite likely, in view of the foregoing evidence, that Paul and the author of Hebrews have independently arrived at the conclusion that in the promise-gospel nexus is to be observed a sort of gospel-span from prophet to Christ whereby as a norm the purpose of God for man's salvation may be gauged. It is, one imagines, equally likely that Manson is right in seeing a close connection between the thought of Stephen and Hebrews and that Stephen, rather than Paul, is the mentor of the author of Hebrews.[12] An alternative suggestion would be that behind all three (Paul, Stephen, and Hebrews) lies a common heritage in the primitive tradition relative to the gospel content of the prophetic teaching of the Old Testament, and that in drawing upon that heritage Stephen and Hebrews are closer to one another in their interests than either is to Paul.

8. *The Herald-Christology and the Other Traditions*

IT REMAINS to inquire whether there is any observable correlation between the use of the terms studied in the Synoptic tradition, on the one hand, and in either the Pauline or Stephen-Hebrews tradition, on the other. The answer all round appears to be an almost certain negative. The evidence appears to suggest general independence between these streams of contemporary early Christian teaching.

In the first place, the terms " promise " and " to promise " occur but twice in the Synoptic Gospels — once in Luke's special source (L) at Luke 24:49, where the promise refers not to the gospel per se but to the coming of the Spirit (cf. Acts 1:4; 2:33, 39) ; and a second time in Mark 14:11, where the reference has no connection whatever with the problem of interest here. The only other instances of promise (both noun and verb) in Acts are found either in Stephen's speech, ch. 7:5, 17,

[12] Oscar Cullmann appears to note the similarity between Stephen and Paul but to ignore that between the former and Hebrews; cf. his *Christ and Time* (1950), pp. 90, 110, 118.

or else in the reported preaching of Paul (chs. 13:23, 32; 23:21; 26:6). Obviously, then, the two traditions found in Paul and Stephen-Hebrews have in no general way influenced the Synoptic tradition here. It is true, however, that the thought of the promise of the Spirit occurs at Gal. 3:14 and there may, therefore, be some genuine connection at this point between the Luke-Acts and Pauline traditions, but at all events the thought has not worked itself into the fabric of the gospel tradition.

Again, in the matter of the Herald of Second Isaiah and the adoption of this line of thought by the sources of the Synoptic Gospels, there appears to be no certain connection with either of the other two traditions. Reference to Lists A and B with which we have been working shows that at Rom. 10:15 and Eph. 2:17; 6:15, indeed, Paul does associate the preaching of the gospel with one of the Second Isaiah passages (that in Isa. 52:7). But in the Romans reference the introduction of Second Isaiah is almost casual; it comes as a part of Paul's argument that Israel has had an opportunity to hear the gospel and so to receive or reject it, and there is no suggestion whatever that the herald is Jesus. On the contrary, the plural is employed (heralds — *evangelizomenōn*) and the reference in Paul's thought will be rather to the prophets as the preachers intended.[1]

This leaves only the two Ephesians passages as possible support for a suggestion that the Synoptic tradition as to the herald of the gospel stems from Paul. And one may assume, I think, that such evidence will scarcely be pressed by anyone who is aware of the present uncertainty attaching to the Pauline authorship of this epistle. Even though it be conceded that Paul wrote Ephesians — as I am prepared to do — yet it is evident that the thought of our Lord as the herald of the gospel did not enter deeply into the matrix of the apostle's thought. And to suggest that the Synoptic tradition which makes so much of the idea stems from such a slight reference in a disputed epistle,

[1] The statement of C. H. Dodd made in the wider context of the Synoptic problem as a whole may be applied here: " Pauline influence upon the Synoptic Gospels is often alleged, but the evidence for it amounts to very little "; cf. his *The Parables of the Kingdom* (1936, Third Edition), p. 77, note 2.

while at the same time that same tradition ignores completely the genuine Pauline emphasis upon the promise-gospel nexus connecting Abraham with Christ, is unthinkable.

The above-noted cleavage between the three traditions is the more remarkable when one recalls the great stress placed by both the Stephen-Hebrews and Pauline thought upon the eschatological element in the gospel.[2] One might have expected to find in both these traditions, accordingly, the Herald of the New Age standing in the very forefront of their teachings. Possibly the explanation is that for Paul, Jesus is above all else the crucified and risen Redeemer and Lord, while for the Stephen-Hebrews tradition he is the great High Priest by whom the true worship of God is carried through and men are brought nigh to God thereby. Be this as it may, the point seems clear that in the matter of the gospel and its proclamation the Synoptic Gospels have attached themselves to a late stratum and therefore to the very pinnacle of the prophetic teaching in interpreting Jesus' person and work in the manner of the Second Isaiah's herald, whereas both Stephen-Hebrews and Paul look rather to the over-all prophetic teaching about the gospel, finding in that message a gospel-span that takes us back into the patriarchal period and to Abraham and his descendants.

In all three traditions, however, it is to be observed that *the gospel has become the central theme of the prophetic message as understood by the New Testament Church.* No doubt this could be seen most clearly only in the afterglow of the tremendous events of the fourth decade of the first century. The Hebrew prophets in their day lacked the necessary perspective from which to observe the entire sweep of revelation from Abraham to Jesus Christ. Yet, as we observed at the beginning of this section of the book, they were early aware of God's redemptive purpose for mankind. Perhaps the Stephen-Hebrews line of thought most nearly approximates their view. For here as with them the promise of entrance into the Promised Land under Joshua furnishes a good example of the redemptive activity of God as a whole. This sort of promise may appear to us a

[2] Cf. William Manson, *op. cit.*, pp. 184, 187.

very materialistic conception of the nature of God's saving purpose. But their thought was that the God who saves in one aspect of man's life eventually will save in every aspect of the same, and surely the gospel in which Christians believe today can be no less inclusive in its view of the universality of God's redemptive purpose.

But it was only, so to speak, piecemeal that the prophets received and knew the divine Word which came to them to deliver to the fathers in their time (Heb. 1:1). Looking backward from the standpoint of the ministry and work of Jesus Christ and his Spirit, the Church should be in a better position to observe that the gospel embraces the totality of Scripture's teaching regarding God's relation to man. At all events our study has made plain that such is the thought and teaching of the three strands of tradition found in the New Testament Scriptures. Those Scriptures, accordingly, present us with the positive claim that gospel, and not law as the Pharisees taught, is the major theme of the prophetic revelation throughout.

THE THEME OF SCRIPTURE'S
PROPHETIC REALISM

B. God's Purpose in History

" Then God said, Let us make man
in our image, after our likeness:
and let them have dominion . . ."
— GENESIS 1:26.

The Theme of Scripture's Prophetic Realism

B. God's Purpose in History

SYNOPSIS

THE GOSPEL-SPAN, whose nature was developed in the last section as normative for God's dealings with men on the plane of history, is in this one applied to the entire sweep of history with a view to discovering his universal purpose. Paul is quoted in Rom. 8:19 ff. with a view to showing that the prophetic realism of the Scriptures claims the gospel to have such universal application as is here proposed.

In developing the argument it is shown: first, *that God, the* Creator, according to the Scriptures prepares a stage (creation), *upon which his historic purpose may be consummated; he is God-behind-nature, inasmuch as it is he who is responsible for all that is, and also God-before-nature, in the sense that nature is made to serve his ultimate will;* secondly, *that as God-in-*history he now proceeds to work on the stage *which he has made, bringing with himself another who acts with him, viz., man;* thirdly, *that activity on the stage of creation is* ex hypothesi *both* purposeful and actual, *i.e., motivated toward a goal and serious about accepting the value of what is done within history;* fourthly, *that a real distinction exists between general history and redemptive history, the latter being the sum total of God's acts in working out his redemptive purpose relative to man;* fifthly, *that Jesus Christ is the supreme divine act in the redemp-*tive history line, the *imago Dei, the exemplar of what God would have man become, and so the focal point of all history both before and after.*

9. *God, the Creator, Prepares a Stage*

I N THE LAST CHAPTER it was remarked that the Hebrew prophets were at a disadvantage in possessing a knowledge of
the promise only, while lacking entirely that of its fulfillment
in Jesus Christ. It must now be said that the Christian Church
is in a growingly disadvantageous position of an exactly opposite kind. If the Hebrew prophets perforce looked forward to
fulfillment, we likewise are compelled to glance backward at it.

Jesus Christ, as Cullmann has remarked,[1] was somewhere near
the " mid-point " in history, not at its end. There is a real sense
in which this is true, not only in a normative but also in a
chronological way. Only the favored few who stood at the foot
of the cross and who were at the empty tomb were, so to speak,
privileged to take their stance beneath the keystone of history's
arch and to look equally in both directions — to see both beginning and end in the light of the " fact of Christ." These, it
is true, signally failed to pierce the mists extending in either
direction, relying as they did at the moment on their own initiative and powers of insight. It was not until the Holy Spirit came
upon them — that same Spirit which spoke to the Hebrew
prophets before them and which speaks to us today — that the
requisite insight into the meaning of the central events of history became theirs.

We of the Christian centuries have a certain vantage point, it
is true, from which we are able to look back and see the arch

---

[1] Oscar Cullmann, *Christ and Time* (1950), pp. 81 ff.

of history's farther quadrant — that is to say, the entire period
of the promise. Then, too, a knowledge of the keystone of fulfillment in Jesus Christ is ours also. And we have the further advantage of knowing that portion of the nearer quadrant extending from the arch's center to the point of history at which we
stand. But actually as regards insight into the gospel and the
meaning of Jesus Christ for the life of man, there is no real advantage accruing to anyone by reason of the particular spot
which one occupies within history. Discernment comes, not by
reason of advantage of place or time, but rather — as both
Scripture and experience testify — by the Spirit of the living
God and by man's responding faith.

   " We walk by faith, not by sight " (II Cor. 5:7) . Even today
we must " see " even as Abraham saw, of whom the Johannine
Christ remarks, " Abraham rejoiced that he was to see my day;
he saw it and was glad " (John 8:56) . At the present moment it
happens that we are about equidistant with Abraham from the
historic Jesus of Nazareth, he on one side of history's archway
and we on the other! Abraham had knowledge of a very little
segment of the promise quadrant of that arch, whereas we appear to be much advantaged in knowing both that and a large
part of the gospel quadrant as well. But that this impression is
illusory is seen in the mists which now gather about the keystone at the arch's center — mists that appear to be growing as
thick for us as those through which Abraham had to gaze. Witness the preceding chapters of this book. But for these mists
their involved argument employing the various arts of literary
and historical criticism would have been quite unnecessary.

   It is quite wrong, therefore, to assume that it will become
increasingly easy to write a Christian theology. There is genuine
danger rather — danger already clearly apparent in certain
quarters to judge by its fruitage — that as the centuries take us
away from the keystone at the center of our faith it will become
harder to write one. Only the theology of prophetic realism
found in Scripture — theology, that is to say, possessing by faith
the insight into God's dealings with men throughout the normative gospel-span from Abraham to Jesus Christ — will ever

be really possible. This the ravages of time cannot efface, for it is grounded upon faith's apprehension of the significance of that gospel-span for the life of mankind generally.

In the present section, accordingly, we shall endeavor to apply the yardstick of this theology's gospel-span to the facts of crea-

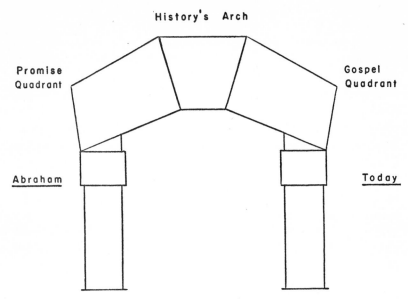

Diagram Showing History's Arch

tion and history as a whole, with a view to discovering the God-intended significance of them. As we have seen, the story of God's dealings with men from Abraham to Jesus Christ includes his purpose to save all mankind through the choice and educating of a particular people to become the medium of accomplishing that purpose. Is this simple gospel sufficiently comprehensive to serve as a norm for evaluating all God's activity in his universe? Is it possible that the prophetic gospel is somehow related alike to the farthest star and to the lowly slave, to the amoeba and to Pharaoh, to the cave man with his celt and to twentieth century man with his atomic fission? Such is the quite astonishing claim of this prophetic theology for its gospel and that gospel's yardstick!

" For the creation," writes the apostle Paul, " waits with eager longing for the revealing of the sons of God . . . because the creation itself will be set free from its bondage to decay and obtain the glorious liberty of the children of God " (Rom. 8:19 ff.). That is to say, every created being, so to speak, is seen standing on the curbstone of the universe's " main street," the while there passes by a great parade. It is the " March of Time " and in this parade are all the events of history depicted in the form of pageants. Those that stand on the curbstone watching this procession include all created beings — the stars and planets, the mineral and vegetable and animal kingdoms, together with all men, great and small, rich and poor, learned and unlearned, the kings and the outcasts of mankind. All are present and all are watching breathlessly for the last pageant of this great display, the appearing of the " sons of God." This interest on all creation's part, says the apostle, is because all God's creatures are to share in the blessings of the salvation to be granted these " sons." In other words, God's plan of salvation as formulated in the gospel is of cosmos-wide significance. It is our present purpose, therefore, to indicate how Scripture's prophetic realism endeavors to set forth this cosmic reference of the gospel.

God, the Creator, Prepares a Stage

The prophetic Scriptures open with a glimpse of God at work. He is creating a universe. " In the beginning God created the heavens and the earth." For the Hebrew prophets there was a beginning, as presumably there will also be an end. God, accordingly, is at once God-behind-nature and God-before-nature. " For from him and through him and to him are all things " (Rom. 11:36) — these words of Paul form a convenient summary of the prophetic view on this topic in all ages.

That view assumes and even specifically states that God is a person, in the sense that he is an intelligent, moral will, planning and achieving meaningful ends through the proper coordination of might and right (Gen. 1:1 ff.). God is neither that *chance concatenation of events which brought cosmos out of chaos by accident* — which, to judge by much that is said or remains unsaid, appears to be the view of some shallow moderns; nor is he *the primal stuff* out of which emerged a series of spontaneous emanations — the view of the older and more profound Gnostics and Neoplatonists. The God of Scripture is different from both of these. He is a knowing, purposing, personal Being who creates all things through his unlimited powers and to serve good ends. " And God saw that it was good " (Gen. 1:4, 10, 12, etc.) .

It is not specifically stated, as the Church of a later age under the dominance of Greek philosophy has averred, that this was a *creatio ex nihilo.* Nor is this expressly denied. Such speculation is far too philosophical for the Hebrew prophets. It is enough to note, as Driver remarks, that the Hebrew verb here *(bārā)* " in the simple conjugation . . . is used exclusively of God, to denote . . . the production of something fundamentally new, by the exercise of a sovereign originative power, altogether transcending that possessed by man." [2] The emphasis of the prophetic narrative in the creation story is upon God, upon his goodness and power, and upon his creative activity, rather than upon the nature of the stuff upon which he works and the exact manner of its coming into *being* or whether it was ever *not-being!* These latter are metaphysical considerations and the Hebrew prophets were not metaphysicians. Their interests were rather theological, religious, ethical, even practical.

The Scriptures, therefore, claim it to be possible for man to discern God at work behind the created universe. Paul even goes so far as to suggest that men are to be judged because of their failure to discern His " eternal power and deity " (Rom. 1:20) , through his activity in the world, and to give him glory therefor. Nonetheless, the prophetic theology leaves no room for imagining that inanimate nature as such exhibits the divine *purpose* in creating. " God saw that it was good " — such is the highest meed of praise accorded nature anywhere in the prophetic Scriptures. Nature, when left to itself, conforms to the

[2] S. R. Driver, *The Book of Genesis* (1948, Fifteenth Edition) , *in loc.*

divine will and to the divine plan — of this there can be no doubt. But of the character of that will or plan, nature can give no hint.

It is only when man comes onto the scene of nature that meaning begins to appear. Such is the prophetic teaching, for example, in a passage like Gen. 1:26: " Then God said, ' Let us make man in our image, after our likeness; and let them have dominion over the fish . . . the birds . . . the cattle, and over all the earth.' " With the appearance of man in God's world the divine motivation relative to the whole begins to make itself evident. God wants a mirror of himself in his sovereign majesty, a mirror that will properly portray him as exercising his might in righteousness. Only man, and not nature, can become that mirror.

Creation, then, is but a stage, the scene of God's purposeful activity. He makes it to serve this end and no other. All its component parts, with the single exception of man, are the *stage props* which form the background against which God's active will works itself out to a consummation. There can be no doubt that in the thought of the Hebrew prophets the universe which God makes is necessary to him in the sense that without it he could not accomplish his moral purpose. Whatever that purpose be, he could never have brought it to fruition without a stage for his activities. But this is not to say that the universe, after its creation, turns round, so to speak, and imposes a limitation upon God or his active working out of his will. Nor is God dependent upon his universe as it is upon him. Else it would be as truly God as the Creator himself! God to the end remains transcendent, sovereign Lord over all his creatures. This is the unspoken, but frequently implied, assumption of the Scriptures. It is at all times implicit in their declarations of God's majesty and holiness.

That God can do with his universe whatever his righteous will dictates is also an assumption everywhere in the prophetic writings. God's universe never, so to speak, is allowed to get out of hand. On the contrary, any limitation upon his might or authority is first and last self-imposed for his own holy purposes.

" The earth is the Lord's and the fullness thereof,
The world and they that dwell therein " (Ps. 24: 1) .

" Who then is he that can stand before me?
Who hath first given unto me, that I should repay him?
Whatsoever is under the whole heaven is mine " (Job 41:10 f.) .

" Shall the thing formed say to him that formed it,
Why didst thou make me thus?
Or hath not the potter a right over the clay, from the same lump
to make one part a vessel unto honor, and another unto dis-
honor? " (Rom. 9:20 f., A.S.V.) .[3]

This implication of God's entire independence of his created
world is first and last the teaching of the prophetic Scriptures
throughout. God never surrenders his Lordship for any cause.
He does, however, limit his exercise of the same to serve his own
ends. Such is the teaching, not alone of Scripture, but of all
Jewish and Christian literature springing from it.[4]

God's beneficent care is over all this stage of his creation. He
tends its flowers and birds as a Master Gardener (Matt. 6:26–
30), and its animal life generally as a Master Shepherd (Ps.
50:10 f.; cf. Ps. 104 as a whole, particularly vs. 16–30) .

But creation's stage is in no sense an end in itself. Nor did
God make it for its own sake. Else there would be no talk of its
subjection (Gen. 1:26). Nor would there be mention of man
as alone of all creation being made in the divine image. Man is
obviously made the pinnacle of all creation. All else is made for
his sake and, therefore, over all he is given authority that he
may bend it to his purposes. And yet — not alone for his own
sake nor yet for his own purposes! For man is himself but *the
reflection of God,* and the reflection must always bow to and
serve that which is primary. Man, therefore, who alone possesses
the " image of God " stamped upon his brow, is the under-
gardener and the undershepherd appointed to act as God's viceroy in exerting dominion over His universe and to mediate to it
His beneficent rule.

[3] Cf. also Ex. 19:5; Deut. 10:14; Job 9:5–10; 26:6–14; Ps. 50:12; Jer.
18:6; *et al.*
[4] Cf. George Foot Moore's *Judaism,* vol. i, pp. 379 f. (1927) .

10. *God at Work on Creation's Stage*

IN THE LAST CHAPTER we noted that God is behind and before nature as nature's Creator and as One who sets before
it the goal of his own devising for its achievement. But God is
not only behind and before nature. He is also God-in-history
and God-before-history and God-behind-history.

He is God-*in*-history: he is *not* God-*in*-nature. This latter is
sometimes affirmatively stated and it is thereby meant that God
is immanent in his world. But God's immanence is an immanence in history, not in nature. That is to say, God is present in
the purposeful activity that proceeds upon the stage of creation
and not in the stage itself. The latter sort of immanence has no
meaning whatever except for a pantheistic philosophy. If God
were in his creation, he would be a part of it — a *deus ex
machina,* mixed up in the cogs of his own making! The typical
prophetic attitude toward this subject appears in the account of
Elijah's experience of Yahweh at Mount Horeb. There Yahweh
was found to be "not in the wind . . . not in the earthquake
. . . not in the fire," but rather in the "still small voice" of
revelation (I Kings 19:11 f.).

God, then, is present *in* history. By this one means that his
moral person is found exerting power and accomplishing his
purposes, just as other moral persons are seen to do within history. And when one says so, one means by history not a mere
succession of events. For this we reserve the word "occurrences," and for their narrating, "chronology." History per
contra is the same series plus the declaration that they have
meaning, that they are in some sort of cause and effect nexus
which exhibits a rational will, that they represent at least a
limited or relative motivation and serve at least mediate ends.
Thus, a history of the English people is an account of the events
associated with the establishment and ongoing development of
the English culture and its institutions, assuming that the historian senses and tries to display the inner logic and hidden mo-

tivations that have been responsible for this development.

C. H. Dodd has said this so well that we shall quote his words at some length:

"History in the full sense consists of events which possess not merely a private but a public interest, and a meaning which is related to broad and permanent concerns of human society. . . . Historical writing differs . . . not in the fullness or precision with which it records occurrences, but in the clarity with which the record brings out the meaning of events. We might indeed say that a historical 'event' is an occurrence *plus* the interest and meaning which the occurrence possessed for the persons involved in it, and by which the record is determined." [1]

Scripture's prophetic realism would add to Dodd's definition that in the Scriptures we have *the " plus" that history has for God,* rather than for man or for any other of God's creatures.

It is God, then, who is behind history's meaning, who through its meaningful events is working out his will of which the prophets speak. A good example of this viewpoint of the Hebrew prophet is to be seen in the conversation between God and Moses at the burning bush in Midian (Ex., ch. 3). When Moses asked God his " name," he was asking God to communicate to him a complete theology in a moment of time, or, if you prefer, to grant him a complete revelation of himself in the course of a single conversation! For the Semite the name always stands for the person and serves as an index to that person's entire character. This fact is illustrated, as is too well known to require demonstration, throughout the pages of the Old Testament, and in the New Testament it is seen in such names as Peter (Matt. 16:18), Boanerges (Mark 3:17), Barnabas (Acts 4:36), and the like — the generally accepted meaning of each name being supplied in the references indicated.

Accordingly, God's answer to Moses in this place — " I am

---

[1] Cf. his *History and the Gospel,* pp. 26 f. Charles Scribner's Sons, 1938. The current literature on the meaning of history is voluminous; one may refer here with appreciation to Herbert Butterfield's *Christianity and History* (1949), Oscar Cullmann's *Christ and Time* (1950), E. H. Harbison's *Religious Perspectives of College Teaching — in History* (1950), and John Marsh's *The Fullness of Time* (1952).

that I am," or probably better, ' I will be that I will be ' — represents a thoroughgoing denial of Moses' request. God will not reveal himself and his character in a moment of time to any man. Rather he will make himself known to his people through the years and by means of an ever richer fellowship. Throughout their history they shall come to know him as he is.

Moreover, a start has already been made, it is suggested. For, as God goes on to observe, he is none other than " The Lord, the God of your fathers, the God of Abraham, of Isaac, and of Jacob " (Ex. 3:16). To the Israelite this could mean nothing other than that Yahweh is that God who gave the promises to the patriarchs and who, through fulfilling them, was at once proving himself to be a faithful God and at the same time working out his purposes on history's plane.

In further illustration of this point, it should be noted that God's name significantly changes after each eventful redemptive act of his performing. This is particularly striking in connection with the Exodus from Egypt and the event of the incarnation. After the former of these, God's new name is declared to be — ' Yahweh thy God, who-brought-thee-out-of-the-land-of-Egypt, out-of-the-house-of-bondage ' (Ex. 20:2),[2] a name that rings like a refrain throughout much of the Pentateuch and elsewhere. His name is also " God of Hosts," signifying that on the stage of nature and within history he is performing his righteous will with mighty power, the power of a host of troops. George Adam Smith, contrasting Amos 4:13 with ch. 5:27, in both of which passages this descriptive phrase is used of God, remarks that " as there [i.e., in ch. 4] His hosts were the movements of nature and the great stars, so here [in ch. 5] they are the nations of the world. By his rule of both he is the God of Hosts." [3] Above all in the Jewish Gospel of Matthew the incarnate Lord takes the name " Immanuel, God with us " (ch. 1:23) or " Jesus " (i.e., salvation — ch. 1:21), both names being indicative of the fact that in Jesus Christ God is entering history as man's Redeemer.

[2] Cf. also Deut. 5:6; 6:12; 8:14; 13:5, 10; Josh. 24:17; Judg. 6:8.
[3] Cf. G. A. Smith's *The Book of the Twelve Prophets,* vol. i, p. 173; see also Jer. 46:18; 48:15; Isa. 47:4.

As God proceeds to work out his will in history, a characteristic way employed by the Hebrew prophets of adverting to his activity is found in the two clauses, " My name shall be there " and " God put his name there." [4] The first occurrence of this is to be found in Ex. 20:24 (the Book of the Covenant). Here, as Driver suggests, " In every place where I will cause my name to be remembered " means, " In consequence of some manifestation of my presence." [5] Commenting further on passages that associate the divine name with the sanctuary at Jerusalem, this writer remarks, " The sanctuary is the place of Jehovah's ' name,' because he there vouchsafes the special tokens of his presence and graciously responds to his servants' devotions." [6] That is to say, God's name is himself in the prophetic vocabulary; wherever his name is known, this is because at that place the living God has made himself felt in the affairs of men and especially of his people.

The characteristic prophetic way of praising God takes its rise from the same series of ideas with which we are here dealing. This is to run through a catalogue of his redemptive acts throughout history. Thus, according to Deuteronomy, Moses does this in song toward the close of his long career. He opens his recital of the outstanding acts of Yahweh with the words " I will proclaim the name of Yahweh: Ascribe ye greatness unto our God " (ch. 32:3 ff. in the A.S.V.). The like account of Yahweh's marvelous works which show him to be God-in-history is found in numerous psalms (cf. Ps. 105; 106; 107; 135; 136, for example), and in Ps. 75:1 the principle is enunciated:

> " We give thanks unto thee, O God;
> We give thanks, for thy name is near:
> Men tell of thy wondrous works."

The Oriental potentate sitting aloof from his subjects in lofty splendor and accomplishing his will through his agents or slaves,

[4] Cf. Deut. 12:5, 11; 14:23 f.; 16:2, 6, 11; 26:2; I Kings 8:29; 9:3; 11:36; II Kings 21:4, 7.

[5] Cf. S. R. Driver, *A Critical and Exegetical Commentary on Deuteronomy* (1895), *in loc.*

[6] *Ibid.*

therefore, bears no remote resemblance to this living God-who-
acts-within-history of the prophetic Scriptures. The transcendence of the God of the Bible is one of moral stature, not of aloof-
ness from his world. This God is ever willing and eager to share
in the affairs of men for their betterment, and it is his actually
doing so that constitutes the Bible's so-called " plan of salvation."

History's Aspects of Purposefulness and Actuality

It has already been remarked that creation is a mere stage and
that history is the action upon that stage. Now, it is only in the
action that purpose is to be discovered, above all else the divine
purpose. Such purpose is exhibited only by the actors on the
stage, by God and man. Professor Butterfield, while not losing
sight of the ultimate part played by God in history, defines it
after this fashion: " History," he says, " is a human drama, a
drama of personalities, taking place as it were, on the stage of
nature, amid its imposing scenery." [7] This is well said but for
the fact that as a definition of history it leaves out the principal
actor, God — a mistake that, however, Butterfield never really
makes. Man alone of all God's creatures may share in history's
drama, because he only can observe the meaning of events and
so actually play a part in them. Man alone is able to sense com-
parative *values* residing in events, in institutions, in other persons, in abstractions. Man only is capable of working for recognizable goals and seeing purpose in life.

All this is said from what one conceives both to have been
the prophetic point of view in Israel and to be the normative
prophetic view at all times. It is the *first* aspect of history which
the prophets of all time have stressed, the moral aspect — by
which we mean that history exhibits design, planning by a holy
will to attain recognizable good goals. It is possible to illustrate
this by showing that creation by contrast, when left to its own
devices, neither is moral nor does it exhibit purpose.

Creation is able to attain to purposefulness, to meaningfulness, and so to some sort of moral status only as it serves as the

[7] *Op. cit.,* p. 7.

stage for God's and man's activities. It is only thus that it succeeds in securing a footing relative to the moral interests of God or of man or of both together. Paul makes much of this point in the eighth chapter of Romans, where he is speaking of creation's awaiting anxiously its deliverance from the ' bondage of corruption ' (v. 21) and from " futility " (v. 20) . And he quite aptly remarks that the " futility " and the " corruption " are in no way due to creation's own will (v. 20) , for of itself it can have none, nor can it serve any voluntary purpose of its own conceiving. But he goes on to state — what is relevant to our thought here — that creation's " deliverance," its salvation so to speak, is dependent upon " the revealing of the sons of God " (v. 19) , that is, upon attaining a status relative to man and so to moral purposiveness.

Examples of the chaotic futility which is creation's present lot and of the manner of its deliverance from it are all about one. It is the archaeologist's spade that in the past several generations has turned up the evidence for us to make a judgment regarding this condition of the inanimate universe. One illustration that has recently come to our attention concerns the city of Phoenix, Arizona. That city derives its name from the mythical bird which, according to the Greek and Egyptian legend, lived for five hundred years, then perished in flames produced by its own act, and thereafter rose alive from its own ashes. The city of Phoenix received this name because in 1867, at its birth, men digging for a canal project upon its future site unearthed a prehistoric Indian village to which was given the name of Pueblo Grande. Like the legendary bird, therefore, the new city rose upon the site of the older village.

The more remarkable and pertinent fact that emerged, however, was that the Indian village had been itself the center of a canal project by which primitive man had converted the desert into a garden of Eden! Twice over, therefore, by man's industry the earth at Phoenix had been made a paradise, while in the intervening centuries through man's profligacy, or perhaps even by reason of his innate cruelty against his fellow man, the garden had gone back to the desert. Thus had this spot of God's creation-stage been subjected to futility by man.[8]

The like incident, of course, has occurred times without number in the history of the rise and fall of civilizations. Numerous examples are to be found in the sand mounds which cover the cities of the Levant, the Mesopotamian valleys, and the valley of the Indus in Sind (modern Pakistan). Harappa in the latter area represents the superimposition of six cities one upon another, each rising from the ashes of the previous one through the course of centuries, while Mohenjo-Daro in the same region probably had nine cities built each upon the ruins of the last during the period of its occupancy.[9]

Professor Stuart Piggot, writing of the nature and final end of this great civilization (which incidentally the present writer has been privileged to examine at first hand), says, "There is a terrible efficiency about the Harappa civilization which recalls all the worst of Rome, but with this elaborately contrived system goes an isolation and a stagnation hard to parallel in any known civilization of the Old World."[10] Sometime about 1500 B.C., he continues, "the long-established cultural traditions of northwestern India were rudely and ruthlessly interrupted by the arrival of new people from the West," the result being the "sack of the ancient cities by the outer barbarians" and the end of civilization in those parts.[11] And the point is that, from the time of the destruction of the Indus Valley culture down to the early decades of the twentieth century (when the then-British Government in the province concerned put through several magnificent canal projects which literally made the desert blossom as the rose, as I can personally bear testimony), the entire district had lain in futile sterility. These cities in consequence, piled high with the drifting sands, have been preserved to the present day quite untouched, their former culture entirely intact and without the superimposition of later cultures, in a sort of natural museum of nature's devising!

[8] I am indebted to Rev. Herbert B. Smith, Jr., for this illustration.
[9] Cf. *Prehistoric India* (1950), by Stuart Piggot, p. 140.
[10] *Ibid.*, p. 138.
[11] *Ibid.*, pp. 238 f.

Arnold Toynbee gives numerous illustrations of such futility caused to creation by man's stupidity, vice, or general degeneracy. He cites, for example, the " abandonment of the Roman roads in western Europe " as an example of decline consequent on " the society which required them . . . [having] gone to pieces." [12] Similarly in the seventh and thirteenth centuries respectively, the partial lack of reconditioning and final abandonment of the irrigation system in the Tigris-Euphrates valley — a system that had been functioning for some four thousand years — was due, he declares, to " social causes," namely, to the overrunning of the Syrian Christian civilization by the Moslem Arabs in the former century and to " the Mongol invasion of A.D. 1258 which dealt the Syriac society its *coup de grâce* " in the latter.[13]

Robert Fitch has much the same to say of the dissipation of the might that was Rome's in his *The Kingdom Without End* (1950). In view of the forceful nature of his writing it will be worth our while to quote from him at length:

" If eventually the Roman power declined, then it was not because of the operation of some mysterious law of cycles, or because of some purely material factor which was suddenly too much for the Roman virtue. It was not because her economy automatically disintegrated; nor because her communications fell of themselves into disrepair; nor because the barbarians were later of a stouter valor than had been vanquished by the first legions. It was because Rome, now drunk with power and softened by prosperity, cared no longer to maintain the benefits she had given to the world, but cared only for the luxuries and the perquisites of her position. When the Roman passion for righteousness disappeared — the passion for law and for equity and for self-discipline — then Roman might disappeared." [14]

Creation, then, is proved both in the prophetic theology and in man's experience to be merely an inert stage upon which either God and man act to achieve harmonious and purposeful (i.e., moral) ends or else by their failure to do so permit the stage

---

[12] Cf. Arnold J. Toynbee's *A Study of History* (1947), p. 256.

[13] *Ibid.,* pp. 256 f.

[14] P. 34.

itself to degenerate in frustration and a futile round of idiotic activity leading nowhere.

By contrast with this inability of creation of itself to exhibit purposefulness, it is easy to show from the prophetic Scriptures that man's activity in history is intended in God's plan to be characterized by such. The story of the Fall in Gen., ch. 3, is essentially the story of God's granting to man the privilege and responsibility of such purposeful activity and of man's failure to measure up to God's purpose in the matter.

Amos, so far as our records go, was the first prophet to discern God's universal interest in and demand upon man's obedience. Accordingly, he sees in the movement of the nations — of " the Philistines from Caphtor and the Syrians from Kir," as well as of Israel " from the land of Egypt " (Amos 9:7) — the purpose of God. These movements were the result of God's " call " to the peoples concerned to " come forth " to a new Land of Promise of his bestowing. In line with the privilege so entailed, these nations have as well a certain responsibility to obey God's commands at every point, and so Amos believes himself charged with a word from God equally for Philistia (ch. 1:6–8), for Phoenicia (ch. 1:9 f.), for Edom (vs. 11 f.), for Ammon (vs. 13 f.), for Moab (ch. 2:1–3), as for Judah (ch. 2) and for Israel (ch. 3). This word is in each case a warning and a call to the people in question to obey the divine will by completing his plan in history for its destiny.

This same prophetic distinction between creation and history — the latter only being conceived as capable of exhibiting a striving for the achievement of moral ends — appears quite clearly in the account of the struggle of Yahwehism with the old Canaanitish Baal worship. It was, of course, the prophets who valiantly attacked that worship in favor of the worship of the true and living God. Its significance is entirely lost if one fails to observe that this struggle was essentially one between a nature cult on the one hand and the God-of-history on the other. As C. H. Dodd has pointed out, Baal's was a " fertility cult " and so associated with " the powers of nature." Accordingly, the religious feud set up between Baal and Yahweh assumed the character of a fight between a nature deity possessing no such thing as either personality or moral character and the personal, ethical God of the Hebrew prophets. " The God of the Old Testament," as Dodd observes, " even at relatively primitive stages, has personal character, which is expressed in his actions toward men, and in his demands upon them, and these actions and demands determine the meaning of history, which is therefore the proper field of his self-revelation." [15]

One could show the same motif with which we are here dealing running through The Psalms as well as the remaining prophetic writings.[16]

Only in history, then — the history of both individual men and women as well as that of groups, of whole societies, and of nations and peoples — with its moral, meaningful element, is God to be found present and at work according to Scripture's prophetic realism, and not in nature or creation as pantheism and poetic mysticism (and even a vapid sort of Christian piety) hold. *Communion with God is to be had, accordingly, not in nature, but rather in the market place, in the factory, in the shop, in the mine — wherever, indeed, persons are to be found, persons with the stamp of God's image on their brow and who throughout their lives by their work and creative activity are " making history."*

The *second* prophetic distinction between creation and history that is to be observed in a prophetic theology is the character of actuality possessed by the latter and denied to the former. H. Wheeler Robinson was the first, one imagines, to point out this characteristic of history. By the attribute of *actuality*, this author means that God has imparted to history and to the events that occur on creation's stage through the activity of persons that character of finality which pertains to events in eternity. One may, therefore, speak of the coinage of earth passing current at its face value in heaven and vice versa. There is a *once-for-allness* attaching to historical events even as to eternal

---

[15] *Op. cit.,* pp. 31 f.
[16] E.g., Ps. 22:28; 33:14; 65:2, 5; 66:4; 68:29 ff.; cf. Rom. 8:28; Gal. 3:28; Eph. 2:11 ff.; Col. 1:27 f.

ones, and an event in either order may be equated with one in
the other as of equal value. It is for this reason that the series of
decisive events through which God-in-history works out his will
are not repeatable and need not be repeated in order to acquire
final worth. It is for this reason that the Hebrew prophets conceived of the "call" of Abraham as a matter of the greatest
moment in God's dealings with man. It is for this same reason
that Christian prophetic theology lays the greatest store by such
historical happenings as the crucifixion and resurrection of our
Lord, Pentecost, and the birth of the Christian Church. These
events are not repeatable because they are events of final worth
in themselves, rather than mere ideas or ideals of the Platonic
type which may be punctured with a contrary ideological pin!
Historical events like these have a solidity imparted to them by
the creative purpose of the living God and nothing can rob
them of the worth attaching thereto.[17]

Both Oscar Cullmann and John Marsh have in slightly differing ways also given expression to their conviction that for the
Hebrew prophets and the Scriptures of both Testaments generally the events of time and history have a validity that is of
the utmost significance for the life of man.[18] These two scholars
have made a study of the terms used for time in the Scriptures
— 'ōlām, kairos, aiōn, and the like — and on the basis of these
word studies they have arrived at much the same conclusions as
Robinson and Dodd regarding the seriousness with which the
living God views the passing events which make up the march
of time. These events, they hold, have a final value for God
which he both declares and stamps upon them. This is quite
other than the casual manner in which the pagan thought of
Greece after Plato looks upon historical happenings as mere
copies of eternal realities, or Hindu philosophical thought regards all of history as maya (illusion) and therefore of no great
significance.

[17] Cf. H. Wheeler Robinson's Redemption and Revelation in the Actuality of History (1942).

[18] Cullmann's book is Christ and Time, and Marsh's The Fullness of
Time, both referred to already in this volume.

Both Hindu and Greek thought, discovering as just indicated a genuinely qualitative difference between historical and eternal events, attributed to the former a series of recurring cycles endlessly repeated and leading nowhere. Hebrew prophetic thought, contrariwise, conceived of time as bounded *before* and *after* by eternity, so that the events of history taking place within time ran forward toward an eternal goal predetermined by the living God who had thus set time between the eternities (as Barth would say, *zwischen den Zeiten*). A diagram will serve to make this plain.

Eternity ⟶   T I M E   ⟶ Eternity
_____
                P l a n e   o f   H I S T O R Y

As will appear, the events within time and on history's stage necessarily have direction — direction motivated by God from behind and directed toward his foredetermined goal. This is not to say, of course, that God is to be held responsible for each event that occurs: it is to commit the prophetic thought merely to a general acceptance of the thesis that history has a goal and that the totality of temporal events is somehow in God's providence tending toward the achievement of that goal. How far latitude — freedom of the human will, for instance — exists within the total series is not here in question.

The thought in Lord Tennyson's line, " Yet I doubt not through the ages one increasing purpose runs," is that had in mind here. In the series of events within time the purpose of God appears like a golden thread which binds them all together, gives each its separate worth, and somehow in the end accomplishes that they shall lead on to an appointed finale. The Arabic of Islam reflects at this point the Hebrew prophetic thought of the relations between the eternity *before* and that *after* time, or that out of which God's purpose comes and that toward which it is directed. For Arabic possesses two distinct words to express this " before-eternity " (*azl*) and " after-eternity (*abad*) distinction, and in consequence in that Semitic tongue one may express the concept " forever " by means of an expression equivalent to " from the before-eternity to the after-eternity." Obviously, such an expression will include in its purview all of time and eternity at a single glance, and the straightforward prophetic view with its *nexus of purpose = event = determined goal* will be seen to have captured the Semitic imagination even in the Islamic aberration from the Biblical faith.

The activities, then, of both God and man within history and on creation's stage have the same abiding meaning and actuality as attaches to activity in eternity. This is because God himself has attached to these activities the character of " once-for-all-ness," of " purposefulness," of " meaningfulness." It is for this reason, if for no other, that man should take life with the utmost seriousness. The God of the Scriptures is not a " playboy " God. Nor will he tolerate a " playboy " man on the stage of history. One of our most eminent psychologists has recently remarked that there is no longer any room in our world for immature people. It needs to be understood that in God's world there never was room for such. We live in a world which has always been hovering on the edge of the abyss: every act, every decision, every motivation in such a world has significance, for it leads somewhere — either up or down.

11. *General History and Redemptive History*

WE HAVE BEEN SPEAKING of the significance of history as being derived from its character of purposeful action on the part of persons, on the one hand, and the actuality imparted to it by a serious God, on the other. It has been our thought throughout that both of these have as their creative and final cause the saving motivation which God entertains relative to man.

With a view to elucidating this idea it is now apropos to point out that there exists within history a significant cleavage which is logically implicit in all that we have thus far said about it. To begin with, it requires no argument that every event in a purposeful series cannot have equal ultimate significance with every other event. This is implicit in the quality of *uniqueness* which attaches to events in history and of which we have already spoken in the previous chapter. That is to say, it is of the very essence of uniqueness that one event should differ from another in importance. Uniqueness means exactly once-for-all-ness and applies only to that which may be said to be one of a kind (*sui generis*, to employ the usual Latin phrase for this phenomenon). That events differ from each other in importance is also a necessary consequence of the fact that, as we have already seen, the God behind and before and in history imparts to each of them the character of actuality or value that it possesses and so to each event its legitimate importance.

We may go farther and declare that an entire series of events may have more significance than another series. " The particular, even the unique," writes C. H. Dodd, " is a category entirely appropriate to the understanding of history; and since one particular event exceeds another in significance, there may well be an event which is uniquely significant, and this event may give a unique character to the whole series to which it belongs." [1] We shall return a bit later to this thought of the one event giving its own unique tone to the entire series in which it is found. Here we are concerned only with the imparted significance pertaining to the series.

We should now be prepared for the discovery that Scripture's prophetic realism posits within history a cleavage of major importance which divides all its events into two such series. These are usually designated respectively " general history " and " redemptive history " (*Heilsgeschichte*).

The first of these is the larger category by far. It embraces, indeed, all the events of history as such, or rather all that represent man's purposive activity on creation's stage as distinct from

[1] *Op. cit.*, pp. 29 f. H. H. Rowley, in *The Relevance of Apocalyptic* (1947, Second Edition), writes to much the same effect, p. 154, as does also Oscar Cullmann, *op. cit.*, pp. 121 ff.

God's and apart from any contribution made by him to human life. This series knows no boundaries of race or people and it includes within its purview all of history's allotted portion of time. General history is the history of all peoples everywhere when that history is viewed in the light of man's mediate aims and purposeful activity. More particularly it includes even the history of the Hebrew and Jewish people, as well as that of the Christian Church and of so-called Christian peoples, so long as this history is told with the limited design of presenting man's — even Christian man's — activities and motivations only. For there is, for example, no greater significance attaching to the accounts of the rise and fall of the monarchies of Israel and Judah in themselves than to a similar one relating to the heavenly kingdom of Tibet!

Redemptive history, on the contrary, is that series of events or those series of events to which God is pleased to assign redemptive value. It is any and all history through which God works his redemptive purpose relative to man. It is even general history, or any part thereof, when this has been taken up into God's saving purpose and when he has attached saving significance to it for the reason that at this point he has become God-in-history and so man's Redeemer.

A very homely illustration will serve to make this cleavage plain. One flower in my garden does not differ from another flower in significance so long as it is attached to the bush which forms one of the stage props on creation's stage. This is because as a stage prop it is no part of history and does not participate in the activity which transpires upon the stage. When, however, a carnation is plucked by man to become an emblem for Mother's Day, it enters into history, becomes by so much an event of significance through its relation to the purposive activity on the part of the man who plucked it. When, further, Mother's Day, through the guidance of God's Spirit who ever lives in communion with his Church and communicates to it his will, is placed upon the Church's calendar of significant events, then this carnation becomes an event in redemptive history and its significance is enhanced accordingly.

This illustration, it should be noted, is only in the nature of an analogy. It is given with a view to indicating how man's activities acquire significance or value through their relation to God's redemptive purpose for man. Actually an impersonal object, such as a carnation or animal, can never acquire more than a *symbolic* significance of the type just indicated. Its importance is never *actual* after the pattern of the actuality which God attaches to historical events, for the reason that, strictly speaking, to the end it can never become an *event* in history but must remain a stage prop on creation's stage. The symbolic significance which it acquires in the manner shown in the illustration has led to the use of what the Church terms its " sacraments." A sacrament is nothing more nor less than an act whereby one of the stage props lying near at hand is brought into a symbolically significant relation to history and to God's purposes for the latter through one of the actors on the stage picking it up to employ in his act. Thus, our Lord made a sacrament out of the bread and wine used in the Communion service by lifting them from the table to serve his purpose at the moment.

It is the dual character accorded to some events rather than others — significance for man in history which they share with all other historical events, *plus significance for God-in-history* in his role of man's Redeemer — that gives redemptive history its distinctive quality. And that Scripture's prophetic realism has always recognized this selective process at work on the plane of history there need be no doubt. The book of Genesis, as is well known, has been planned in a manner to exhibit this selective process at work in the matter of the history of early man.

Following upon the accounts of Creation and the Fall in this book (Gen., chs. 1 to 3) , the selection begins: *first,* of Adam's two sons, Cain and Abel, the latter would have been taken for consideration (ch. 4:4) , but in view of his death God perforce raised up Seth to take his place (v. 25) ; *then,* of the line of Seth, Noah appeared and much is made of how pleasing he was to God and of his consequent salvation from disaster (ch. 5:32 and chs. 6 to 10) . Thereafter, to quote Driver, " all the descendants of Noah disappear, except the line of Shem " (ch.

11:10 ff.) , following whom Terah is selected (v. 31) , and again from his progeny, Abraham (ch. 12:1 ff.) . Thereafter " Ishmael disappears, and Isaac alone remains," and again, after ch. 36, " Esau and his descendants disappear, and only Jacob and his sons are left." Thus, as Driver continues, " the attention of the reader is fixed upon Israel, which is gradually disengaged from the nations and tribes related to it." [2] Paul's argument also in Rom., chs. 9 to 11, in favor of the eventual salvation of the Jews as a people is based on this principle of selection (cf. ch. 9:6–13) and his assurance that the Jews have been chosen by God for redemption (ch. 11:1 ff.) .

These are merely representative examples of a generally recognized principle in Scripture. The activity of God in choosing out a particular people (Ps. 33:12) , a saved and saving remnant (Micah 4:6 f.) , an Anointed One — whether he be priest, king, or Messiah (Ex. 30:30; Ps. 2:2) , the Suffering Servant of Second Isaiah (Isa. 42:1, *et al.*) , a prophet chosen to speak God's message to mankind (Isa. 6:6 ff.) , and eventually the Christian Church itself — all this activity serves to illustrate the same principle of a selective process proceeding within history under God's direction and giving to some events greater eternal significance than to others.

Cullmann has written in a striking manner of this series of redemptive events which, taken together, constitute what we have termed redemptive history. Starting with the definition of the Greek word *kairos* (occasion or opportunity) , as used in secular circles to mean " the moment in time which is especially favorable for an undertaking . . . the fixed day, which in modern jargon, for example, is called ' D day,' " he proceeds to show that the New Testament usage is much the same. Only " here . . . it is . . . a divine decision that makes this or that date a *kairos*," an occasion, that is to say, " a point of time that has a special place in the execution of God's plan of salvation." [3] He then points out how the totality of this series of *kairoi*, the line, that is to say, formed of these significant points, consti-

[2] S. R. Driver, *Commentary on Genesis*, p. ii.
[3] *Op. cit.*, p. 39.

tutes redemptive history as a whole. All these points on the redemptive line and, indeed, the whole line so formed now has the significance which God has appointed for it.

In view of the great significance of these redemptive events for the purpose of God in creating his world, this series, so to speak, constitutes the *core* or norm of history throughout. It becomes the norm by reference to which all of general history is to be viewed and evaluated. In the most literal sense this series is made up of God's own acts within history. It is the series of events through which God becomes God-in-history. Obviously, then, it is to be identified with the gospel-span of the Pauline, Synoptic, and Stephen-Hebrews traditions within the New Testament Scriptures. It is the series of events that serves to fill out the gospel's content and message, the stuff of which the Scripture's theology of history is made up.

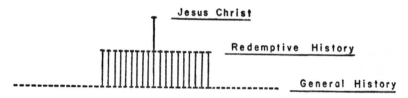

Diagram Illustrative of the Relation Between Redemptive and General Histories, Together with the Paramount Importance of Jesus Christ [4]

The relative significance of the two series of events which we have been discussing in this chapter (those which respectively constitute general and redemptive history), is well set forth by an illustration which I owe to Dr. Paul Wright. Remarking on the futility of man's life when man is left to his own devices, he instanced the habits of the Eskimos, a people whose lives are generally taken up with a round of securing and eating blubber.

[4] The *one-to-one correspondence* between certain points in redemptive and general history indicates that here both God and man have a part to play in such events. It is, of course, God's part in them that imparts to them their character of newness and of creativity — a character which weaves them all together into the pattern of redemptive history. Jesus Christ, then, is an event in both series and the norm or mid-point of both.

Blubber, it would appear, is the principal food eaten at breakfast and thereafter they rush off to fish or harpoon a seal or fish
or whale which will provide them with more blubber. This
constitutes the major activity of their day and they raise children
for no better employment than the eating and hunting of blubber! Life, it seems, is for them an eternal round of blubber.

But, said Dr. Wright, lest we imagine that in a more favorable clime our lives are quite superior to the Eskimos, let us
take stock of our own activities. We rise in the morning to a
breakfast of ham and eggs and thereafter quickly rush off to
office or factory for no other objective than to acquire money to
buy more ham and eggs. So that if the Eskimos' life is a round
of blubber, ours would appear to be one equally of ham and
eggs! What clear pictures of the futility in which man's life on
the plane of general history is involved! Contrariwise, redemptive history is made up of that series of acts wherein God steps
into the stream of human history with creative purpose. When
he does so, then a new thing appears: the ceaseless round of
man's futility is arrested and the creative act of God occurs. It
is this cyclic movement of man's futilities alone with which
pagan thought is acquainted; hence the Greek and Hindu teaching that history is composed of nothing else than this futile
round. But this is general history. The prophetic realism of
Scripture is acquainted with that revelation which gives the insight to observe God's acts in the redemptive series. It is such
insight or contrariwise the lack of it that makes all the difference
between the two philosophies of history that are involved here.[5]

JESUS CHRIST — IMAGO DEI AND SUPREME ACT
OF GOD IN HISTORY

Just as one series of events may prove of more significance
than another, so it is in keeping with our argument that one
event shall have pre-eminence over all others. The Hebrew
prophets long looked forward to the coming of one through
whose activity the saving power of God should be manifested

[5] Cf. an article on " The Bible as Revelation " in *Theology Today* for
July, 1945, pp. 455–469.

toward mankind in a climactic fashion. As is too well known to require elaboration, he was variously termed the " Branch " (Isa. 11:1; Zech. 3:8), " Ruler in Israel " (Micah 5:2), " God's son " (Ps. 2:7), " Prince of Peace " (Isa. 9:6), " Messenger of the covenant " (Mal. 3:1), " Herald of the gospel " (Isa. 52:7), " Suffering Servant of Yahweh " (Isa. 42:1 ff.).

This expectation was eminently fitting, considering the fact that in the prophetic Scriptures God becomes God-in-history only through the mediation of the activity of men. This statement by no means contradicts the thought with which our last section closed. Every historical event in which God shares is at once an act of man and an act of God. It is no doubt conceivable that it should have been otherwise, but so God has appointed that it shall be. When we search the Scriptures and human experience, we discover that if there be a God who acts at all on the human plane and within history, then that God works his will through men.

This is not the place to discuss the mutual relations of the divine purposing and human freedom of action; it is sufficient to remark that Scripture's prophetic realism has always found room for both without contradiction. But as the activities of men of even prophetic stature are at best halting, faulty, lacking in complete commitment, disinterestedness, and self-discipline, it is fitting that in " the fulness of the time " God should bring into the world one wholly so committed.

He did this according to the Scriptures in the person of Jesus Christ. The latter was God-in-history in climactic reality. He was the redemptive act of all redemptive acts. He was, to adopt Cullmann's terminology, the " mid-point " of history in the sense of being history's arbiter and norm. All the *kairoi* of the redemption-revelation line or of redemptive history lead up to him or else fall away from him. He is the alpha and omega of the line because he is also its mid-point and subsumes the whole.

As so often happens in Biblical studies, as in others in which earnest men are giving of their best to a common task, C. H. Dodd among others had anticipated Cullmann's insight at this point. I venture, therefore, to quote him: " Christianity," he says, " takes the series of events recorded or reflected in the Bible, from the call of Abraham to the emergence of the Church, and declares that in this series the ultimate reality of all history, which is the purpose of God, is finally revealed, because the series is itself controlled by the supreme event of all — the life, death, and resurrection of Jesus Christ." [6]

This means that redemptive history is not oriented with reference to the *end* of the age (*Endzeit*), as both Jewish theology and Christian millenarianism — including American fundamentalism and to a degree the " dialectic theology " — would have us believe. Rather, its focus is the *mid-point* of history, which is Jesus Christ in his historic manifestation. This prophetic orientation of history is quite original with it. Not only does it differ from that of the Jewish and Christian thought just mentioned, but it is also poles apart from that of pagan mythological speculation. For the latter characteristically looks to the ancient past or even to the prehistoric age for its " golden epoch," just as the former looks to the posthistoric for the same. But with Scripture's prophetic realism it is the Figure at the center of history who is its lodestar!

There are, if I mistake not, two reasons for this. In the first place, *only this prophetic realism really takes history seriously.* Only this theology really believes in the actuality of the historic events and so in the redemptive value of God's activity within history. A little reflection will show that this is so, however startling it may at first appear. Paganism is characteristically either pantheistic or else deistic, for the reason that it cannot believe in a God who is at once *above* and *in* his world. He may be one or other but not both. If he be *in* the world, then, says the pagan imagination, he must be identified with it — that is, he must be in creation's stage, and the result is pantheism. But if God be *above* the world, then obviously, so the pagan imagines, he must be pushed quite off the stage. In this latter case, man may have known God in prehistory before creation was, or alternatively so far back in the mists of the " olden times " as makes no difference.

[6] *Op. cit.,* p. 30.

Greek and Roman mythology chose the second of these two alternatives, though the philosophy which transplanted it from Plato onward tended to interpret the old myths in terms of the first. In neither case did Greek speculation come to grips with the theism of the prophets of Israel, who needed no mythology, on the one hand, to teach them of the transcendence of God, nor philosophy, on the other, to tell them that he was immanent. For knowing him to be a personal Spirit, they could not conceive him as other than both at once: *above* his world in the sense that he was not mixed up in the creation-stage which he had made, *in* it, as we have seen, by his historic activity accomplished through his rapport with man. This latter attitude alone takes history seriously because it alone sees God at work in history in genuine spiritual (that is, personal and moral) actuality.

Apocalypticism too has always found the true values only in the eternal order; hence, its eye must ever be upon the beyond-history. The "absolutely otherness" of God sets him apart from man and history in a manner suggestive of second century Gnosticism, and it becomes at least doubtful whether its professed allegiance to doctrines like the incarnation, the atonement, and man's justification, as well as God's self-vindication within history, is not mere lip service due to the presence of these teachings in Scripture. It does seem that apocalyptic theology ought to get on very well with a spiritualizing of all the down-to-earth doctrines of the faith, even as paganism would have no trouble with them so long as it could mythologize them, the difference being that the latter runs them off the stage of history in a pre- and the former in a post-history direction! It is, if one mistake not, because of his repugnance with reference to the mythologizing tendency which Bultmann finds in popular Christian circles contemporary with the origin of the Christian movement that he would now *demythologize* the Christian Scriptures.[7]

The prophetic Scriptures, however, know nothing of either

[7] Cf. *Kerygma und Mythos, Ein theologisches Gespräch*, edited by Hans Werner Bartsch, vols. i, ii (1952) and *Kerygma and Myth* (1953), being the translation of vol. i by Reginald H. Fuller.

this pre- or post-historical otherworldliness infecting paganism and apocalypticism. These Scriptures are quite frankly *this-worldly* in that they take the redemptive working of God within history at its face value and accept it as of equal importance with anything occurring in eternity in either its pre- or post-historical sense. In consequence of this prophetic viewpoint, it becomes natural for those who hold it to believe that God would redeem his people by a supreme redemptive act somewhere about the mid-point of history to give vivid and dramatic expression to the significance of history and particularly to the conclusive import of redemptive history for man's salvation.

The second reason for the central figure in history being the norm for all history is not a theoretical one like the first, but rather a statement of an observed fact. One is speaking, of course, from the standpoint of the prophetic Scriptures when one terms the present reason " a fact." This fact is that Jesus Christ is in very truth the " *imago Dei*," the " Son of God." Whatever one may think of the theoretical reasons for the focal point of history being at the beginning, middle, or end of the same, it is a simple matter of *witness* on the part of the prophetic Scriptures that the person, work, death, and resurrection of Jesus Christ constitute in fact that mid-point. This witness is to be received on faith and through faith as the medium of its apprehension.

It must remain for succeeding chapters to develop certain aspects of the thought in mind here. This much, however, should be said at this point in explanation — God's purpose, as the Hebrew prophets saw that purpose, has been from the beginning to make man in his image that the latter may enjoy high moral and spiritual fellowship with his Maker. This is in reality God's purpose in history. He desires to bring forth " sons of God " so like himself that men may look at them and remark, " Like father, like son," because they see his image unmistakably reflected in their faces. This, says the priestly author of Gen. 1:26, was God's original motive in making man, and the Scriptures give us every assurance that he has never forgotten his original motivation. In one way and another they suggest that salvation for man means his achieving this goal and enjoying as a consequence the fellowship which is its reward.

The significant contribution which the New Testament makes to Scripture's prophetic realism at this point is that through Jesus Christ God's saving purpose for man has been achieved on the plane of history. God has raised up his own Son who is the perfect image of his person in order that he may bring with him "many sons unto glory" (Heb. 2:10; Rom. 8:29).[8] This he does through a process of transformation whereby these latter become "the same image" as himself (II Cor. 3:18). To those who accept this witness of the Scriptures about Jesus Christ, he becomes in the best sense the Mediator between God and man. For he at the same time *mediates* to such the divine image by degrees, step by step, or, as Paul puts it, "from glory to glory," and at the same time *restores the fellowship* which sin had destroyed between man and his Creator.

It is *from faith* that the prophetic Scriptures bear witness to this fact of Jesus Christ and it is *to faith* on the part of the hearer or reader that they speak. For those believing Scriptures, therefore, on the one hand, and the believing reader, on the other, Jesus Christ is the focal point of history. It is toward him, they testify, that all previous history points forward; it is toward him that all subsequent history looks backward. It is in this sense only that he is to be spoken of as the "mid-point" in history — not as though he were chronologically placed there with exactitude. Rather, that he is, so to speak, so located in midstream as to make it dramatically evident that everything in history first and last is to be evaluated by reference to him. He is what God has willed that man shall become; therefore, he is the norm for all men, the norm of the *imago Dei*.

[8] Cf. also II Cor. 4:6; Col. 1:15; John 1:14; Heb. 1:3.

THE CONTENT OF SCRIPTURE'S PROPHETIC REALISM

A. The Gospel of Jesus Christ

'All things are from God
who reconciles us to himself
through Christ.'
    — II CORINTHIANS 5:18.

The Content of Scripture's Prophetic Realism

A. The Gospel of Jesus Christ
SYNOPSIS

*T*HE DESCRIPTIVE PHRASES *that are attached to the word* gospel *in Scripture give us a surprisingly complete account of its content. Four of these are chosen as titles of this and the succeeding sections as they are sufficiently comprehensive to include the entire sweep of the field of Biblical theology.*

In Second Isaiah the herald proclaims the gospel of the coming eschatological time. In the New Testament, particularly in the Synoptic Gospels, this herald becomes the content of his own gospel message. Accordingly, in this section under the caption of " The Gospel of Jesus Christ," we discuss: (1) the place of the incarnation in Scripture's prophetic realism — *its purpose is to show man what God is like and what God expects man to become;* (2) the place of the atonement in this theology — *it is shown that this was necessary to God's being the kind of God who would give his best for man's salvation and for man to be drawn to God in at-one-ment through the* communication *of God's love;* (3) the place of the resurrection — *God was behind this as also behind the incarnation and the atonement; in it his power and purpose are seen; it serves to raise Jesus Christ to the position of Lord over men's lives and to place him in a position to carry on his function as man's Redeemer. Man's resurrection occurs in two senses — the* ethical, *within the Church fellowship; the* corporeal, *for service to God throughout eternity. Both are accomplished only " in Christ."*

12. *The Incarnation and Prophetic Realism*

O UR THESIS to this point has been that the gospel is the sole theme of the divine revelation and so of Scripture's prophetic realism. There is much more in Scripture than that revelation and there is much besides the gospel. But this " plus material " is all by the way, so to speak — interesting, no doubt, and informative, but of no normative value. Only the gospel, which is the theme of the revelation-redemption line and so the golden thread running throughout history, together with its central figure, Jesus Christ, is of crucial significance for our faith.

In the present and succeeding chapters we shall analyze this gospel with a view to exhibiting its specific content. But first a word is in order about the defining phrases which attach to the term " gospel " in both testaments. It is surprising how numerous and comprehensive these are and how they serve in the aggregate to define the word. For the Old Testament they include " gospel of good," and by implication " of peace " and " of salvation " (Isa. 52:7; Nahum 1:15), and ' gospel of righteousness ' (Ps. 40:9). For the New Testament they are among others — " gospel of Christ," " of Jesus Christ," " of our Lord Jesus Christ," " of the glory of Christ "; " of God " and " of the glory of the blessed God "; " of the kingdom of God "; and " of peace " and " of our salvation." It will be convenient to gather up all the implications of these phrases in this and the chapters that follow under the four heads — " The Gospel of Jesus

Christ," " The Gospel of God," " The Gospel of the Kingdom," and " The Gospel of Our Salvation." In this section we begin with " The Gospel of Jesus Christ."

This phrase together with its equivalents — " gospel of Christ," " of our Lord Jesus Christ," " of the glory of Christ," and " of His Son " — occurs twelve times in the New Testament.[1] The noun *kērygma* also occurs once in the equivalent phrase " the *preaching* of Jesus Christ " (Rom. 16:25), as does *epangelia* in 'the *promise* of life in Christ Jesus' (II Tim. 1:1). The two verbs meaning " to preach " and " to preach the gospel " also at times have Jesus or Jesus Christ as their direct objects,[2] the most striking example being in Eph. 3:8 — ' to me . . . has this grace been granted to preach to the Gentiles *the gospel of the unsearchable riches of Christ.'* In the Old Testament the practical equivalent of these phrases is — ' the herald of the gospel ' (Isa. 40:9; 41:27; 52:7), ' the publisher of peace,' ' the herald of good,' and ' the publisher of salvation ' (Isa. 52:7; cf. for the verb Isa. 60:6; 61:1).

There is, however, a marked difference between the two sets of passages from Old and New Testaments. In those from Second Isaiah the gospel is the subject of the Herald's proclamation. In the New Testament generally the relationship between Herald and gospel is reversed and Jesus Christ, the Herald, has become himself the content of the gospel he proclaims.

There is no suggestion in the Second Isaiah passages that the herald will thus become the content of his own gospel message! The way in which the Servant Songs are interspersed with the Herald passages might well have suggested as much in pre-Christian times, and Skinner has made the suggestion that in Isa. 61:1 f. the herald's office and person are described in terms previously applied to the Servant,[3] a phenomenon that might

---

[1] Mark 1:1; Rom. 1:9; 15:19; I Cor. 9:12; II Cor. 2:12; 4:4; 9:13; 10:14; Gal. 1:7; Phil. 1:27; I Thess. 3:2; II Thess. 1:8. Probably Rom. 1:16 and I Cor. 9:18 did not originally contain a reference to Jesus.

[2] Thus, *evangelizesthai* — Acts 5:42; 8:35; 11:20; 15:35; 17:18; Eph. 3:8; *kērussein* — Mark 5:20; Luke 8:39; Acts 8:5; 9:20; I Cor. 1:23; 15:12; II Cor. 1:19; 11:4; Phil. 1:15.

[3] Cf. J. Skinner, *The Book of the Prophet Isaiah* (1898), *in loc.*

certainly have led some to identify the two. But even the Aramaic Targum of Jonathan bar Uzziel, which identifies the Servant (*sans* suffering) with the Messiah at Isa. 53:10 *et al.* and so might well have made the further identification, Herald = Servant-Messiah, never does this.[4]

The idea that the herald of the gospel proclamation is also the content of the gospel he proclaims seems, therefore, to have originated in New Testament times, and there can be little doubt that it was in some way made as the result of the impact of Jesus' person, or teaching, or works, or all three combined, upon his contemporaries. For that Jesus was for the Early Church at once the proclaimer of the gospel and its content seems certain.[5]

Two of the clearest passages in proof of this suggestion are Rom. 1:3 ff. and II Cor. 4:4. The gospel, says Paul, is God's gospel in the sense that he is sponsor for it, but it pertains to his Son, who is its theme: it is the ' gospel of the glory of Christ.' When one recalls that for the Hebrew-Christian tradition *glory* stands for the real character of a person as it is revealed to others through self-expression, Paul's contention is seen to be that *the gospel's content concerns the nature of our Lord's very being and its meaning for the world.*[6]

Gerhard Friedrich has suggested, rightly one imagines, that Mark 1:1 by the phrase, " The beginning of the gospel of Jesus Christ," means essentially the same. The gospel of Jesus Christ is in Mark's meaning the gospel *about* him and it is Mark's purpose in writing down that gospel to write about Jesus. Mark 1:14 f. again makes Jesus the Herald of the gospel in accord with the Synoptic tradition generally, as we have seen. But for Mark himself that gospel comes through what Jesus *is* as much as by what he says. Consequently, it is not only for him a gospel about " the kingdom of God," but also in the end a gospel about Jesus himself and his relation to the Kingdom. It would be easy

---

[4] Cf. J. F. Stenning, *The Targum of Isaiah* (1949), *in loc.*

[5] Cf. T. W. Manson, *The Servant-Messiah* (1953), *passim;* also C. H. Dodd, *According to the Scriptures* (1953), especially pp. 108–110.

[6] Cf. Friedrich in Kittel's *Wörterbuch,* II, p. 730, lines 24 ff.

to show that the same thought about Jesus' relation to the gospel he proclaims emerges in the other passages cited above.[7] But we shall not labor the point by attempting an exposition of each of them. Assuming rather that for the New Testament community generally Jesus was both Herald and content of the gospel, we shall proceed to a consideration of the three most significant aspects of his person and work — that concerned with the beginning of his earthly life (the incarnation), that at the close in which his work comes to a climax (the atonement), and the seal of God upon the whole (the resurrection).

It is quite likely, as has just been intimated, that Mark 1:1, in which the author gives us the title of his book (" The beginning of the gospel of Jesus Christ "), marks the turning point from the Second Isaiah's thought of the gospel which a herald proclaims to the Church's conception of the Herald as himself the gospel's content. If this be so, then this is because the Church believed itself to be encountering in that Herald the redemptive activity of the living God. The incarnation, it held, was God's definition of himself in terms of human personality.[8] Reference to the relevant passages shows that there is little duplication of the terms used to describe our Lord on the part of the authors of the New Testament. This is because each has endeavored in his own words to testify to a commonly acknowledged experience. Stereotyped terminology is evidence of regimented thinking, and there is none of this surely in the New Testament Scriptures.

The incarnation as a first part of the gospel about Jesus Christ is intended to give expression to what the Church has called *his prophetic office*. That is to say, Jesus Christ through the incarnation speaks for God, as it was every prophet's function to do.

This significance of the incarnation has two facets. First, through God's becoming man in the person of his Son and prophet, Jesus Christ, we learn what God is like. This is what

---

[7] *Ibid.,* II, p. 726, lines 3 ff.

[8] Cf. Matt. 1:23; Mark 1:11, 35; John 1:14, 18; Col. 1:13–15; II Cor. 4:6; 5:19; Heb. 1:3 ff., *et al.*

the term " Son " is intended to say. The Hebrew Scriptures and the Jewish literature following upon them had spoken of God as " Father." [9] The Christian ones now give us the complement of that term.

We need not, therefore, go outside the Jewish ethos to discover why the Christian Church speaks of Jesus as the Son of God. " Son " means God-in-history, God manifesting himself to man, even as " Father " means God-in-eternity, God the Creator and Provider of all man's needs. Wherefore we say, " Our Father who art in heaven," but of " his Son, born of woman, born under the law " (Gal 4:4), the proper characterization is " image of the invisible God, the first-born of all creation " (Col. 1:15).[10]

The Son's function is to manifest the Father on the plane of history. In II Cor. 5:19 (" God was in Christ reconciling . . ."), Paul gives us, not a static picture of a person, but rather the thought that it is in the activity of Jesus Christ, the Son, that the Father is to be seen. This idea in its historical perspective may be expressed as follows — God's people had long been acquainted with his redemptive activity as that was interpreted to them by the Hebrew prophets. But that prophetic revelation had been at best ' piecemeal,' ' chunky,' ' uncorrelated ' (Heb. 1:1). The so-called " theophanies " were ephemeral, one might almost say chance, revelings of himself on God's part to men of insight. By contrast, the incarnation unites all their meaning in the substratum of a single personality — Jesus Christ, the Man of Nazareth.

When Rabbi Kohler wrote his well-known book on Jewish theology in 1918, he remarked, " It may seem rather strange that no such work has hitherto been written by any of the leading Jewish scholars of either the conservative or the progressive school " (p. vii). He went on to observe that this was due to certain fundamental differences between Judaism and Christianity in the matter of the hope of attaining to something like

[9] Cf. T. W. Manson, *The Teaching of Jesus* (1935, Second Edition), pp. 91 f.; Deut. 14:1; 32:6; Ps. 103:13; Hos. 11:1; Mal. 1:6; 3:17.
[10] Cf. also John 1:14, 18; 14:9; II Cor. 4:4, 6.

" final truth " (pp. 1 ff.) . One inclines to the belief, however, that the rabbi has overlooked that most significant difference between the two faiths which furnishes us with the real reason for the phenomenon of which he wrote. This is the rejection on the part of Judaism of the doctrine of the incarnation.

Judaism and Christianity alike stem from the Hebrew prophetic teaching. Accordingly, both know of God's justice, righteousness, holiness, truth, grace, and love. Moreover, both faiths testify to the personal experience of these various facets of God's character on the part of one and another individual prophet and saint throughout the years. But for a consistent, satisfying, well-rounded theology there must be found some single substratum in which God's varying qualities may be seen to cohere as well as come to their rightful expression.

The Christian faith has from the beginning found this bond of cohesion in the person and work of Jesus Christ. He was in his person the answer to Moses' question at the burning bush — " What is Thy name? " what is Thy nature like? The answer is, " Like Jesus Christ, the Son and image of God." The justice, love, truth, righteousness of the Father are manifest and cohere in the Son who is God-in-history. In his person they find their manifestation on the plane of history, in his person they are shown to be actual.

In the second place, in the incarnation Jesus Christ as God's prophet par excellence shows us what God would have man become. Jesus is not only perfectly human, he is also perfect man. He is man at his highest and best, he is man as God would have man become. This is Paul's meaning at Eph. 4:13, where he writes of " mature manhood, to the measure of the stature of the fullness of Christ."

It is sometimes objected that Jesus' true humanity could be and was a matter of observation, but that his being perfect man in the sense of being all God would have man become is something that only God could know. The rather obvious reply to this objection is — of course, only God could know it and it is for this very reason that it must become one of the subjects of his revelation to man. The thesis of this volume is that the content of revelation is the gospel and that the supreme gospel fact is that which we are now discussing — viz., the person and work of Jesus Christ. The "gospel of Jesus Christ" is the gospel about him, about his person and work. If the New Testament Scriptures, then, are right in making him an integral part of the revealed gospel message, it follows that this part, like all the rest of the gospel, is to be apprehended by faith on man's part.

What Jesus Christ was and what he is today are not facts to be *deduced*. Nor may man's reason decide what he may have been nor what he may now be, though these matters are like all other matters of faith amenable to reason and capable of being made intelligible to it. Such matters as these are to be arrived at by induction, not by deduction, the induction namely of objective revelation. For these facts are a part of the given data of God's self-revelation on the plane of history. As such they are just as intelligible and amenable to the human reason as other historical facts, but no more so. What Jesus Christ may have been or may be is no more to be deduced by logic than is the problem of who or what Julius Caesar may have been or may now be.

Such data are *given* to human experience, not to be deduced by the human mind. The statement of the New Testament, accordingly, that Jesus Christ is God's Messiah or the Servant of Yahweh or that he represents "mature manhood" as God would have it — these are not the results of the Church's speculation about his nature. They represent rather the spontaneous expression of the prophetic *word* of revelation definitive of the *work* of God which Jesus Christ was and is. There is never genuine revelation unless God's word and work converge after this fashion on a particular moment in history. Hence, Luther's famous dictum that unless the Word is heard in the Lord's Supper, there is no sacrament! Unless God's Word is heard in definition of his act, there is no revelation at any time. The Church, then, in its witness that the incarnation gives us a picture of perfect manhood is merely declaring the word revealed to it in the event of Jesus Christ. And that Jesus Christ was perfect man fulfilling the Father's will to perfection is as proper a subject of revelation as any other of its subjects. Accordingly, those who hold the view that we may not speak of Jesus' perfect manhood do so either because they really reject the concept of revelation itself or else do not understand it.

The perfection intended is to be understood in one respect only, however, namely, as regards the character God expects of man and Jesus' allegiance to his Father's will in consequence of his possessing the former (Matt. 5:48; Phil. 2:5 ff.; Heb., ch. 2). The *imago Dei* of the Genesis story also had this one reference only, as its simple perusal makes clear. Man reflects the divine likeness as he obeys the divine will.[11]

It is futile, however, to argue, as is often done, from what sinful man is to what Jesus' knowledge or wisdom or intellect must have been like. Sinful man is no pattern for the *imago Dei* on any side of his being, and we have now become clear on one point at least in this connection — namely, that man's life is so unitary that, when it is vitiated in one part (as by disease or sin), the whole is vitiated in all its parts. The psychosomatic nexus is recognized today even in medical and psychological circles: with how much greater reason in theological ones!

There can be but one way to discover what utter trust in and obedience to his Father's will can do for man and that is to observe what these actually did in Jesus' case. It is true that perfection in Jesus' manhood does not imply perfect knowledge on his part; it is equally true that the norm for Jesus' knowledge is not the knowledge of sinful, imperfect man; nor the norm for his wisdom and powers, sinful man's wisdom and powers. It is at this point, therefore, that our methodology as we study the meaning of Jesus Christ for human life must be in the most absolute sense empirical.

But matters have long been otherwise. The old school of " liberalism," in the interest of a theory of *kenōsis* derived from an unlikely interpretation of the meaning of Phil. 2:5 ff., held that Jesus " emptied himself " of his divinity at the incarnation and therefore could not have known or done many things recorded in the Gospels. Of this theory, two things are to be said.

[11] For elaboration, see below in Section D.

In the first place, the passage in question is not so much a theological one as ethical in its import. This appears from its introduction, where such words as these occur; " Do nothing from selfishness . . . Let each of you look . . . to the interests of others. Have this mind among yourselves, which you have in Christ Jesus." Thereafter there follows the example of how our Lord humbled himself, becoming obedient unto death. To say, then, that Paul means to suggest that men are to emulate Jesus in emptying themselves of their personalities — the equivalent of his pouring out his divinity — is to commit him at once to a *non sequitur* and a patent absurdity. What Jesus is said to have " emptied himself " of was *self* (Greek, *heauton*). He poured out self, says Paul, by pouring the world in, by making the world of mankind, so to speak, his other self. This is the language of ethics, not of metaphysics nor of theology. Neither Jesus nor man generally is capable of becoming someone other than he is, and neither here nor elsewhere does Paul's thought lend itself to such an absurdity.

Again, of what one can do who in agreement with the divine will thus empties himself of self, neither this nor any other passage in Scripture presumes to give us absolute theoretical certainty. For such information in Jesus' case we are entirely dependent in empirical fashion upon the Gospel narratives, together with such additions as are made by the apostle Paul and The Epistle to the Hebrews.

The historical data, witnessed to by the primitive Church, bear testimony to Jesus' remarkable knowledge of human nature, his ability to probe men's souls to the utmost, his keen sense of their frustrations and their own realization of and shame at their failures, together with their earnest wish to turn from such failures toward higher aims and motives, and his powerful healing touch which could at once banish disease and transform character. The same Gospel records represent to us a man possessed of moral and spiritual insights far transcending those of sinful mortals, a man who so far discerned the meaning of history and of God's ways with men as at once to foresee the calamity about to fall upon his people and the cruel end to which man's sinful stupidity would bring himself.

The same insight into the meaning of life and of man's destiny taught him, so the Gospels of the Church declare, what was his own place in the Father's plan for man's redemption. He knew — through his intimate spiritual fellowship with his Father on the one hand, and on the other by reason of his equally deep insight into his oneness with all of sinful, suffering humanity — that he was both man's Lord and man's Redeemer. It is the Church's testimony in its Gospels, not only that it believed him to be these things, but also that he knew himself to be such.

It is now possible to quote the characteristically striking and authoritative writing of C. H. Dodd to the above effect. For in a rather remarkable passage in his recently published *According to the Scriptures* (1953), he has this to say:

"... the New Testament itself avers that it was Jesus Christ himself who first directed the minds of his followers to certain parts of the Scriptures as those in which they might find illumination upon the meaning of his mission and destiny. ... I can see no reasonable ground for rejecting the statements of the Gospels that (for example) he pointed to Psalm 110 as a better guide to the truth about his mission and destiny than the popular beliefs about the Son of David, or that he made that connection of the ' Lord ' at God's right hand with the Son of Man in Daniel which proved so momentous for Christian thought; or that he associated with the Son of Man language which had been used of the Servant of the Lord, and employed it to hint at the meaning, and the issue, of his own approaching death. To account for the beginning of this most original and fruitful process of rethinking the Old Testament we found need to postulate a creative mind. The Gospels offer us one. Are we compelled to reject the offer? " (p. 110).

It seems unbelievable that modern scholarship in the interest of a theory of *kenōsis* — supported as this now is by a radical hypothesis regarding Gospel origins, that of form criticism — should find it possible to deny the validity of this testimony cited by Professor Dodd.[12]

[12] Cf. the late Clarence T. Craig in *The Interpreter's Bible*, vol. vii (1951) and Rudolf Bultmann, *Theology of the New Testament*, vol. i (1951), pp. 26 ff.

There are, of course, not wanting numerous voices that are raised in protest against the extreme conclusions of the form-critical school at this point.[13] In any case it ought to be clearly understood that the problem does not concern the undoubted fact agreed to on all sides of the true humanity of our Lord.[14] The dispute concerns rather simply what a true man who has wholly committed himself to the Father's will may and may not know by way of prophetic insight into the meaning of life, of man, of himself. For it is not argued that our Lord knew these things because he was the " Son of God." If he had the insights of which we have been speaking, then he had them because a perfect man can have them. He had them because he was and is the *imago Dei* and therefore the proper exemplar of what sinful man is to become, because from the beginning God has intended man for a unique authority over all his creatures (cf. Gen. 1:28 with Heb. 2:5–9). The present writer, agreeing with Professor Dodd as above quoted, would add but one word of his own to the witness of Scripture's prophetic realism about Jesus Christ — namely, that employing the best literary and historical techniques now at our command, we appear to have no reason for believing that Jesus Christ was not possessed of the insights and the powers ascribed to him in the Gospels.[15]

THE JESUS-OF-HISTORY AND THE CHRIST-OF-FAITH

We have described the incarnation as God's definition of himself in terms of human personality. Two inescapable corollaries appear to arise from this definition. In the first place, it seems

[13] Cf. William Manson, *Jesus, the Messiah* (1943), ch. vi; G. S. Duncan, *Jesus, Son of Man* (1949), chs. x–xii; Vincent Taylor in *The Interpreter's Bible*, vol. vii (1951), pp. 116, 130; and the author's *Intention of Jesus* (1943), *passim*.

[14] F. C. Grant thinks that those who hold to Jesus' having a so-called " messianic consciousness " savor of Docetism (*The Interpreter's Bible*, vol. vii, p. 654). But this is hardly a fair charge: belief in Jesus' true humanity and Docetism are incompatible.

[15] Cf. an article in *Theology Today*, for July, 1954, on " From Schweitzer to Bultmann," in which the present writer argues that Jesus *as a prophet* ought to have had as deep a consciousness of his own place in God's purposes as other prophets, like Isaiah, Paul, Luther, and Kagawa.

clear that the so-called " Jesus-of-history " and the " Christ-of-faith " are one and the same person. We have already noted how the older liberalism rent asunder the seamless robe of our Lord's person along these lines. That school of criticism declared that when by its methodology it succeeded in getting " back to Christ," it found him to be, not the Christ of the Church's creeds, but a simple, rather heretical Jewish rabbi, a purveyor of a plain and rather practical social ethic, but devoid of any claims for himself, his person, or his work.

Accepting the same methodology and an even more drastic improvement of it in the direction of form criticism, the Continental theology of " crisis " and American Neo-orthodoxy find no fault with this dichotomizing of the person of Jesus Christ. But whereas Harnack and Hermann of the older school accepted the simple rabbi as the " real Jesus " the school of the crisis theology prefer the Christ of the Church's faith and upon him erect their creed.

Both these schools have given us an abortive Christ. Each has taken the half of his person that pleased its fancy and each is bereft of the half of the truth possessed by the other. The Jesus-of-history of liberalism is the creature of a literary technique that had its roots in a humanistic philosophy of history. This philosophy could conceive of Jesus only as a religious genius who appeared at a particular point in the evolution of the race.

The theologians of " crisis " have seen how barren such a Christology is. But, instead of attacking it at its source with an improved technique of literary and historical criticism, they have accepted the picture of the Jesus-of-history as historically accurate and so have had no other recourse than to take refuge in the Christ-of-faith. The simple Jewish rabbi of the liberals, we are now told, was the Son of God come to earth incognito: it is for this reason that he presents to us such a shabby appearance! And though he did not believe himself to be Messiah, Son of God, Son of Man, Suffering Servant, or anything else in particular that we can discover by our best literary and historical methods, this need not trouble us. After all such methods can " only establish a historical fact, not prove an article of faith," and "faith, being personal decision, cannot be dependent upon a historian's labor." [16]

In his latest book, *Criticism and Faith* (1952), John Knox gives us one of the clearest expositions of this Neo-orthodox Christology to be found anywhere. The general thesis of his book is that of the Neo-Catholicism now taking hold within American Protestant circles, which professes itself content with the Church's memory (i.e., with tradition and hence authoritative recollection) as this is stimulated by the Spirit (or alternatively, by the " Christ ") — a memory that places it above the harassments of the scientific inquiry of the historian and his conclusions regarding the events recorded in the Gospels. The Church knows in advance that historical research can only verify its memory. Criticism, therefore, cannot destroy faith.

In elaborating his thesis, Professor Knox sets forth three propositions relative to the person of Jesus Christ which he endeavors to prove. These are: first, " our knowledge of Christ does not depend upon what can be known about the life of Jesus "; secondly, " our knowledge of the authentic words of Christ does not depend upon what can be established as Jesus' words "; thirdly, " the truth about the meaning of Christ does not depend upon what was present in the self-consciousness of Jesus." [17]

Naturally one accepts much that is said here, however much one would like to place the emphasis in places where it is not put in this statement of Neo-orthodoxy's case and however much one would wish to challenge some of its underlying postulates. But, be this as it may, our only concern at the moment is with its apparent rending of the seamless robe of our Lord's person. This seems to be clearly evident in such statements as those quoted above in which " Jesus " and " Christ " stand over against each other as not one entity but two. Several further illuminating quotations along similar lines may now be added: " The words which are of greatest and deepest concern to us as

[16] Cf. Bultmann, *Theology of the New Testament,* Vol. I, p. 26. Copyright, 1951, by Charles Scribner's Sons. Used by permission.

[17] *Op. cit.,* p. 47.

Christians are not the words of Jesus but the words of Christ "
(p. 51); " The words of the Spirit are as certainly the words of
Christ as are the words of Jesus " (p. 52); " The meaning of
Christ is not limited to the terms in which Jesus conceived that
meaning" (p. 56); and "This living, present, and creative
reality — sometimes called the Spirit in the New Testament,
sometimes Christ — is continuous with Jesus of Nazareth but it
is not to be simply identified with him " (p. 52).

While one is in agreement with Professor Knox's desire to
bring together into intimate unity " Word of God," " Christ,"
and " Spirit," and in general sympathy with his thesis regarding
the Church's " memory " as far as it goes, one cannot fail to de-
tect here a serious dichotomizing of our Lord's person. Two
rather obvious replies appear justified to the sort of thinking
that has gone into his expression of his case.

In the *first* place, it places too heavy a strain on the critical reconstruction of the Church's memory about Jesus. How is one
to know that the shabby rabbi — accepted by this school as
well as by liberalism as the Jesus of the Church's *memory* —
is not all there is to Jesus Christ as liberalism said he was?
How is one to believe that somehow he is to be identified with
the Christ, the Spirit, the Son of God? Or if one does not like
the term " identify " — and Professor Knox does not — how
shall one at any rate believe that Jesus of Nazareth is so " continuous " with the heavenly Christ as to give validity to our
belief in a genuine incarnation of the Son of God? Indeed, is
there sufficient continuity between " Jesus " and " Christ " to
allow of our still believing in God's historical revelation of himself in the former at all? Or rather, has not the bond between
these two figures become so tenuous that Christian theology
may get on very well without Jesus?

As we have already observed, Donald Baillie, Dean Willard
Sperry, and others have recently declared that the theology of
crisis and American Neo-orthodoxy at this point seem to be
presenting us with a new " Christ myth." This for a religious
faith claiming to be based on a solid historical foundation is
definitely taboo. Bultmann's above-quoted statement about the

relation between faith and the work of the historian — a statement with which Knox appears to be in complete accord — is disturbing from one who is an authority on New Testament history. If faith and the historian's labor, as Bultmann asserts, are to be utterly dissociated from each other, then would it not seem that Christianity has ceased to be a historical religion, that the series of redemptive acts that constitute the theology of history testified to by the Hebrew prophets is of no consequence to our faith, and that Christian theology has become a vapid sort of mysticism alongside the other theosophies?

Nor does it help matters to call on the Church's memory, as Knox's thesis allows. For, on the showing of the type of criticism that he accepts, what the Church remembers is only the shabby rabbi. It does not and cannot remember the heavenly Christ incarnate as the Son of God and Son of Man, for according to this view it never recognized him as such when he walked in its midst. And it must be said in all candor, that as long as the crisis theology and American Neo-orthodoxy accept the findings of the form critics and the like destructive literary and historical criticism, this is all that the Church will ever be able to recall of its impressions of Jesus of Nazareth.

Jesus Christ the Norm for God

The *second* answer to this view is that it is quite un-Biblical. The crisis theologian's acceptance of the poor rabbi of Nazareth is due, not only to his adopting the critical findings of the form critics, but also to his inheritance of a low view of human personality from his mentor, the Danish philosopher and theologian, Sören Kierkegaard. Together with the latter, these theologians hold that human personality can do nothing but veil divinity. They cannot believe that it is the best possible medium, in fact the only adequate medium, for *revealing* God. Hence, they conclude that Jesus did not reveal God. Rather, his humanity served only to obscure Him.

But the New Testament is very clear that such is not the case. Its witness is to the effect that Jesus of Nazareth revealed God, and nowhere does it say anything to the contrary. All the quotations on pages 116 through 123 above say as much, and these could be multiplied tenfold. To cut the Gordian knot at this point as quickly as possible, permit me like our Lord to resort to the analogical argument to be derived from the literary form known as parable — The Parable of the Blind Man and the Painting:

The crisis theologian, one is constrained to believe, is like unto a visitor at an art gallery who beheld a blind man shuffling with his cane across the floor in the direction of a painting of note which was hung upon one of the walls. When the blind man had detected that he stood immediately in front of the painting of his search, he lifted toward it his sightless eyes. Then in consternation he raised his voice with the cry, " But, I cannot see it." Hearing his cry of despair, the visitor shouted out for all to hear, " Behold, will you, that painting before the blind man is veiled! "

No one who possesses eyes to see will agree with such an observer. The New Testament is equally clear that the veil lies upon the heart of the person who cannot see the Son of God in Jesus of Nazareth (II Cor. 3:15) and that his humanity did not constitute a veil upon his divinity. Our Lord's human flesh was a revealing medium, not a veiling one. And this has always been God's intent for all human flesh according to Scripture's prophetic realism. Witness Gen. 1:26, where it is said that man is to become the " image of God " and his " likeness." Human personality is qualified, as other aspects of nature are not, to reveal God. It is for this reason that the remark has already been made in this book that to find God and to have communion with him one must go, not to the woods or seashore, but wherever men are to be found — into the shop and factory, to the school and the home. For it is men who have the image of God, however imperfectly, stamped upon their brows.

Those theologians who take their stance with the older liberalism, accordingly, and see in Jesus of Nazareth the poor, heretical rabbi, are in reality allying themselves with the secular world of Jesus' day which could see in him nothing more than this. That world followed him, if at all, " for the loaves and fishes." Eventually it crucified him. That world it was which saw "no form or comeliness," "no beauty," in him that it should desire.

But there is another view of Jesus of Nazareth — that of Scripture's prophetic realism — which sees him manifesting his Father by his blameless life; by his compassionate industry on behalf of the homeless, the diseased, the wretched, the social outcaste; by his giving himself unstintedly to save the lives of men at every level of life's interests and needs. *It is a divine thing to be like this and thus to live one's life in time.* God is not veiled thereby but set forth and manifested. And it is this Jesus of Nazareth who actually lives in the Church's memory, if we may trust the records, not that Jesus of modern critical reconstruction adopted by the crisis theology and Neo-orthodoxy. Witness Acts 2:22, " ' Men of Israel, hear these words: Jesus of Nazareth, a man attested to you by God with mighty works and wonders and signs which God did through him in your midst . . .' "! in conjunction with Mark 2:10, " ' But that you may know that the Son of man has authority on earth to forgive sins ' — he said to the paralytic — ' I say to you, rise, take up your pallet and go home.' "

This Jesus of the Church's memory is one who knew himself to be the Son of Man, the Son of God, Messiah, priest and prophet of his people, and who performed the works and taught with the authority attaching to such knowledge. It is futile, then, to declare that modern literary and historical criticism verify this memory of the Church; rather it has reconstructed for us a picture of the historical Jesus that is diametrically opposed to that memory. We must make a choice accordingly at the present moment between the memory on the one hand and the reconstruction on the other. And the point cannot be too sharply expressed that the chief desideratum today in New Testament scholarly circles is a re-evaluation of the methods and findings of a type of criticism that has faced the Church with this dilemma and the counsel of despair which is its only recourse.[18]

[18] My colleague, Professor Surjit Singh, has called my attention to Emil Brunner's apparent desertion of the Christological view of the crisis theol-

The second corollary arising from the definition of the incarnation as God's revelation of himself in terms of human personality is that *Jesus Christ is the norm for what God must be.* This surely is John's meaning in ch. 1:18 when he remarks, ' The Unique Divine One who is in the closest fellowship with the Father, he has shown Him forth.' The oft-repeated query, " What is the difference between saying that Jesus is *the Son of God* and that saved men are *sons of God?* " is a quite legitimate one. In the Semitic idiom, " son of " means merely " like." For instance, " son of righteousness " means " righteous "; " son of peace " means " peaceful "; and the like. Does not the expression " Son of God," then, as applied to Jesus Christ mean " godlike "?

In reply it should be said, first, that as regards saved men this is exactly what the expression means. Our Lord's teaching in a passage like Matt. 5:43–48 is the ground for saying so. Here, to be " sons of your Father," as the passage makes clear, means to be like that Father in attitude and motivation.

But the case is quite otherwise with Jesus Christ.[19] To say that an ordinary man is a " son of God " is to utter the homely proverb, " Like father, like son." But to say that Jesus Christ is " the Son of God " is to reverse the proverb and declare, " Like Son, like Father." One is aware of Donald Baillie's objections to one's saying that " God is like Jesus," " Jesus reflects the character of God," " Christianity gives us a Christlike God," and the like.[20] But I am here speaking of a deeper level of appre-

ogy in his latest work, *The Christian Doctrine of Creation and Redemption* (1952), which appeared after the above pages were first written. Thus, Brunner writes: " The historical Jesus is no other than the Christ to whom the apostles bear witness. In his action and his speech he stands before us as the only one, the Man, who, with divine authority . . . claims us for himself. Those who do not close their eyes to the actual Jesus of history . . . can do no other than confess with Peter: ' Thou art the Christ, the Son of the living God ' " (p. 327). Modern form criticism knows no such Jesus-of-history!

[19] In what follows I am not forgetting that " Son of God " may in some instances be no more than the equivalent of " Messiah " as applied to Jesus (cf. Matt. 16:16). But that there is a deeper note struck in the New Testament as a whole will hardly be denied; cf. Rom. 1:4 and Heb. 1:1 ff.

[20] *Op. cit.,* p. 66.

ciation of Jesus than that of which Baillie is thinking.

Permit me a personal reminiscence. Some time ago I was reading from the Gospel of Luke with a young man who had been raised in a fundamentalist environment and had afterward, so he thought, lost his faith. (I have become skeptical of these people who have " lost their faith " and come to me to regain it!) When we came to Luke 23:34, " Father, forgive them; for they know not what they do," he looked up quickly and remarked, " But the Father could not forgive sin that readily "! One knew, of course, that he had in mind the thought that the Father, an angry God, required to be appeased by the Son. And, knowing this, I remarked: " Do you realize what you are saying? Both Scripture and modern psychology conspire together to teach us that it is exactly the superior person who can forgive. In reality, therefore, you are saying that of the two — the Son and the Father — the Son is the superior. You are saying that if a person must make a choice between gods, then he must prefer the One who died on the cross to the One in heaven! "

Of course, we are not faced with any such alternative. It is only a wholly inadequate theology that would make it ever appear to be so. But the incident does help to point up the sense in which I now say, in spite of Baillie's strictures, that in place of liberalism's " godlike Christ," the New Testament gives us rather a " Christlike God." That is to say, *Jesus Christ is the norm of what God the Father must be.* This is exactly what the incarnation says to us. It is, moreover, precisely what it is intended to say. Either God, the Father, is like his Son, or else we shall be forced to choose the latter as the better of the two! This cannot be, of course, but it is well to place the matter in this paradoxical light that we may see just how meaningful the incarnation is.

This discussion should help us, one imagines, to sound somewhat of the profundity attaching to the statement that Jesus Christ is the norm of redemptive history as a whole, that is, that he is the norm of God's self-revelation to man. He is so because in the deepest sense which the words are capable of meaning

Jesus Christ is God-in-history. He is God come down into our midst — *Immanuel*, to employ the Hebrew word. Like every other event on history's plane he has within his person the *actuality* with which the Father has endowed him. In his case this is the actuality of God functioning among men.

13. *The Atonement and Prophetic Realism*

THE MEANING of the phrase which we are studying in this section of the book — " the gospel of Jesus Christ " — is by no means exhausted by the part which the incarnation has to play in that gospel. We have seen that the herald of Second Isaiah comes heralding the 'gospel of peace,' the 'gospel of salvation' (Isa. 52:7). In the Synoptic Gospels, from being merely the Herald of that gospel, the historic Jesus becomes himself the content of the gospel which he heralds. The peace referred to in Second Isaiah is between God and man, as is generally agreed. It is the product of the cementing of a genuine fellowship between the two. In the Synoptics, Jesus Christ becomes in his person and work the medium by which this reconciliation is accomplished.

And so we are led directly from Second Isaiah's " gospel of peace " to a study of reconciliation or atonement between God and man. These two English words stand for the same term in Greek (*katallagē*). The second of the two is the more impressive to English-speaking people, as it is a formation of the English itself rather than of the Latin. In the Middle English before 1500 it appeared as " at on " or " at one," and it means, therefore, quite literally *at - one - ment*. The atonement is accordingly the process by which at-one-ment between God and man is achieved.

This is what the Church has always termed the *priestly* work of Jesus Christ. But the witness of the New Testament makes of it strange work for a priest. Pagan priests, believing in an angry

god, have often brought to him a gift or sacrifice by way of appeasement. Or else they have thought of their offering as a
means of cementing fellowship between themselves and their
god through partaking in a common meal which they set forth
before him. C. H. Dodd and Vincent Taylor among others have
shown that no thought of appeasement of an angry deity attaches to the sacrifices of the Old Testament. It still remains,
however, in the Hebrew ethos that *it was man who brought
something to God* — as either gift or means of cementing fellowship — that the reconciliation might be achieved.[1]

In the New Testament Scriptures a new element is introduced. This is of such a subtle nature that it may easily be
overlooked. Here it is no longer *man* who brings the gift or
effects the reconciliation. It is rather God, or, perhaps better,
God-become-man, who does this. The logic behind this fact may
be found in the thought that, since by man the rift in the fellowship between God and man was made, so by man it must be
bridged. But as man of himself cannot overcome the breach,
God becomes man to do it in his name and on his behalf. It is
nowhere said by the New Testament writers that this is so, but
the doctrine of the atonement as they present it seems to pre-
suppose or postulate such logic.

In any case it is to be remarked as deeply significant that the
exemplar for the atoning work of Jesus Christ is not to be found
in the sacrifices of the Levitical system. At most this sacrificial
system lends to the New Testament some of its terminology for
a doctrine of the atonement. But the *stuff* out of which that
doctrine is formed comes rather from the several interpretations
of the work of Jesus Christ in terms of his *personal devotion* to
the will of God. Thus, as we have already seen in glancing at the
three major strands of New Testament tradition, *first,* in the
Synoptic Gospels the Herald of the gospel becomes its content
on his own part by assuming the role of the Suffering Servant
of Yahweh; *secondly,* in the teaching of the apostle Paul the

---

[1] Cf. C. H. Dodd, *The Epistle of Paul to the Romans* (1932) at 3:21 ff.
and in JTS, vol. xxxii, pp. 352–360; also V. Taylor, *Jesus and His Sacrifice*
(1937), pp. 49 ff., 53 f., 296.

Son of God gives himself as a willing sacrifice because behind that act is the Father's approbation and even personal desire (Rom. 5:8; II Cor. 5:19; Phil. 2:5 ff.); and *thirdly,* in The Epistle to the Hebrews the Son is shown to be the genuine high priest and so worthy to be the " mediator " between God and man (ch. 1:2 ff.; 4:15; 5:8 ff.).

In all these interpretations of our Lord's work it will be obvious that one factor remains constant — namely, Jesus Christ in his priestly or atoning work acts on behalf of God; God is the instigator of what he does. Thus, the Suffering Servant is Yahweh's servant and does his bidding. The Son is God's Son and of him Paul is constrained to write, " God was in Christ reconciling the world to himself " (II Cor. 5:19). The high priest is again God's Son, and it is because he dedicated himself to the doing of his Father's will (Heb. 10:7), that " by that will we have been sanctified through the offering of the body of Jesus Christ once for all " (v. 10).

Jesus Christ's priestly work, then, is to be seen in the dedication of his entire life, in the self-dedication exhibited in all that he said and did during his ministry. The experience of the cross represents merely the culmination of the whole: it is not the whole in and of itself. For our Lord had dedicated himself wholly to the doing of his Father's will at the very start of his ministry and he was from the first prepared to go wherever that dedication of himself should lead. Whenever Jesus met a " pharisee " — to employ the term in its popular and so derogatory sense — he was pilloried anew upon a cross. That on Golgotha was, therefore, in a real sense but the largest and most climactic cross of all. The prayer, " Not my will, but thine, be done," was symbolic not alone of this final act of sacrifice but of the tenor of his whole life. Our Lord's whole ministry, therefore, was a priestly one from its beginning to its end, and it found its source and motivation, not in man nor in man's purposes, but in God and in the will of God for him.

Since, then, Jesus Christ was so to speak " acting under orders," it would seem obvious that the atonement is one of man to God, never the reverse. God does not require to be reconciled. He is ever ready for renewal of the fellowship which man's sin has disrupted.

In support of this contention, C. H. Dodd has shown conclusively that in neither Old nor New Testament are the Hebrew and Greek verbs referring to atonement ever made to have God their object.[2] The thought that God requires to be propitiated or appeased is a pagan idea quite foreign to the prophetic Scriptures. *Expiation* consists rather in these Scriptures in the removal of that stumbling block between God and man which has destroyed their mutual fellowship. This stumbling block has always been man's rebellion against God's will (Gen. 3:1 ff.). Its removal accordingly is accomplished by displacing man's rebellion with obedience through the persuasive work of Christ (II Cor. 5:19). And it is always God who is the active agent in initiating the removal of this stumbling block. " God was in Christ reconciling " — such is the invariable teaching of the New Testament. It is God who yearns over his children who have departed into the far country (Luke 15:20), who searches out his lost sheep (Matt. 18:10–14), who sends his servants the prophets to reclaim his wayward people, and who at the last sends his unique Son, saying, " They will respect my son " (Mark 12:1–11).

The history of Christian theology is not lacking, it is true, in theories of the atonement that have held that Christ on the cross was endeavoring to appease his Father's wrath by the sacrifice of himself. In such theories stress has been laid on the passages in Paul which speak of the believer's being " bought with a price." [3] But, in the light of the teaching at which we have been looking, such language can have but one meaning, viz., that *the atonement has cost God much*. It has cost him, indeed, the very best he had to give, his unique Son.

To suggest that the price of our Lord's atoning death is paid to God, or alternatively to the devil, as such theories have held, is to turn the language of metaphor into crude prose. Paul's

---

[2] *Op. cit.*

[3] Cf. I Cor. 6:20; 7:23; and see also Acts 20:28; Eph. 1:7; Rev. 1:5; 5:6; 14:1–5.

words here are like those we employ in speaking of one boy's rescuing another and drowning in the attempt. The remark is often heard, " That brave deed cost the boy his life." If one were to ask, " To whom did he make the payment? " one would be put down as either lacking in imagination or as speaking jocularly out of turn. It is with such metaphorical language that we are dealing here in Paul beyond question. We have been " bought with a price " in the profound sense that God was prepared to spend the best he had — his own Son's life — in winning man back from rebellion against him. Such theories as we have mentioned are unworthy of this character of God and quite contrary to the prophetic teaching about his redeeming love. God does not require to be bought off. Indeed, his grace is not for sale, not even to his own Son! Nor can man do anything, nor need he do anything, to obtain it. It is his free gift in Jesus Christ (Eph. 2:8–10).

Was our Lord's atoning death necessary then? If the Father was prepared for it, was himself the instigator of it, was it not a useless piece of divine exhibitionism for Jesus to die on the cross? The answer to these and like questions is twofold: *First,* Jesus' death was necessary to God. *It was necessary to his being that kind of God,* the kind who would spare nothing that men might be restored to fellowship with himself. The point may be illustrated by means of a parable — The Parable of the Motor-car Factory:

The Kingdom of God is like unto the superintendent of a motor-car factory who conceived an idea for a new model of the car he manufactured. He called together his draftsmen and the heads of the various departments of his factory, therefore, and explained to them, employing diagrams and small models which he had made, just what the new car should be. Then he said to them, " Go back now to your offices and work out the several details that this new model may take to the road six months hence."

But one of the draftsmen was a Platonist and so, calling his fellows together, he said to them: " See here, it is the idea that is the real. Our superintendent has conceived the idea of this new model. Is it not, then, as good as made already? Why waste our time and effort in executing plans to achieve what now exists? " This seemed good to his associates; so they went back to their offices and did nothing.

But another of the department heads was a man of prophetic insight, and on careful scrutiny he discovered the defect in the other's argument. So he too called together his associates for conference and said to them: " Be assured that we have made a great mistake. The idea is not the only real. Not until it is worked over by an active personality and converted into steel and rubber may we rightly say that a new model car has come into existence! "

This also appeared to his colleagues to be true. So they went back to their drafting boards and the assembly line, and in due course the new model was rolling out of the factory's doors!

The point of this modern parable is one that we have already made in connection with our study of the theology of history. God has so ordered the universe in which we live that what happens on the historical plane is characterized by *actuality*. The historical event on earth has the ring of genuineness in heaven (Matt. 16:19; 18:18 f.). Consequently, it was not enough that God should *conceive the idea* of giving his Son to redeem man. The idea, to achieve actuality in terms of concrete effectiveness for man, had to be worked out on the historical level.

Let us suppose that having entertained the idea of suffering with a view to man's redemption, God had stopped short somewhere along the way — what then? He might, for instance, have found the thought of incarnation itself repugnant to him. Or being incarnate, the Son could conceivably have succumbed to the temptations which came his way — temptations that indicate quite clearly that redemptive suffering was, indeed, a matter of the greatest trial to his spirit. What if, at any of these points, Father or Son had recanted and gone back? Clearly, to be the God portrayed for us in the prophetic Scriptures, God was compelled by an inner necessity of his being to go through with the ordeal to the bitter end.

The historical, then, has meaning for God. Through Christ's death on the cross our reconciliation with him becomes an *actual* fact consummated for eternity. Clearly it could not have been achieved otherwise, not because God was not ready for the reconciliation to occur. We have already seen that there is no

Scriptural basis for such a supposition. Rather because reconciliation between persons is not achieved by ideas, by right
attitudes, by readiness to have it so, but only *by deeds,* by *paying
the cost,* and not alone by willingness to pay the cost. By the
historic event of the cross, accordingly, God actually achieved
his eternal purpose to pay to the full what it should cost to redeem man.

Again, the atoning death of our Lord was necessary to man.
It was required in order that man might be reconciled to God,
and we may be certain that nothing short of that death would
have served to achieve this end. In the death of Jesus Christ
there was present that strange, intangible, personal drawing
power which we associate with all spiritual mysteries.

It was surely of this that Paul was writing when he remarked
to the Corinthians, " The love of Christ constraineth [R.S.V.,
controls] us " (II Cor. 5:14). It was this also that he had in
mind when he wrote to the Romans, " For I am not ashamed of
the gospel: it is the power of God for salvation to every one
who has faith " (Rom. 1:16), and again, " The righteousness
of God has been manifested . . . in Jesus Christ . . . whom
God put forward as an expiation . . . to be received by faith "
(ch. 3:21–25).

Anderson Scott has made a genuine contribution to our understanding of these passages through a careful study of the
words involved. He has, for example, made it clear that Paul
means here by " manifested," not demonstrated, but rather
communicated. God manifested his love in Christ, then, in the
sense that on history's plane it became an active love carrying
through and impinging upon the individual and drawing him
irresistibly to himself. It is only so that according to the Scriptures " at-one-ment " can be achieved for man — not through
man's acquiring knowledge of a concept or idea of God's love,
but rather through its coming to him as an active force and
working by means of personal contact between Christ and the
believer in him.[4]

[4] This teaching of Paul is not to be confused with the " moral influence
theory " of the atonement. It is far richer and more meaningful than that

THE AT-ONE-MENT A SUCCESS

As in the case of the doctrine of the incarnation, so here there are two corollaries arising out of what we have been saying. The *first* of these is that on the view of prophetic realism the atonement really accomplishes the end in prospect relative to affecting personalities for their salvation. This is because this prophetic theology makes God the sponsor and instigator of the entire atoning program. In every other theology it is man who takes the initiative and man who carries through the actions involved in the whole matter. This is true even of those theologies labeled " Christian " wherein the Son purchases the good will of the Father. For in such theologies it is the Son *as man* who takes the initiative of which we speak. Otherwise the point they seek to make has no meaning whatever.

With the prophetic theology it is quite otherwise. Here the thought that God originates and carries through the atoning work from first to last is taken with the utmost seriousness. And the result is that the atonement is a success! For man can be frustrated, but God never. If God could ultimately be frustrated in his purposes, he would clearly have resigned his Godship.

This is one of the insights that it is the purpose of the author of Hebrews to elaborate. In the heart of that epistle the work of our Lord as the great high priest is contrasted with that of the Levitical priesthood at just this point (Heb. 9:13; 10:10–14, 19–25). The latter, through the sacrificial system of the *cultus* carried on by man and for man's salvation, endeavored to do what man could do toward this end. The result was a round of futility concerned with the " washing of pots and pans," " the sprinkling of the ashes of a heifer " on an unclean people, the

---

theory supposes. Moral influence is that merely of an *idea*. But Paul's teaching, as we have just seen, is based on the *active impinging of the person* of God in Christ on the individual. There can be no stronger force in all the world than this personal reaching out of a personal God to encircle other persons with his love. The reference is to C. A. Anderson Scott's *Christianity According to St. Paul*, pp. 62 ff. Cambridge University Press, 1927.

offering of bulls and goats. And in the end all that was achieved was the maintenance of the *cultus* itself with a view to its starting, so to speak, from scratch with each New Year. Even the Day of Atonement — the only day's ceremonies with which Hebrews is concerned — had no other effect than this. The entire system had the sole merit of acting as a perpetual motion machine which required no other power than that provided from within itself to keep it running! But the work of Christ for this epistle's author, as for all the New Testament, had behind it the originating and generating power of God himself (chs. 2:10; 5:8 ff.; 9:13 f.). In consequence that work was effective for the end which was had in view. It has made it possible for us to " draw near to the throne of grace . . . with confidence " (chs. 4:16; 10:22).

Paul is treating of the same insight, though with a slightly different terminology, in Rom. 3:21 ff. The word translated " expiation " here is *hilastērion* in the Greek, the term used in the Septuagint to translate the Hebrew *kapporeth,* which is often employed to refer to the " mercy seat " on the Ark of the Covenant. Whether or not Paul's meaning here is to be taken so dramatically as to imagine with Ritschl that he speaks of Jesus as our mercy seat, or rather more simply with Deissmann that the word in question is an adjective meaning " of expiatory value," in any case the point is that Jesus Christ is the meeting place between God and man. He is this, says Paul, because it is he " whom God put forward as an expiation by his blood, to be received by faith " (v. 25). Again, the initiative is seen to be God's and only his, and because this is so, the reconciliation intended is effected.

MAN IS A PARTNER TO GOD'S REDEMPTIVE PURPOSE

The second corollary of the prophetic doctrine of the atonement is that *man on this view is drawn into the orbit of God's redemptive activity.* According to the prophetic Scriptures of both Testaments, when God acts on the plane of history, he always acts through men — either a prophet or another, in this case through his own Son become man. This is the theme of

Hebrews, ch. 2, as it is also of Paul in Phil. 2:5 ff. and of the Synoptic Gospels and their sources.[5] But as Jesus walked in Galilee he called other men to join himself in this saving work, employing the characteristic expressions, " Follow me," or, " Come after me," to accomplish this end. And he warned those who followed him, " Whoever does not bear his own cross and come after me, cannot be my disciple " (Luke 14:27).

This bearing of the cross was not, then, according to our Lord something reserved for the great martyrs of the faith. It was for every disciple of his. All Christians are potential " martyrs " in the English sense of the word, even as all are by their call and profession " witnesses " (the Greek sense of the same word).

Paul has shown how this idea of sharing in the redemptive activity of God in Christ came to practical expression in his own evangelistic and administrative work for the Christian Church. In Col. 1:24 he wrote, " Now I rejoice in my sufferings for your sake, and in my flesh I complete what is lacking in Christ's afflictions for the sake of his body, that is, the church. . . ." This principle of participation in God's redemptive activity may be generalized and applied to every member of the body of Christ. This is to adopt with reference to the entire redemptive community the concept of the Suffering Servant — a concept which was in the first instance corporate rather than (or as well as) individual, as is generally agreed among Old Testament scholars.

This adaptation of the Servant concept to the entire community enables us to see how thoroughly prophetic in spirit the New Testament Scriptures really are as regards the matter of the atonement. For it brings the prophetic concept of " corporate personality " into the picture in a real way. This is a view of man which, much like modern sociology, sees him, not as an individual isolated from the community, but rather living his life in a series of groups (social, intellectual, economic, religious, and the like) in which with the groups in question he

[5] Cf. Mark 10:45; Luke 19:10 (L); 22:14–23 (L; cf. Mark 14:22–25); Matt. 1:21 (M); John 6:35–40; Q is the only source not having the motif.

experiences a mutuality of privilege and responsibility.[6]

T. W. Manson has shown that the prophetic doctrine of the *remnant* is not that of a redeemed society but rather of a *redeeming one* according to the best insights of the Hebrew prophets. Further, he has pointed out that it is this redemptive remnant which in the New Testament becomes the Christian Church.[7] Accordingly, it is at this point of *corporate participation* that the doctrines of the atonement and the Church coalesce and become one in Scripture's prophetic realism. We shall have occasion to elaborate on this theme in chapter 23 below.

Meanwhile, it will suffice to close this chapter by stating explicitly what has been implicit throughout our discussion, that the priestly doctrine embodied in the Levitical system had no genuine contribution to make to New Testament teaching on the atonement for the reason that, as *Hebrews* points out (ch. 9:9 f.), that system was framed at a subhuman level and so as regards man's spirit resulted in a mere round of futility. The Suffering Servant and remnant concepts elaborated by the Hebrew prophets, contrariwise, had in them the germ of a truly great doctrine on the divine-human level. It was this prophetic teaching, then, and not the Levitical priestly one which was perpetuated in and elaborated by the New Testament doctrines of the work of Christ and the Christian Church.

14. *The Resurrection and Prophetic Realism*

THE RESURRECTION of our Lord was the major point of emphasis in the gospel as preached by the Early Church of the book of *The Acts,* even eclipsing, though not entirely displacing, the story of the cross (Acts 2:24–36). One reason for

---

[6] Cf. H. Wheeler Robinson, *Redemption and Revelation* (1942), pp. 149 f., 258 ff.

[7] Cf. T. W. Manson, *The Teaching of Jesus* (1948, reprint of Second Edition of 1935), pp. 178 ff., 227 ff.

this is that the Church at the first was stunned by the *mysterium tremendum* of the resurrection experience. It was not psychologically prepared for either our Lord's death or his resurrection, though, on the testimony of Mark, Jesus had on three occasions at least warned his disciples to expect these two events.[1]

Bultmann and others have sought to explain this psychological unpreparedness by suggesting that Mark was undoubtedly unreliable in his recording of the facts of our Lord's teaching at this point. Jesus' prophecies of these events are all, in Bultmann's judgment, *vaticinia post eventum* — fancied prophecies placed on Jesus' lips by the Evangelist in the light of the events.[2] An alternative and more likely explanation is to be found in the fact that the disciples of Jesus were Jews, who shared the common Jewish expectation of a political messiah. This expectation formed for their minds a psychological *block* against which the teaching of Jesus at this point made no impression. To the last they were heard inquiring, " Lord, will you at this time restore the kingdom to Israel? " (Acts 1:6). It can scarcely be doubted that such spiritual obtuseness really characterized Jesus' little band. This is a phenomenon that has recurred many times throughout history in the presence of the great, and notably in the case of those of prophetic stature on the Hebrew scene.[3]

Accordingly, when the resurrection occurred, it blotted out everything else before the Church's mind for the moment. And it became at once the all-important factor in the latter's apologetic regarding the cross — the " stumbling-block " for contemporary Judaism as it had been at first for the disciples themselves (cf. Mark 8:32 with I Cor. 1:23). A " crucified Messiah " made no sense to any Jew who had been nourished on the idea of a political hero, scion of the house of David, whose most noteworthy anticipated achievement was to be the routing of the enemies of Israel. Perhaps the best contribution of form criticism to our understanding of this period has been to establish the fact that the " resurrection narratives " were the earliest

---

[1] Cf. Mark 8:31; 9:30–32; 10:32–34.
[2] *Op. cit.*, p. 30; per contra see Vincent Taylor, *op. cit.*, pp. 85 ff.
[3] Cf. Matt. 23:29–32; Luke 11:47 ff.

portions of our Gospels to be written down — and that for the reason that the Church almost immediately sensed their apologetic value in portraying the resurrection as God's *seal* on the work of the crucified Redeemer.[4]

We need not wonder, accordingly, that for the moment the Church was unable to see this event of the resurrection in its proper historical perspective and in its relation to the other events — life, ministry, person, teaching, death — which make up the total meaning of Jesus Christ for mankind. The fact that for them the resurrection was temporarily out of focus is the best possible proof of the reality of the experiences which they report. The later New Testament writers do not neglect the resurrection, nor minimize its importance, though it is apparent that their accounts are not so charged with emotion as the earlier narratives. Thus, in I Peter 1:3 we read that God " has begotten us by his great mercy unto a lively hope through the resurrection of Jesus Christ from the dead." The apostle Paul too, for all his greater stress upon the redemptive value of the cross, when the occasion requires can write a chapter on the integral part which the resurrection plays in the gospel preached both by himself and the " apostles who were before " him (I Cor., ch. 15) . That he is aware of its penetrating to the very heart of the message that he must proclaim is shown in his use of it to exhibit the source and dynamic behind Christian ethical living also.[5]

But, in addition to the apologetic value that the Early Church attached to this event, there is another reason for its emphasis upon the resurrection of our Lord. This is the fact that in it the Christian community saw a tremendous exhibition of the power of God at work in and through his Son. This is the point of stress in Peter's Pentecostal address according to the account in Acts, ch. 2. " But God," says Peter, " raised him up, having loosed the pangs of death, because it was not possible for him

---

[4] Cf. Vincent Taylor, *The Formation of the Gospel Tradition* (1933) , pp. 47 f. and *The Gospel According to St. Mark* (1952) , pp. 524 f.; also M. Dibelius, *From Tradition to Gospel* (1934) , pp. 178–217, *et al.*

[5] Cf. Rom. 6:5 f.; Eph. 2:6; Phil. 3:10 f.

to be held by it. . . . Being therefore exalted at the right hand of God, and having received from the Father the promise of the Holy Spirit, he has poured out this which you see and hear. . . . Let all the house of Israel therefore know assuredly that God has made him both Lord and Christ, this Jesus whom you crucified " (vs. 24, 33, 36).

This emphasis upon the power of the resurrection is still that of Paul in his epistles. To the Romans he writes that Jesus Christ was " designated Son of God in power according to the Spirit of holiness by his resurrection from the dead " (Rom. 1:4). To the Philippian Church he says that even so late in his ministry his fondest wish is to " know him and the power of his resurrection " in his own life (Phil. 3:10). Much, too, of the Epistle to the Ephesians is written about the thought of " the immeasurable greatness " of the power of God which was manifested in Christ " when he raised him from the dead " (Eph. 1:19 f.).

It is highly significant in this connection that Paul invariably makes God the active agent in the resurrection of his Son. The latter does not spontaneously rise up but rather is " raised from the dead by the glory of the Father " (Rom. 6:4; cf. 8:11, 34; 10:9; I Cor. 15:12 ff., 20, etc.). Just as God the Father is found to be behind both the incarnation and the atonement, therefore, so he is behind the resurrection. This fact has great and important implications, not alone for Christ and his labors, but also for the salvation of mankind.

Kirsopp Lake pointed out that *Luke-Acts,* and possibly *John,* maintain a distinction between the resurrection and ascension of our Lord.[6] Paul on the other hand, he suggested, fuses the two events into one, or perhaps better makes no real distinction between them.[7] Whether Lake's observation is valid or otherwise, it serves at all events to underline the fact that both these events (resurrection and ascension), in the Early Church's Scriptures stand for God's exaltation of Jesus Christ to his right

[6] Cf. *The Beginnings of Christianity* (1933), vol. v, pp. 17 ff.

[7] Cf. Luke 24:39; Acts 1:9–11; John 20:27 ff.; Rom. 8:9 ff.; I Cor., ch. 15; II Cor. 3:17.

hand to receive moral and spiritual sway over the lives and destinies of men as his viceroy. In the thinking of the Early Church, accordingly, the succession of ideas clustering round the resurrection of our Lord will run: this event is God's seal upon his work; the affixing of that seal has brought into operation the immeasurable power of God; and that power has released our Lord for further active service under the Father's direction and in man's behalf. The resurrection, it may then be said, points up what the Church has termed the office of Christ's *kingship*.[8]

The Prophetic Psychology and the Resurrection

It seems clear that the doctrine of the resurrection is a logical necessity if one accept as a postulate the Hebrew prophetic psychology. That psychology denied the Greek idea that man was a dichotomy composed of two mutually exclusive principles (soul and body), which could be so far separated that the disintegration of the latter could occur simultaneously with the preservation of the former. The Hebrew psychology taught rather that the individual was an essential unity composed of a body into which the spirit (as an animating force) had been blown by the breath of God (Gen. 2:7).

According to this teaching the body *is* the person on his active side and is altogether essential to his activity and continued existence. Without the body a person would be unable to function in any particular, and to the Hebrew prophet a functionless, living person would be a contradiction in terms! Such a person also would possess no individuality whatever, for spirit as such is not conceived as possessed of the principle of individuation.

Wheeler Robinson, to whom we are indebted in large part for an analysis of the Hebrew psychology, writes that to the mind of the Hebrew prophet " his body was a complex of localized functions, and his body was himself. Hebrew has no proper word for, and no organic idea of, ' body.' Nephesh, the animating principle of the body, is really a quasi-material aspect of its life." " If we realize this feature of the Hebrew psychology," this

[8] This thought goes back to Mark 12:36, where Jesus quotes Ps. 110:1 f., a passage suggestive of the kingly office.

author continues, " it helps us to understand the reference to the offending eye or hand or foot in the New Testament (Mark 9:43 f.), the Pauline parable of the body and its members (I Cor. 12:12 ff.), the Pauline doctrine of sin, as the invader of the psychically conceived flesh."[9] Against the background of such a psychology, it is obvious that a doctrine of the immortality of the soul without reference to the like saving of the body would have no meaning!

It is Paul who adapted this psychology to the needs of the Christian faith. He did this particularly in his correspondence with the Church in the Greek city of Corinth. Here the *nature* of the resurrection body is discussed by him only because the *fact* of the resurrection itself has been challenged on the ground that it is impossible to conceive of any sort of body that would be useful in the eternal order (I Cor. 15:35 ff.). The argument appears to lend itself to statement in terms of a syllogism like the following: first, a resurrection presupposes a body to be raised that would be useful in the eternal order; secondly, but such a body is unthinkable; therefore, thirdly, there is no resurrection.

This sort of argument is quite obviously one raised from the standpoint of Greek thought. All Jews untinged by such thought believed in the resurrection of the body in a quite literal fashion, particularly such as were influenced by Pharisaic teaching. This would include almost everyone in the Jewish circle with the single exception of the Sadducees, who denied the doctrine presumably because it was not specifically taught in the Old Testament, as well as for the reason that they had been tinged with Greek cultural ideas from the time of the Seleucids.[10]

In dealing with the problem as it presented itself at Corinth, Paul had to steer a narrow course between the Scylla of the Hellenic doctrine of the immortality of the soul and the Charybdis of Pharisaic materialism. Plato had taught that " every soul is immortal "[11] and that when it comes in contact with matter (or " something solid," as he calls it), " it settles down,

---

[9] *Op. cit.,* pp. 140 ff.
[10] Cf. Mark 12:18; Josephus, *Antiq.* 18, 1, 3; *Jew. Wars* 2, 8, 14.
[11] Cf. *Phaedo* 105.55.E; *Phaedrus* 245.24.D, *et al.*

taking upon itself an earthly body." " The whole," he then declares, " compounded of soul and body, is called a living being." [12] But, he proceeds, " soul, considered collectively . . . governs the whole world," and so is pre-existent to the incarnate life which it may live. Feeling itself imprisoned, therefore, in the body, it endeavors to escape from the latter as soon as it inhabits it, and in doing so it may go either up or down, that is, may transmigrate into lower forms of life or else may return upward to God.[13]

The Stoics took over much of Plato's thought and identified the individual soul with the *Reason* which is found in God. They termed it *spermatikos logos* (seedlike reason, literally), or the "generative *principle* in organisms." [14] At death this principle found release and flew back to the divine from which it had come forth. This is pure pantheism, of course, and it appears to have been a logical development of the Platonic doctrine when followed through to a conclusion. Such was the Greek thought current in Paul's day at Corinth and elsewhere.

On the other side, the Pharisaical, Paul had to deal with a doctrine of the resurrection that was frankly materialistic. That the dead " might be recognized, it seemed necessary," so thought the Jews contemporary with Paul, " to assume that they would rise with the defects and deformities they had in life: the lame, lame; the blind, blind. . . . It was also believed that the dead would rise clothed as they had been in life, as the witch of Endor saw Samuel; or in the garments in which they were buried." [15]

Steering a course between these two extremes — pantheism and materialism — Paul taught that there was both a continuity and a discontinuity between man's earthly life and that beyond. To show this he chose the analogy of the seed which the farmer plants in the ground. The continuity appears in the fact that " like begets like ": you sow wheat and reap the same, not barley nor corn (I Cor. 15:38) . Similarly — so the argument would

[12] *Ibid.*, 246.25.C.
[13] *Ibid.*, 246.25.C. through 249.29.D.
[14] Cf. Liddell and Scott, *op. cit.*, art. *logos*, III, 7, b.
[15] Cf. George Foot Moore, *Judaism* (1927) , vol. ii, pp. 380 f.

run — when you bury John Doe, you expect John Doe to rise and rightly so. But the discontinuity appears in the undoubted fact that there is no single portion of that which is sown in the grain as reaped (v. 37). So it is with the resurrection of believers. The body that dies is not the body that rises (vs. 37 and 42 ff.). The material stuff of which a man is made will be changed " in the twinkling of an eye," though his identity will persist. Thus there is continuity in discontinuity.

Obviously Paul's doctrine is based on the teaching of the Hebrew prophetic psychology that the body is not just so much flesh and bone, but is rather the active individual himself, as he is distinct from all other individuals. And what he is concerned to preserve in the afterlife is this identity of the individual as such.

While Paul followed the Hebrew psychology, therefore, in arguing for the resurrection of Christian believers, it is equally clear from this same chapter of I Corinthians that the thought of our Lord's resurrection was not a matter of deduction on his part. He merely states this latter as a well-known fact, giving an account and a fairly complete one of the resurrection appearances (vs. 1–8). The argument at this point runs along these lines: that Jesus Christ has been raised from the dead needs no demonstration beyond the simple testimony of those who saw him afterward. Some " five hundred brethren " and more are involved. Most of these are " still alive " (v. 6), and anyone who doubts the facts involved may inquire of some of them.

From this known fact, however, one may argue to the unknown — namely, to the question of the resurrection of believers in Jesus. Consequently, to the argument from the Hebrew prophetic psychology Paul adds a theological one in proof of believer resurrection. Believers, he argues, will be raised for the reason that " as by a man came death, by a man has come also the resurrection of the dead. For as in Adam all die, so also in Christ shall all be made alive " (vs. 21 f.). It is clear, then, that it is fundamental to the prophetic doctrine of the resurrection that (a) the resurrection occurs only by the power and will of God, and (b) results in the perpetuation of the individuality of the believer who is united to Jesus Christ in a life-giving fellowship. The individual, so the prophetic doctrine teaches, is not swallowed up in a pantheistic sea called "the divine" at death, nor does he rise to a life whose requirements are such as to demand the persistence of his present flesh-and-bone body. He will find, however, that he is still himself, that he is still *an active personality qualified to carry on* in the new order, and that he is capable through his close association with his Lord to complete tasks that previously were impossible for him.[16]

The Resurrection of Believers in Jesus Christ

It will have already been apparent that the connection between the resurrection of Jesus Christ and that of his followers is so close and intimate that we must pass imperceptibly from the one to the other. However, a concluding word needs to be said at this point about the resurrection of the latter. Cullmann's thesis of the redemption-revelation line includes among other novel features the idea that the teaching of the New Testament Scriptures divided the Messianic age as taught by Jewish eschatology into two parts. The Christian faith early saw ahead two future ages instead of Judaism's one, namely, one on earth beginning with the incarnation, ministry, death, and resurrection of our Lord, and a second that was to begin with the Parousia (the so-called "Second Coming") and extend therefrom throughout eternity.[17]

The first of these eschatological periods is equivalent to what C. H. Dodd has termed the epoch of "realized eschatology"[18] and Albrecht Oepke, "the new phase of redemptive history into which believers have been transferred along with Christ" (*Glaubensrealität*).[19] The second is that usually referred to by Christians as the "future life" and as after the "Second Coming" of our Lord.

[16] It is interesting to note how close the Hebrew psychology is to certain modern developments in this field from William James, the *Gestalt* psychology and Behaviorism to the present day. It is clearly closer to modern psychology than either is to that of Greek thought.

[17] Cf. Cullmann, *op. cit.,* pp. 82 ff., 144 ff.

[18] Cf. C. H. Dodd, *The Parables of the Kingdom* (1936).

[19] Cf. Kittel's *Wörterbuch,* II, p. 335, lines 25 f.

In both these eschatological periods the Christian's life is manifestly affected by the fact of our Lord's resurrection. In consequence Paul, for example, uses the term " resurrection " with reference to the Christian's experience in both periods. In the *first* period — that upon earth and in the fellowship of the Church — the resurrection of believers is of an *ethical* nature.[20] This results from believers being alive " in Christ," says Paul, in living fellowship with the Lord of life and with the consequent dynamic issuing from this relationship. This idea of an ethical resurrection was elaborated by Paul alone under that name, though no doubt the conception was generally taught in the Early Church.[21] This ethical resurrection following upon and in living communion with Jesus Christ was a historical fact remarked by both Christian and pagan writers alike in the early Christian centuries.

In the *second* eschatological period — that in heaven or eternity — believers who have been raised with Jesus will live and reign with him. This resurrection of the entire individual along the lines above sketched out, that he may carry on in eternity, is the logical product of the concept of " corporate personality " to which reference has previously been made. Again, it is Paul who elaborates this doctrine and holds that it is those who are now " in Christ " — that is, in living communion with him — who will be raised up (I Cor. 15:20–22). But the rest of the New Testament assumes the same logic while expressing its result in different terms.[22]

[20] Cf. Rom. 6:1 ff.; Eph. 2:1 ff., *et al.*

[21] So Oepke, *op. cit.*, lines 16 ff.

[22] Cf. John 6:39 ff.; Heb. 6:2; and the " Bride, the wife of the Lamb " concept to be found in Rev. 21:9 as well as in Eph. 5:21 ff. In his *Preface to Personality* (1952), Surjit Singh has in rather unique fashion developed the thought of this chapter. Starting with the resurrection of Jesus Christ and of the believer in him, he shows how " the historical *koinonia* " became the basis of the " disciples' fellowship with their master " and how this " created in them a sense of personal worth and destiny. They became personalities — the children of God. Moreover they received a vocation from this fellowship, and that is to awaken in men and women everywhere a high sense of personal destiny which God in his infinite mercy has bestowed upon them " (p. 2).

THE CONTENT OF SCRIPTURE'S
PROPHETIC REALISM

B. The Gospel of God.

'And God said to Moses,
I will be what I will be:
And He said, *You shall say
to the children of Israel,*
I will be has sent me to you.'
— EXODUS 3:14.*

---

* The translation of God's name in the quotation on the title page of this section is perhaps the most commonly adopted. If, however, the verb is taken as a causative and rendered ' I cause to be what I cause to be,' this equally fits my thought in this chapter. Cf. W. F. Albright, *From the Stone Age to Christianity* (1940) , pp. 198 f.

The Content of Scripture's Prophetic Realism

B. The Gospel of God

SYNOPSIS

*T*HIS TOPIC *was reserved for presentation at the point at which we have now arrived for the reason that our knowledge of* God *is one that comes to us in historical sequence. We know him through his working within history and as we observe his redemptive activity. In this section, accordingly, we discuss first the functional or historic-pragmatic definition of God as God-in-history. In the course of the discussion it is pointed out that of the two terms used by the Hebrew prophets to indicate the totality of God's nature, they were more interested in his* sedaqah (*righteousness, or right dealing with men*), *than in his* qodesh (*holiness, or what God is in himself apart from his world*) *. This* sedaqah *concept of God-in-history is next analyzed along three lines. (a) God is Creator and Father, (b) God is Teacher, and (c) God is Redeemer and Friend. It is shown by a multiplicity of illustration that this analysis covers the ideas of the prophetic revelation in both Testaments relative to the nature of God.*

Finally, *the section closes with the suggestion that for Scripture's prophetic realism God-in-himself and God-in-history are the same God. It is true that the Hebrew prophets stopped short of a speculative endeavor to prove this. So did the New Testament Church. It was not until the Christian faith came to the formation of the creeds within the Greek ethos that a doctrine of the Trinity was formulated. Nonetheless, the data for this doctrine lie at hand within the pages of the New Testament and the formulation is in accord at once with prophetic realism and with modern sociology and social ethics.*

15. *The Functional Definition of God as God-in-History*

THE CENTRAL PROBLEM of Biblical theology concerns the nature of God. It may appear strange, therefore, that the discussion of this question has been delayed to this point in the present volume. It has been usual, indeed, for Biblical theologians to open such a study as we are here making with this topic. But this has not been the order of revelation nor is it that of Scripture's prophetic realism. We have already observed that, according to the writer of Ex., ch. 3, God refused to disclose himself in his fullness in a single conversation with Moses, and the suggestion has been made that this is illustrative of his usual attitude. Adopting a like procedure we have not written first of God but rather of " God's Purpose in History," and of " The Gospel of Jesus Christ " before discussing " The Gospel of God."

We have done this because God discloses himself to man — as the prophetic writer hinted that He said to Moses — in historical events rather than by means of personal photographs.[1] Even Moses was not permitted to see God's " face," but could only behold his " back " (Ex. 33:23) . It is true that in v. 11 it is said

[1] Cf. E. Stauffer's remark in his *Die Theologie des Neuen Testaments* (1948, Fourth Edition) : " Hence in the N.T. the phrase *peri theou* never occurs (only *peri patros* in John 16:25) . . . If God speaks with us, he speaks with us concerning his Son (Rom. 1:2 ff.; I John 5:9) " — p. 280, n. 533. This is as much as to say that God never reveals himself as he is, but only as he is prepared to show himself on the plane of history, and that is in his character of the Son of God.

that " the Lord used to speak to Moses face to face, as a man speaks to his friend," but the prophetic writer did not mean by this that Moses could " see " God, else he would not have gone on to remark in God's name, " You cannot see my face; for man shall not see me and live " (v. 20). The Hebrew prophets " saw " God only in his activities in history. At most they " heard " his voice speaking to them by way of interpreting these acts of his as other men were never privileged to hear him speak. But they never saw him.

There have been those like Jacob and Isaiah who after some intimate disclosure of God's nature, because of the very intensity of the experience, have thought themselves able to say, " I have seen God face to face, and yet my life is preserved " (Gen. 32:30), or " my eyes have seen the King, the Lord of hosts! " (Isa. 6:5). But in reality they have not seen God. What they have seen is rather some sort of intermediary of his — such as the " man " with whom Jacob wrestled all night or the " seraphim " of Isaiah's vision. Even these latter as was customary in the prophetic writings covered their faces before God! [2] Such is the prophetic teaching generally, and John has given us a conclusive summary in the words, " No man has ever seen God; the only Son, who is in the bosom of the Father, he has made him known " (John 1:18).

According to the prophetic Scriptures, therefore, man knows God by His activity in history before he knows Him. Or, better perhaps, man discerns God's handicraft on creation's stage before realizing that it is God who is at work. It is to this that Paul refers in Rom. 1:19–21. And he roundly condemns man for beholding God's works of creation (" the things that have been made ") without acknowledging the Creator behind them (" his invisible nature . . . his eternal power and deity "). Paul is no doubt right in criticizing man for his lack of insight and faith. Yet the sequence inevitably must be in the order indi-

[2] Isaiah says specifically of the occasion, " I saw the Lord . . . high and lifted up " (v. 1). But, as George Adam Smith remarks, " Isaiah describes no face, only a Presence and a Session . . . ' a sweepy garment vast and white ' "; cf. his *The Book of Isaiah* (1900, Twelfth Edition), vol. i, p. 63. Note also John's description of the Lord on his throne in Rev. 4:3.

cated — man sees God's act *first;* the word of insight whereby God is known as being behind his works follows only thereafter, either immediately or upon reflection. The only God whom we know, accordingly, is the God who reveals himself in his historical activity and pre-eminently in Jesus Christ who is " the incarnate Word of God," that is to say, the Word revealing itself in God's activity through a person whom he has wholly identified with himself.

This thought is expressed in the phrase with which this section is headed — the gospel of God. It occurs some eight times in the New Testament in just this form.[3] A study of these passages indicates that probably all of them should be interpreted in the light of two (Mark 1:14; Rom. 1:1). For these two appear to give the key to the understanding of the others.

In the two passages taken as determinative for the group, God is clearly the subject or author, and not the object or content, of the gospel.[4] This is shown in Mark 1:14 by the direct statement that the gospel as preached by Jesus Christ concerns the fulfillment of the time and the Kingdom of God being at hand. Likewise Paul in Rom. 1:1 ff. through the use of the phrase " concerning his Son," makes it quite evident that by the " gospel of God " he does not mean that God is the gospel's content or that the gospel is about God, but rather that God is its prime mover or executor.[5]

The other six passages do not so readily indicate their meaning in the use of the phrase in question. However, nothing in their contents appears to suggest anything contrary to the interpretation just made for the two whose meaning is clear. Accordingly, we may assume that in all cases of its use in the New Testament the phrase, " Gospel of God," means, " the gospel

[3] Cf. Mark 1:14; Rom. 1:1 ff.; 15:16; II Cor. 11:7; I Thess. 2:2, 8, 9; I Peter 4:17.

[4] Cf. also Friedrich in Kittel's *Wörterbuch,* II, p. 726, lines 9 ff., and p. 729, lines 18 ff.

[5] Perhaps I Tim. 1:11 should be added to the list in note 3. Its probable translation is, " The glorious gospel of the blessed God " (R.S.V.), and not, " The gospel of the glory of the blessed God " (A.S.V.): *per contra* cf. Friedrich, *op. cit.,* p. 631, lines 34 f.

whose originator and sponsor is God." [6] And in the present chapter we shall endeavor to discover somewhat of the nature of God in the same manner that revelation itself proceeds — viz., by indirection, by observing what sort of God God is as we see him at work.

GOD REVEALED IN EXPERIENCE

What we have just been saying about the phrase, " Gospel of God," amounts to this: we need not expect to find a metaphysical definition or knowledge of God in the prophetic Scriptures. The gospel which is the definitive content of Scripture does not contain a description of what God is in himself. It does not endeavor to describe God in abstract fashion as, so to speak, a *Ding an sich*. Karl Barth was right, or at any rate he was speaking in accord with the point of view of the Scriptures, when he wrote many years ago that God can never be made the *object* of man's investigation or experimentation. To the very last God remains a (indeed, *the*) *Subject*. He cannot be placed like a protozoan beneath a microscope, nor like a beetle under a dissecting needle, nor yet like a planet at the end of a telescope. To the very end God remains the true and living God, Sovereign Subject over and never object of man's most clever scrutiny, showing himself to man only by a series of saving acts.

All this is so because God is a Sovereign Person and it is the distinguishing characteristic of persons that they must reveal themselves if they are to be known. It would, therefore, be contrary to all that we have thus far said about the prophetic revelation to suggest that the gospel of God means categorically the gospel *about* God. God never gave any of his prophets a message about himself any more than he revealed himself directly to them. Rather he gave them a message about his working, about the salvation which he afforded man, about his Son and his Son's atoning work and resurrection, about his love and gracious activities. And it is precisely in such activity, in such

---

[6] In the O.T. also God is never the content of the gospel message. Cf. for example, Isa. 52:7.

saving work, in such gracious dealings with men, that he is to be known and only so.[7]

The Hebrew prophets said all this in their own way. They had two special terms by means of which they endeavored to state all that could be said about God — viz., *qodesh* (holiness) and *sedaqah* (righteousness). The first of these is from a stem meaning *separateness*. It therefore lent itself to use wherever and after whatever fashion God was to be spoken of *in himself* or in opposition to or over against his world. This *qodesh* of God was, as Burrows has remarked, " the ' numinous ' quality of Deity, the *mysterium tremendum,* or, more particularly, the ' otherness ' of God, his separation from everything ordinary, earthly, or human." [8] *Qodesh,* then, brings us as near to a definition of God in metaphysical terms as the prophets ever came in their thought of him.

The Priestly Meaning of " Holiness "

The meaning of this word *qodesh,* however, underwent a development in two directions and these tended to lead away from the original metaphysical sense which it had. One of these developments was due to the influence of the priest in Israel. At his hands *qodesh* acquired a ceremonial connotation and came to mean " set apart " or " dedicated " for ritualistic purposes in connection with the worship of Yahweh in the Temple. The attribute of separateness, therefore, which was originally a metaphysical one attaching to Yahweh, now attached itself to *things* — to the Temple and the furniture and sacrifices pertaining to the same (Lev. 16:27; 22:4; Num. 4:15; Ps. 11:4; Matt. 24:15;

[7] H. Richard Niebuhr, in *The Meaning of Revelation* (1946), means, I think, much the same when he remarks — " Revelation means God, God who discloses himself to us throughout history as our knower, our author, our judge, and our only saviour " (p. 152). Oepke, in Kittel's *Wörterbuch,* also defines revelation in the N.T. sense as, " The self-tendering of the Father of Jesus Christ to the Community " (III, p. 596, lines 7 f.), and in the O.T. sense as Yahweh revealing himself " as the Lord of history, as the Holy and Merciful One, as the Creator of the World " (*ibid.,* p. 574, lines 19 f.).

[8] Cf. Millar Burrows, *An Outline of Biblical Theology* (1946), p. 68.

Heb. 9:1). Animals, produce, money then became *qādosh* according as they were "separated" to the service of Yahweh (Num. 4:4, 19; 18:19; 31:6; 35:25). The garments of the priests too were holy in this sense (Ex. 35:19; Lev. 16:32), as were also the various parts of the tabernacle and Temple (Lev. 6:16; I Chron. 29:3), and the fellowship meals with God which were to be eaten in them (Lev. 6:17 ff.).

THE PROPHETIC MEANING OF "HOLINESS"

The other development of *qodesh* occurred under the exclusive influence of the Hebrew prophet. Here the thought of separateness indigenous to the term took on an ethical meaning quite unlike that given it by the priest. This appears already in the vision of Isaiah to which attention was directed above. Note the prophet's reaction to what he saw and particularly to the hymn of the heavenly beings in which the word thrice repeated is the adjective "holy." "Woe is me!" says Isaiah, "for I am undone; because I am a man of unclean lips, and I dwell in the midst of a people of unclean lips: for my eyes have seen the King, the Lord of hosts!" (Isa. 6:5.)

Skinner's comment on this passage can scarcely be bettered, one imagines: "Although the idea of holiness in the O.T. is never to be identified with that of moral purity, it is clear from Isaiah's immediate sense of guilt that ethical perfection is included among the attributes that make up the holiness or Godhead of Jehovah." [9] I should like to call particular attention to two points that emerge from Skinner's statement: *first,* that the "ethical perfection" of which he speaks is something which only the Hebrew prophet saw and attached to the word *qodesh,* so far as our records go in any event; the people generally no doubt followed the priest in the ceremonial definition of the term to a large extent. Skinner does not say this, but it is obvious, I think, that it is only the prophet or one sharing his insights who would have seen this point. *Again,* Skinner's equation of "holiness" with Yahweh's "Godhead" is advisedly made; for the word to the Hebrew prophet's mind stood for

[9] Cf. J. Skinner, *op. cit., in loc.*

precisely all that God was or could be conceived to be in himself. Its etymological meaning of "separateness" made such a conception possible. One may say, therefore, that the following equations would express with a degree of accuracy the prophet's mind: *qodesh* = ethical character = Godhead (or, God-in-himself). God-in-himself, that is to say, was for the prophet a person the pattern of whose nature was ethical character, and the name for that pattern was *qodesh* or holiness.

The Holiness Code in Lev., ch. 19 through 26, furnishes us with a combination of both priestly and prophetic views regarding holiness — the best to be found in Scripture. For the writer of this portion of the book of Leviticus the dictum, " You shall be holy; for I the Lord your God am holy " (ch. 19:2), is an inclusive statement, indicative of the totality of man's relation to God and to his fellow man. As we read through the code it becomes clear that " holiness " for him includes both the *ethical* (vs. 15, 17 f., 20, 29, 33 f., 35 f.) and the *religious* or *ceremonial* (vs. 5–8, 19, 21 f., 23–25, 26–28, 30) sides.

The New Testament, finally, takes up only the prophetic side of the definition of the term and perpetuates it. All Christians are to be " saints " (holy ones — Rom. 1:7), that is ethically holy, separated, consecrated to God's service (Mark 6:20; John 17:11; Rev. 3:7), that they may have fellowship with a holy God (Acts 9:13; Rom. 1:7; Heb. 6:10; Rev. 5:8).

In the present context these two lines of development of the term *qodesh,* respectively by the priest and the prophet, are significant only in so far as they serve to indicate the interest of the prophetic theology in God-in-himself. And there can be no doubt as to the witness of the Scriptures on the point. For the priestly usage of the word far outstrips the prophetic.

Isaiah's characteristic name for God is " the Holy One of Israel " (Isa. 1:4, *et passim*), and the name is found also in Ezekiel (ch. 39:7 only), at II Kings 19:22, and in The Psalms (e.g., Ps. 71:22). In Ezekiel the phrase, " My holy name," occurs several times (ch. 20:39, etc.), and also occasionally elsewhere (e.g., Lev. 22:32); also the form, " His [or, thy] holy name " occurs (as in I Chron. 16:10; Ps. 103:1). " His holiness " is of comparatively frequent occurrence, particularly in The Psalms (Ps. 30:4; 47:8) . In the New Testament the *noun* (holiness) occurs but four times certainly (Rom. 1:4; II Cor. 7:1; I Thess. 3:13; Heb. 12:10) , the first and last of these referring to God, the other two to Christians; while the *adjective* (holy) , with the exception of its frequent usage to refer to the Holy Spirit (e.g., Luke 1:35; Acts 1:8; Rom. 5:5) , is limited in its occurrences to about a dozen references to the persons of the Deity (Mark 1:24; Luke 1:35; Acts 3:14; etc.) . With these comparatively few exceptions — and they are such by comparison with the multitude of Old Testament examples devoted to the priestly references to holy *things* such as sacrifices, places, and the like, together with the fairly frequent New Testament references to the " saints " (holy ones) — *the prophetic theology makes little of God's " holiness,"* least of all to his metaphysical separateness from his world.[10]

THE MEANING OF RIGHTEOUSNESS

The second Hebrew word used by the prophets with reference to the nature of God is *sedaqah* (righteousness) . This word stands for the whole person of God in relation to his universe, particularly man. *Sedaqah* is God's ethical character impinging on his world. And it quite literally means that God pours into his every act his whole righteous person. He never acts without his love, his justice, his truth, his mercy being involved — all of these function in everything he does. When they do, this is his *sedaqah* (his ethical person) acting. Those theologies, consequently, that would dichotomize God's functioning, as though at one time it is his justice, at another his love, and what not characterizing his activity, can find no support for themselves within the pages of the prophetic Scriptures. All that God is is present in all his actions. This dictum is of the essence of the prophetic understanding of him.

[10] Cf., for the use of " holy " to apply to things, Ex. 3:5 (ground) ; 16:23 (sabbath) ; 28:2 (garments) ; 30:25 (ointment) ; Lev. 14:13 (trespass offering) ; Num. 5:17 (water) ; etc.; and for men in the N.T., cf. Matt. 27:52; Acts 9:13; Rom. 8:27; etc.

Thus the prophets by means of the one word "righteousness" gave expression to the wholeness of the character of God which he manifests on the plane of history in all his dealings with mankind and the other creatures he has made.[11] At times the plural of "righteousness" (translated, "righteous acts") is used with a view to giving an inclusive picture of all of God's relations with his creation (Judg. 5:11; I Sam. 12:7). Accordingly, it is said of him, "The Lord is righteous in all his ways" (Ps. 145:17). But by far the majority of cases in which the term "righteousness" appears have reference to God's saving activity on behalf of his people (Isa. 41:2, 10; 42:6; 51:5, 7 f.).[12]

In both Testaments God's righteousness receives far greater prominence than the complementary concept of holiness. Reference to a concordance will serve to indicate as much at once. We shall not labor the point here by adducing the manifold evidence available to prove it. The entire chapter above on the prophetic theology of history, with its stress on God's righteous acts of redemption (his "righteousnesses" in the Hebrew), and also that to follow immediately, on God's self-revelation as God-in-history, are composed of the materials available in the Scriptures to indicate the prophetic interest in his righteousness.

It should be clear, then, that the prophetic realism of Scripture is far more concerned to know about God-in-history than about God-in-himself. This is just another way of saying that it is in God's redemptive acts (in the *kairoi*, or occasions on which God's righteous acts are performed), acts which taken together constitute redemptive history, that the prophets exhibit their major interest. Following his bent, the Hebrew prophet found that by observing God's ways in history and listening the while to God's own interpretation of them through his Word of revelation he was learning to know God himself by a method of *indirection*. To adopt for the moment the usual theological terms, the prophet knew little about God's "transcendence"

---

[11] Cf. II Chron. 12:6; Ezra 9:15; Ps. 11:7; 116:5; Jer. 12:1; Isa. 11:4.

[12] Cf. Schrenk in Kittel's *Wörterbuch*, II, p. 197, lines 20–39, and Skinner, *op. cit.*, Append. ii. R.S.V. often translates the word "victory."

(just another word for "holiness"), and that little through his
"immanence" (or "righteousness"), through his working on
creation's stage.

Had the writers of Scripture been philosophers, the entire
picture would have been different. For the philosopher's chief
concern has been to discover what God — assuming that there
is one — is like in himself. He has been determined by means
of his limited reason to place himself directly in possession of
the knowledge of God's transcendence. It was of this attempt to
secure a *direct* knowledge of God that Paul was thinking when
he wrote to the Corinthians his views on the futility of their
quest. 'The world,' he remarked with considerable irony,
'through its wisdom has not known God' (I Cor. 1:21). It
was not, so the apostle taught, by this proud method of the philosopher's reason that God could be known. God, Paul went on
to say, can be known only through the *kērygma* — through
listening to that gospel message which is concerned with his
historical dealings with men for their redemption, dealings
which culminate in the work of "Christ crucified" (v. 23).
Doubtless this prophetic method to which Paul subscribed — a
method consisting of patiently observing and listening — demands more in the way of humility on the part of those who
pursue it. But it results at all events in furnishing the prophetic
realism with a satisfying definition of God along functional or
empirical lines — a definition based upon his self-revealing
within history.

16. *Analysis of God's Self-revelation as God-in-History*

IN THE LAST CHAPTER we were concerned to establish the fact
that Scripture's prophetic realism interests itself only in the
functional definition of God that emerges from his self-revelation within history. In the present one we shall examine this

functional definition in detail. And as we do so, we shall turn to that normative series of historic events (redemptive history) that constitutes the gospel message of Scripture and that exhibits how God deals with mankind generally. For it is through his dealing with mankind in these ways that the functional or empirical definition of God emerges.

As this redemptive series constitutes the content of the prophetic revelation, any individual or group that at any time has stood within its circle and to a degree imbibed of the prophetic spirit and shared the prophetic insights is in a position to inform us of this functional definition which God has given of himself. Such groups include, of course, all the Hebrew prophets themselves, but in addition the Hebrew patriarchs, the postexilic Judaism which produced the Psalter, the Hasidic sects, even the Essenes, the Sadducees or Zadokite priests, and the Pharisees of Jesus' day, ancient and medieval Judaism, modern Judaism in its various branches, and the Christian Church from its beginning to the present day. No one of these has ever been lacking in some measure of the empirical knowledge of God of which we speak.

The diagram that follows indicates the relation of each of these to the parent prophetic stock. It is our claim in this volume that the Christian community by its witness to the gospel avoids the tangential tendencies exhibited by the other heirs of the prophetic revelation. The latters' divergence from the straight line of tradition as shown in the diagram on page 168 is intended to suggest this difference.

With a view to furnishing us with an outline for our discussion in this chapter it will be convenient to draw upon a book written by a modern exponent of liberal Judaism — *The Little Sanctuary* (1943) of Rabbi Solomon Frehof — as an example of genuine testimony to God's self-revelation. This book is distinguished both by its prophetic insight and by the simple clarity of its exposition. It purports to be a commentary on the *Union Prayer Book for Jewish Worship* (1940, revised edition), the worship manual of modern Judaism and a direct descendant, as the rabbi rightly claims, of the oldest prayer book in the world. Its ancestor was produced — along with Psalter and Mishnah — by the synagogue of postexilic times and was the precursor of all modern Christian prayer books, Protestant and Catholic.

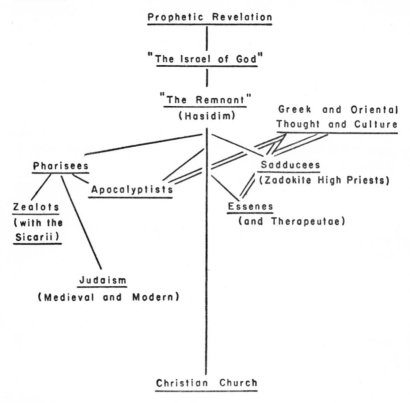

Diagram to Illustrate the Relation of Various Groups to the Prophetic Realism of the Scriptures

Rabbi Frehof's fascinating thesis is, briefly, that every worship service in this prayer manual of the synagogue is written around three ideas concerning God, viz., first, that God is Creator and Father; secondly, that God is Teacher; thirdly, that God is Redeemer and Friend. The author supplies a wealth of convincing illustration from the prayer book itself in support of his thesis. It would be easy to give examples as Rabbi Frehof has done from the entire extent of the manual. God is repeatedly addressed as " Heavenly Father," " Loving Father," " Our Father in heaven," " O Eternal Father "; as the " Gracious Giver of knowledge "; and as " Our Redeemer," " Our King and Helper," " Our Saviour and Protector," and as " Guardian " of his people. It is said, moreover, times without number that " all goodness and truth " are God's. He is praised for his " wondrous redemption in days of yore," for " marvelous have been thy works at all times to the children of men " (p. 197). And the prayer is expressed that Israel may know " the transient nature of earthly possessions," " the insecurity of a life stayed on prosperity without faith in thee," and that " no arrogance may tarnish the joy of success, no self-exaltation debase the love of achievement " (p. 199).

Such teaching about God is so obviously in line with the prophetic teachings of the Scriptures as to require no comment and it provides us, accordingly, with the basic analysis of God's self-revelation for further exploration. For these three concepts of God to which the rabbi refers are beyond any doubt the aspects of God's nature that a study of the Scriptures reveals. One may turn, for instance to Ps. 19:1–6, 7–11, and 12–14 for a statement of these three facets of God's person and work. Here in one psalm the threefold outline lies before us! It is as though the prayer book had taken it bodily from this source. We shall, therefore, follow this outline in stating the prophetic teaching about God's revelation of himself in history.[1]

(1) God as Creator and Father

The first prophetic word about God's working in his world is, " In the beginning God created the heavens and the earth " (Gen. 1:1). God is the Creator of all things that exist, including man. God has made all, God provides for all, God rules over all. God is the alpha and the omega, the beginning and the end.

---

[1] Cullmann also includes God's *creative activity* along with His *teaching* and *redemptive* functions as a part of redemptive history (*Heilsgeschichte*) and, therefore, as a genuine element in revelation; cf. *op. cit.*, pp. 131 ff., 178.

" For from him and through him and to him are all things "
(Rom. 11:36).

The Hebrew prophets, as has been observed, were not metaphysicians. They did not speculate about the nature of things.
They exhibited no interest in what Thales taught about " being
how it is " and " not-being how it is not." They neither inquired
into the constitution of matter as did the ancient Greek atomists
nor did they seek to bring all being into a universal Unity as
did the Hindu monists. However, they did assume a distinction
between God and the universe which he had made. They were
(perhaps unconsciously) metaphysical pluralists, therefore. And
they insisted on the oneness of the true and living God whom
they worshiped. Paul is simply voicing the usual prophetic attitude when he writes, " For although there may be so-called gods
in heaven or on earth — as indeed there are many ' gods ' and
many ' lords ' — yet for us there is one God, the Father " (I Cor.
8:5 f.).[2] The Hebrew prophets thus posited God and his world
for the sole and sufficient reason that they had heard God speak
to them and they were convinced that his voice was not to be
confused with a thousand and one other voices proceeding from
out of his created universe.

The prophetic realism sees God's hand as Creator and Providence in the beauty of the farthest star and the fragrance of the
smallest flower, in the simplicity of the child and the saintliness
of the sage, in the courage of manhood and the purity of woman-
hood, in the frightfulness of the earthquake and the gentle falling of the rain, in wind and wave and sunshine, in the provision
of food for the animals and man, in all the majesty of nature
and in every talent with which man is endowed (Ps. 19; 34; 148;
also Job, chs. 38 ff.). " In keeping with the Old Testament tradition," writes Bultmann, " God . . . is, for Jesus, *the Creator*
who governs the world with his care, feeds the beasts and adorns
the flowers, without whose will not a sparrow falls dead to

[2] When the empirical nature of the prophetic realism is grasped, the
problem of whether the earliest Hebrew prophets were " henotheists " or
" monotheists " is seen to be of little significance. They knew of only one
God, who spoke to them and whose works they beheld; with Paul, therefore, they would have said, " For us there is one God, the Father."

earth, and who has counted every hair of our heads (Matt. 6:25–34, par.; 10:29 f., par.) ." [3]

No statement of the prophetic theology, then, is complete that does not reckon with these facts. God is the God over all his works, the God who cares for them all, who loves them all. Such is the ultimate prophetic *cosmo*logy and at the same time the ultimate prophetic *theo*logy. And no doubt Paul is quite right when in line with such thought he writes that " the creation waits with eager longing for the revealing of the sons of God . . . because the creation itself will be set free from its bondage to decay and obtain the glorious liberty of the children of God " (Rom. 8:19 ff.) . Creation is a product of the " righteousness " of God of which we have spoken, in the sense that into the creative act — as in all his acts — God has poured all of his righteous person. Nor does he ever abandon any one of his creatures to a blind fate. If he creates, he is also the Guarantor of his creature's security and preservation. The fine, ethical sense that insists that no man has a right to make a machine that he cannot control and adequately care for derives from this prophetic insight into the character of the righteous God. The prophetic realism taboos the deistic conception of a god who has so little moral sense as to start a world spinning like a top and then to go off and leave it to its own devices.

So much for the prophetic teaching of God as Creator. Rabbi Frehof is not so happy, however, one imagines, in his linking the term " Father " with that of " Creator." The prophetic teaching makes a real distinction of no little significance at this point. God is Creator of all his creatures: he is not Father of all of them. The problem here is doubtless one in the field of semantics, but it is not to be minimized. For Plato, Zeus was " the father of all gods and men," and many systems among pagans have applied the term " father " to their god. But as T. W. Manson has shown, these pagan mythologies have always held to God's paternity as implying merely his being the *progenitor* of either men's flesh or spirits or of both together. Scripture also has this conception but it applies the term Creator to

[3] *Op. cit.,* p. 23.

cover it, as we have just seen, though, to be sure, even here there is a difference in the moral levels, respectively within and outside the prophetic teaching.[4]

Father, on the contrary, in the Scriptures is a name for the *redemptive* side of God's nature. It is used, accordingly, only with reference to those within the redemptive circle or the "family of the redeemed," of those who have made the filial response which is the complement of that for which the term "father" stands and which the Father's love evokes. " In the Old Testament," says Manson, " God is the Father of Israel in the sense that he is the founder and creator of the nation (Deut. 32:6; Isa. 63:16; Mal. 2:10). . . . The reference in the Old Testament is to a particular historical event in the deliverance of the people from Egypt. Thus the act by which Jehovah becomes the Father of Israel is to be thought of as adoption rather than creation. He is the creator of all the peoples; but Israel is in a special sense his son (Hos. 11:1), even his first-born (Ex. 4:22; Jer. 31:9)." [5]

In the New Testament the same thought of God's Fatherhood prevails. Millar Burrows has put the thought with which we are dealing in a very striking way. " The idea," he writes, " of the universal Fatherhood of God and brotherhood of man comes from Stoicism rather than the Bible. God is man's Creator; he loves men like a father; men are also of one common origin and descent, and are made in God's image. The terms ' Father ' and ' son,' are used in the Bible of a relation which is potential for all men but realized only by those who receive the divine adoption." [6]

The natural corollary arising from such teaching of the prophetic Scriptures is *the motive to evangelism* that from the first has been a prominent feature of the Christian movement. In the light of the foregoing that motive may be stated as one *to convert " neighbors " into " brothers,"* to bring all peoples into the family circle of God.

For the New Testament, beginning with Jesus, the neighbor was not merely a member of one's social, economic, religious, or

---

[4] *Op. cit.,* pp. 90 ff.   [5] *Ibid.,* p. 91.   [6] *Op. cit.,* p. 142.

even racial group. Rather, as the parable of the Good Samaritan teaches, the neighbor is every man (Luke 10:25–37). The point of the Pharisee's question lay exactly in the fact that for contemporary Judaism the neighbor of the commandment "Thou shalt love thy neighbor as thyself" (Lev. 19:18) was one's associate, a member of one's own inner circle of fellows or friends.[7] Such a man in the immediate cultural ethos of Jesus' day could be known by his clothes, which were a badge designating the group to which he belonged. And the point of Jesus' parable was that, when a man lay naked or "stripped" (v. 30), his badge was gone! It is at this point that the teaching of Jesus enters in a challenging manner. For a man without badges is the neighbor in the true prophetic view that all men without distinction are under God's love and care and, therefore, should receive the respect and love enjoined for the neighbor.

But *the family words* — brother, father, son, mother, sister — are in a different category. One is a "son of God" according to the Scriptures who acknowledges his moral responsibility to accept God's will for his life and so become "like the Father" (Matt. 5:45 ff.). One is a "brother" who is such in Christ, the great "elder brother" of the family group (Rom. 8:29). Hence, that love of the neighbor of which Lev. 19:18 speaks should lead every son of God who shares the prophetic outlook to strive to bring all men within the "household of God" (Eph. 2:19).

(2) God as Teacher

Again, God is Teacher throughout the entire Hebrew prophetic, Jewish, and Christian traditions. This idea is basic. Without its truth there would be no real revelation in the sense of which we have been speaking in this book. The conception is that which underlies all such expressions as "Oracle of Yahweh," "The word of Yahweh came," "And God said," and the like. Essentially God is Teacher as he is the Revealer of the divine wisdom and instruction to man.

This appears in all sorts of contexts and situations throughout

[7] Cf. Herbert Danby, *The Mishnah* (1933), p. 20, n. 9, and p. 22, n. 2.

the extent of God's dealings with his " chosen people." In reply
to Moses' complaint, for example, that he is not " eloquent," is
" slow of speech, and of tongue " (Ex. 4:10), God replies,
" I will be with your mouth and teach you what you shall
speak " (v. 12). In Isaiah the peoples of the earth declare that ·
it is God who " will teach us of his ways " (Isa. 2:3). The
psalmist in like fashion prays, " Teach me thy way, O Lord "
(Ps. 27:11), and " thy paths " (Ps. 25:4).

The Hebrew equivalent for the English term " teaching " or
" instruction " is torah. This word, therefore, stands in the Old
Testament for the divine instruction in the most inclusive
sense. In Isa. 2:3, for example, it is in apposition to the phrase,
" The word of the Lord," and is found in the significant context
of the saying of the peoples and nations of the earth:

> " Come, let us go up to the mountain of the Lord,
>   to the house of the God of Jacob;
>   that he may teach us his ways
>   and that we may walk in his paths."

God's torah, his instruction, in such a context can only mean
all that he has to tell man about " his ways " and concerning
walking " in his paths."

It is unfortunate that in the Septuagint and New Testament
the Hebrew word is translated by the Greek nomos, as this has
given a totally wrong slant to the understanding of its fundamental meaning. The latter term means " law " and, accordingly, can be used only in a restricted sense which is by no
means native to torah. In the Hebrew tradition this word is
used to cover God's instruction of whatever nature. George Foot
Moore has an instructive passage on the subject which applies
to the entire history of the word. " ' Torah ' is the generic term,"
says Moore, " rather than commandment (mitswah) or statute
(ḥoq); both of which are indeed included in it, but as particular species or forms that may be distinguished within it (not
from it)." [8]

This view that torah stands not only for law in the strict

[8] Op. cit., vol. ii, p. 81, n. 28.

(Greek) sense, and so equivalent to *nomos,* but also for " the whole content of revelation," [9] holds for the entire Old Testament Scriptures as well as for the later rabbis. William F. Albright suggests that its use with reference to the teaching of Moses may be related to the fact that " the slightly earlier system of Akhenaten was also known as the 'teaching' (*sbâyet*)," a word that shares with the Latin *doctrina* " the two senses of ' system of teachings ' . . . and ' correction, punishment.' Hebrew *tôrâh* has the same meaning." [10] Skinner too points out that in Isa. 1:10 (" Hear the word of the Lord. . . . Give ear unto the law of our God ") the parallelism shows that " the reference is not to the Mosaic law, but to the prophetic revelation that follows (cf. 5:24; 8:16; 30:9) ." [11] And in Jer. 31:33, where Yahweh is said to put his torah in men's " inward parts," it is obvious that the divine instruction, and not law, is meant in view of the sequel: " All shall know me, from the least of them unto the greatest of them " (v. 34) .

When we turn to the New Testament, we discover an earnest endeavor afoot, first on Jesus' part and then on the part of Paul, to recover the essential meaning of torah as divine instruction rather than as law as understood by the scribes and Pharisees. Both of these taught that in order to receive such torah man required to achieve a rapport with God transcending the necessity for all giving and receiving of specific *orders.* The older liberals found it difficult to reconcile the account of Paul's struggle with the Judaizers over freedom from the law with the Synoptic picture of Jesus' attitude of liberality, to the detriment of the latter in their judgment. But the form critics, and particularly in this instance Bultmann, give us a better picture of Jesus' attitude to the torah and one that corresponds with the definition we have been following. " As interpretation of the will, the demand, of God," he writes, " Jesus' message is a great *protest against Jewish legalism,* i.e., against a form of piety that regards the will of God as expressed in the written law and

9 *Ibid.,* vol. i, p. 263.
10 *Op. cit.,* pp. 205 f., 324, n. 30, and 329, n. 96.
11 *Op. cit., in loc.*

in the tradition which interprets it, a piety that endeavors to win God's favor by the toil of minutely fulfilling the law's stipulations." [12] He goes on to say that for Jesus " God requires radical obedience. He claims man whole — and wholly."

When we turn to Paul we discover in his writing what W. D. Davies terms a " ' Christifying ' of the torah " and the thought that " spirit and torah . . . are coincident as it were in Christ." [13] This appears in a passage like Rom. 8:2 — ' For the torah (instruction) of the life-giving spirit in Christ Jesus has delivered you from the sin-inspiring, death-dealing torah (law) .' Here as elsewhere Paul can mean by torah two different things — the old law of ordinances accepted pedantically as so many orders to be obeyed (Eph. 2:15) , and the new spirit to be under whose sway means a new rapport with God. For the torah in the former sense he has nothing but condemnation — not, to be sure, as evil in itself (Rom. 7:7) , but as powerless to produce the character of goodness in man that may hope for God's vindication (Rom. 3:20 f.; Gal. 2:16 ff.) . For torah in the sense of the new spirit of life in Christ Jesus, Paul had only commendation. Those who possess it " set their minds on the things of the Spirit " (Rom. 8:5) and so have no need of specific commands but rather spontaneously do the will of God.

The apostle says all this in a great variety of ways that show how very mature his thought was on the subject. He speaks, for example, of having " the mind of Christ " in a context that makes it clear that this is the equivalent of knowing " the mind of the Lord " (I Cor. 2:16; cf. Isa. 40:13 which Paul is here quoting) . In the same passage he speaks of our having received ' the Spirit that is from God, that we may know the things graciously bestowed upon us by God ' (v. 12) . Similarly, he sets his own ability to discover the right answers to ethical problems over against that of Jesus himself (I Cor. 7:10, 25 ff.) on the ground that he ' has been shown mercy by the Lord ' and so has ' the Spirit of God ' (v. 40) . This *torah* or spirit of God is also equated by Paul with the divine wisdom (I Cor. 2:5 ff.) ,

---

[12] *Op. cit.,* pp. 11 ff.
[13] Cf. W. D. Davies, *Paul and Rabbinic Judaism* (1948) , p. 223.

just as in the Old Testament wisdom literature an equation was made between torah and wisdom.[14]

From the teachings of both our Lord and his apostle, then, it is clear that in the thought of God as Teacher the New Testament position is at one with that of the Hebrew prophets. Throughout the Scriptures it is the *rapport* of the human spirit with the spirit of the living God to which is attributed the insights that come from man's great Teacher. It was that rapport which made it possible for the prophet of God's covenant people to discover his will quite apart from the receiving of a series of dictated commands. It was that rapport which was surely in Jesus' mind when he made the two old commandments of love — toward God and man — the sole rule of life (Mark 12:28 ff.; cf. Rom. 13:8–10).

A *moron* is by definition " one who cannot plan his day." There have been and still are religions adapted to such persons and these may be termed *moronic religions*. They assume that their devotees cannot know God's will for them from hour to hour. Accordingly, they presume to dictate by means of specific injunctions what men are to do each hour of the day. When Judaism descended from the high level of the prophetic revelation with its spirit-guided life to the roundelay of Mishnah and Talmud after the manner indicated in the quotation above from Rudolf Bultmann, it became for the time being a moronic religion. It then became the task of the Christian phase of the prophetic faith to reclaim the Jews to the former level of genuine rapport with God, the supreme Teacher whom they had formerly known. Jesus' two maxims — ' Seek first His Kingdom and His righteousness ' (Matt. 6:33) and ' He that wills to do His will, he shall know ' (John 7:17) — would seem to be all that are required to point the way into the larger life of the spirit and of liberty.

(3) God as Redeemer and Friend

The third prophetic teaching about God is that he is man's Friend and Redeemer. Actually Abraham is called — and he is

[14] Cf. Burrows, *Op. cit.*, pp. 78 f., and Moore, *Op. cit.*, vol. i, pp. 264 ff.

the first in the Hebrew Scriptures to be called — "God's friend" (II Chron. 20:7; Isa. 41:8; James 2:23). It is noteworthy that it is only in late, even postexilic, literature that the phrase is used of Abraham. Probably it means, as Deissmann has suggested, that Abraham was God's favorite. "*Friend,*" he remarks, "was the title of honor given at the court of the Ptolemies to the highest royal officials. 'Greek writers . . . already used this name for the officials of the Persian king; from the Persian kings the practice was adopted by Alexander, and from him again by all the Diadochi; but we meet it particularly often as an Egyptian title.'" [15]

In any literature, then, tinged by Persian, Egyptian, or Greek influence "friend" might mean one whom God wished to honor or one honored by God. In the earlier Old Testament literature Abraham is simply called God's "servant" (Gen. 26:24), which in the Hebrew idiom would have the same sort of semiofficial titular sense as that above indicated for "friend" in another cultural ethos. In both cases the thought would be that Abraham had a status of great importance in God's sight, that man's Sovereign had chosen him for service of real significance in His dominions.

From Genesis to Paul the prophetic writers of Scripture have taught that the relationship that pertained between God and Abraham was fraught with deep significance for both the latter's progeny and the whole human race.[16] This appears very clearly in the name that Yahweh communicates to Moses for transmission to his people at the burning bush (Ex. 3:13–16). It is as 'Yahweh, the God of your fathers, the God of Abraham, the God of Isaac, and the God of Jacob,' that he would be known to Israel. Abraham is the "father of the faithful" — herein lies his importance for Scripture. He is the forerunner

---

[15] Cf. Adolf Deissmann, *Bible Studies* (1923), p. 167; also R. H. Charles, *The Apocrypha and Pseudepigrapha of the Old Testament*, vol. i, p. 547, on the *Wisdom of Solomon* 7:27.

[16] Cf. S. R. Driver, *A Critical and Exegetical Commentary on Deuteronomy* (1895), on Deut. 1:11. For the refrain, "The God of your fathers," see Deut. 1:21; 6:3; Josh. 18:3; Judg. 2:12; II Kings 21:22; I Chron. 5:25; II Chron. 7:22; Ezra 7:27; Acts 5:30; 7:32, *et al.*

of all those who really believe in God, and so " it is men of faith who are the sons of Abraham " (Gal. 3:7; Rom. 4:9, 16 ff.) .

GOD'S FAITHFULNESS ASSURES MAN'S REDEMPTION

This faith on man's part serves to throw God's faithfulness into bold relief. Apropos of the Exodus and of the incident just mentioned in the career of Moses, Driver remarks, " The God who now takes Israel under his care is the same who formerly showed his faithfulness to their ancestors, and was known of them." [17] God had made promises to Abraham and his successors and he had fulfilled those promises. Hence, he is proved to be a faithful God who can be trusted in all his dealings with his people, and it is the very faith of those fathers answering to God's faithful character that throws the latter, so to speak, upon a screen where all may see it.

George Foot Moore comments on Isa. 41:8 ff. in the same vein. " When the prophet," he writes, " would inspire his fellow exiles to faith in the signal deliverance their God was about to work for them, he addresses them, ' But thou, Israel, my servant, Jacob whom I have chosen, the seed of Abraham, my friend . . . fear not, for I am with thee, be not dismayed, for I am thy God.' " And the point, says Moore, lies in this, that " the posterity of Abraham, God's ' friend,' have in that very fact the assurance that the God of their fathers will not desert them in their distress." [18]

This character of faithfulness, then, was the first that God revealed to his people. In Hebrew the word for " faithfulness " is 'emūnāh and it may be translated either " truth " or " faithfulness." Its stem ('amn) fundamentally means " to be firm," or " to be steadfast." As used with reference to the character of God, therefore, the noun means that God is " true to his revealed character and to his promises." [19]

In Jer. 10:10 the prophet makes an acrostic out of the similar

---

[17] *Ibid.*

[18] Cf. *op. cit.,* vol. i, p. 536.

[19] Cf. Driver, *op. cit.,* on Deut. 32:4; also Hoskyns and Davey, *The Riddle of the New Testament* (1931) , pp. 35 ff.

noun *'emeth,* whose meaning is exactly the same as the above. Jeremiah, emphasizing the three consonants which in Hebrew make up the word, suggests that it may be taken to stand for the following — *'E* stands for *'El* (God), *M* for *Melek* (king), and *T for Tāmīd* (eternal); hence, " God, eternal King." Probably Jeremiah's acrostic accounts for the fact that the rabbis held *'emeth* to be God's alone. The word is, so to speak, his signet to their minds. He alone is true and faithful and no man can ever claim to be so.[20] No doubt this accounts for the curious fact that in neither Testament is man ever said to be " true " or " faithful " (cf. Ps. 116:11; Rom. 3:4).[21]

It is on this character of faithfulness in the fulfilling of his promises that the Scriptures predicate their conviction that God will assuredly redeem his people. This was the point of Moses' reminding the Israelites at the Exodus of God's faithfulness toward the patriarchs. His people can trust a faithful God sufficiently to leave the " flesh-pots " of Egypt and follow his servant out into a wilderness! And the same logic will serve to follow Him in all his saving activity. He has promised to save mankind and he will do so because to fulfill his promises is of the essence of his nature (cf. Heb., chs. 3; 4).

It will perhaps be objected that this sort of reasoning about God does not take us very far into the depths of his nature. This is true, of course. But it should be recalled that, as already remarked, the Hebrew prophet characteristically was not concerned to probe the nature of God-in-himself. The prophet's approach to the problems of religion was an empirical one and his motivation was practical. He, therefore, called Israel's attention to the empirical fact that God had proved himself faithful in his dealings with the fathers. From this he argued simply that he could be depended on to be faithful in all his ways with his people. This approach may not satisfy those of a speculative turn of mind. But it must be admitted that it was well calculated to serve the purpose of convincing a hardheaded people

---

[20] Cf. Moore, *op. cit.,* vol. ii, p. 195.

[21] Cf. an article by the writer entitled *An Exposition of the Beatitudes* in JBR, July, 1947, pp. 162 ff.

that God would carry through his redemptive plan on their behalf.

However, as time went on the Hebrew prophet took occasion to point out the deeper reason for God's redeeming mankind. This deeper reason is God's essential love for the man whom he has made. It is love that lies behind God's faithfulness and provides the more remote motive for the same (cf. Ps. 25:10; 40:11; 57:3, 10; 61:7; Hos. 11:1 ff.; Micah 7:20). This love motif finds its most profound pre-Christian expression perhaps in the prophecy of Hosea with its deep theme of the forgiving love of God in the face of man's sin. And if we may trust the best modern scholarly opinion, this teaching of Hosea arose out of his own experience and God's coming to him at the heart of it. It was out of such experience of the prophet that God had said he would make himself known from time to time, on the interpretation of the " burning bush " passage to which we have already subscribed (Ex. 3:14). The like theme of God's forgiveness of his people occurs as well in Jeremiah's teaching about the " new covenant " (Jer. 31:31–34) and for a like reason — Jeremiah too had gone through " bitter waters " in his endeavors to win God's people back to Him and to His obedience, and in their midst he had learned the meaning of the divine forgiveness. The theme of the Suffering Servant and his vicarious atoning for man's sins which we find in Second Isaiah must also have been hammered out on the anvil of the prophet's own suffering and atoning love (Isa. 53:6, etc.).

REDEMPTION A HISTORIC PHENOMENON

It is to be remarked as a corollary to this faithfulness aspect of God's nature that the salvation that it holds out to man must of necessity occur, at any rate to a degree, within history. It is here and now that God shows himself to be the God who reclaims and fulfills his promises. Were this not so, the constant appeal that as God had shown himself faithful to the fathers, so he would be to their descendants, would have had no meaning. Unless it were a known fact that God had fulfilled His promises to those fathers, his faithfulness in the past could not have been held up as a stimulus to faith.

It is because the saving promise is fulfilled by God in history that after each new significant event he acquires a new name, as we have before observed. Thus, " The God of your fathers " becomes after the Exodus " The God who brought you out of the land of Egypt, out of the house of bondage " (Ex. 13:3, 14; Deut. 5:6; Josh. 24:17; Judg. 6:8). Students of the Old Testament have often been critical of the large number of materialistic promises recorded as made by God in those Scriptures, particularly promises relating to the land of Cannan, the " land flowing with milk and honey." But it was only through such realizable promises transmitted through the prophets that God could teach his people of his character of Redeemer and Friend and so advance them to the higher moral and spiritual ground.

Ernest M. Ligon, in *The Psychology of Christian Personality,* dwells on the psychological significance of this last item. " The child," he writes apropos of the first Beatitude (Matt. 5:3), " must be given goals about which he can do something immediately, and reach relatively soon. As each one is reached, a higher one must be discovered for him " (p. 39). So he argues, for the " poor man " of the Beatitude to attain to the " Kingdom of Heaven," this concept must have for him some meaning — though not necessarily a very advanced one from the moral or spiritual standpoint — for him to make a beginning in the Christian way. Similarly, one would suggest, God taught his people of old the sort of God with whom they had to do through a series of promises and fulfillments calculated to take them higher and higher in moral insight — and all this accomplished, be it noted, on the plane of history. It was, indeed, in line with this same prophetic teaching that God's ultimate redemptive act should have been achieved in and through the historic person whom we know as Jesus Christ, as well as by the abiding presence of his Spirit in the historic Christian fellowship.

We shall inquire of the significance of this last statement in some detail in the remaining chapters of this book. Meanwhile, it is important to notice that the two apocalyptic doctrines of the " incognito " Christ and the " beyond-history " Church do not derive from the prophetic Scriptures. The teaching of these Scriptures is decidedly down-to-earth in the sense that it holds God's promises to be fulfilled within history. It is only to faith, it is true, that the insight to see this fulfillment comes, but to faith such insight does indeed come. And apocalypticism shows itself to be lacking in spiritual insight when it declares that it cannot see this. It is exactly within history — in the midst of its calamity, turmoil, " blood, toil, tears, and sweat " — that the prophetic spirit sees God's will achieving its goal and himself experiences the salvation and peace that God offers to them that love him. There will be, it is true, a consummation of all God's purposes, but that consummation holds out no prospect of any qualitative difference between the salvation for God's people now and then, within history and in eternity.

17. *God-in-History and God-in-Himself*

GOD-IN-HISTORY has revealed himself as Creator, as Teacher, as Redeemer. So far we may certainly speak of God as known. He is known through his creative, his instructional, his saving activities within history and in man's experience of him. He is known as he speaks to the prophetic spirits in all ages of these his workings. He is known as he manifests himself above all in his Word become act in his incarnate Son — in that Son's incarnation, atoning work, and resurrection.

It is only by faith that God is thus known to men. " We walk by faith, not by sight " and " we see through a glass, darkly " while within history. But, however he may be known, still *God is known:* such is the central message of Scripture's prophetic realism. And everyone who shares its spirit will voice the prayer for Succos — the Feast of Tabernacles — as found in the Jewish prayer book, which begins, " O Living God, we thank Thee that Thou hast not left us to grope after Thee in the dark; that Thy law has been a lamp unto our feet, and a light unto our path," and ends, "Lift up our eyes that, like our fathers, we too may see, through the leafy bough, the light of sun and star so that our souls may soar to Thee." For we know God, as the prayer indicates, through both his *words* and his *works*.

We know God only partially, it is true: but we do know him. Our knowledge is partial, but it is not illusory. It is not *maya* (illusion). Between the God-in-history and the God-in-himself, then, there is a link of continuity so strong that the burden of proof must always rest on those who claim that to the last God is *the Unknowable* to man. As already remarked, the prophet used the two words *qodesh* (holiness) and *sedaqah* (righteousness) to signify the distinction intended her by the two hyphenated phrases descriptive of God. We have also brought forward sufficient evidence, one imagines, to demonstrate that he was far more interested in the latter — that is, in God-in-history — than in the former.

This interest was conditioned by the Hebrew prophet's great concern for the redemption of mankind, a concern which gave him little or no time for the speculative interest of the Greek philosopher. The latter would no doubt have brushed him aside rather contemptuously with a reference to his shallow "activism." But this same prophet would have been shocked with the suggestion emanating from American pragmatism that this "activist God-in-history" was all there was to God! For the prophet did believe in God-in-himself, however much he would have denied knowing much about him.

It is clear from Isaiah's vision, with its reference to the holy God, and Isaiah's immediate sense of ethical unworthiness that to the prophet's mind the God of his immediate apprehension was the same as God-in-himself. In other words, what God revealed himself to be, that he most certainly was to Isaiah's way of thinking. One might, therefore, say that from God's "righteous acts" (his *sedaqah*), his "holiness" (his *qodesh*) could be deduced. Point for point what God is in experience, that he is in fact. This view would hold, one believes, for all the prophets in the Hebrew ethos.

Those movements or schools of thought, accordingly, both

within and without the Christian Church which from time to time have declared God to be the great Unknowable have no kinship with the prophetic thought or spirit. The prophet does not begin, as does the philosopher, with speculation about the nature of God, it is true. Rather, he awaits God's voice and the divine instruction which it mediates. But once God is known through his activity within history and his interpreting Word of revelation, the prophet takes the leap of faith from God-in-history to God-in-himself and finds them to be the same God. To do otherwise is to doubt God, not to believe in him! Such a leap is not, as is wrongly said, " a leap in the dark," but rather a leap into the arms of that God who has revealed himself in history as the faithful, the loving, the just, the true God.

One cannot say much on this topic from the standpoint of the prophetic realism of the Scriptures — so much is obvious from all that has thus far been said in this volume. It was when the Church came into contact with Greek thought that it began to think through the implications of the data which those Scriptures contain for an understanding of the nature of God-in-himself. The result was the doctrine of the Trinity. That this doctrine carries us beyond the explicit statements of Scripture it is generally agreed.

But that the doctrine of the Trinity represents a valid conclusion from the data of the prophetic testimony about God's working and self-disclosure one is constrained to believe. Trinitarianism — and not Sabellianism — is the natural product of a forthright endeavor to piece together this testimony. For if God has revealed himself within history as Creator-Father, Teacher, and Redeemer-Friend, then the normal conclusion to draw is that these modes of expression of himself stand for something fundamental in the nature of God-in-himself. The Church's doctrine of the Trinity represents an endeavor, however inadequate, to say as much. And it has adopted the category " person " to describe this threefold differentiation in the Being of God only because this is the highest category it knows.

A *person* is an active will showing itself in intelligent activity and striving toward moral goals. But it is more than this: for it is also one part of a nexus that includes other persons inter-twined with itself. Modern sociology has to a large degree suc-ceeded only in underlining the fact with which we have always been familiar that no man lives to himself alone. Even Robin-son Crusoe had to be given his " man Friday " by Defoe, and Simeon Stylites, we may be sure, had his friends beneath his pillar to keep him supplied with the necessities of life. " Man is a gregarious animal ": he lives his life in groups.

Now, this gregarious animal is made in the " image of God." For this reason a personal God living alone and without con-tact with other persons is inconceivable to man, however true or otherwise the conception may be in itself. It is, indeed, this very thought that has led some theologians to suggest that God must have created man for companionship with himself because he was alone and lonely! But this suggestion does not probe very deeply into the heart of the problem nor does it offer a solution that is tenable. If God was *lonely*, how long may this state be thought to have lasted before he bethought himself of making a companion for his loneliness? From the side of social ethics too, comes an argument that fits this one from sociology rather nicely. This is that only the loving person is a truly ethi-cal one. But love requires a social object upon which it may im-pinge, else love is nonexistent. If, then, " God is love," as the prophetic Scriptures have demonstrated through examples taken from his historic activity, it would seem to follow that there must be within his own nature a multiplicity for its exercise.

If God, contrariwise, were a unitarian God, it would appear that he had made man incapable of anything approaching a true conception of him. Indeed, he would appear to have striven to produce a man who, rather than being in his image, was as far as possible unlike himself. And further, he would have taken the trouble to reveal himself for what he was not rather than for what he was. For the revelation of God-in-history suggests that *God-in-himself is like a family group* — being composed of a Father, a Son, and a Spirit — with the mutual relationships of privilege and responsibility which such a group experiences. It is this prophetic faith, be it noted, that has flowered out into the highly ethical religion which we know from the Scriptures and which has borne magnificent results in producing character — that of prophet and reformer, of martyr and saint, of many an unknown and unsung humble follower in the " way of Christ." [1]

[1] For the argument for the Trinity based on the findings of modern sociology and social ethics and an appraisal of the same, cf. Donald Baillie, *God Was in Christ* (1948), particularly the section entitled " Two Trends of Trinitarian Thought," pp. 133–140. I incline to believe that I am a bit more favorable to the argument than Professor Baillie appears to be.

THE CONTENT OF SCRIPTURE'S
PROPHETIC REALISM

C. The Gospel of the Kingdom

'How beautiful upon the mountains
    are the feet of
  the Herald — the Publisher of Peace,
  the Gospel Herald — the Proclaimer
    of Salvation,
Who says to Zion,
  " Thy God has begun His Reign." '
              — ISAIAH 52:7.

C. The Gospel of the Kingdom
SYNOPSIS

*I*S IT " *good news* " *to be told that God is King? The answer will depend upon the nature of the God in question. The answer of the prophetic Scriptures is "yes," because the God they know and to whom they witness is a good God. The idea that God's Kingdom or Sovereignty forms a part of the gospel message first appears clearly in Isaiah at chs. 40:9 f. and 52:7. The same idea occurs frequently in the Gospels and The Acts.*

Accordingly, in this section the "gospel of the kingdom" is presented under the following heads: (1) The basic prophetic concept of the sovereignty of God. *The Hebrew and Greek words translated " kingdom " are actually abstract nouns; the Scriptures teach that God is sovereign over all his universe and particularly over those men who acknowledge his Lordship.* (2) The realization of God's sovereignty. *The* prophets *concerned themselves with* how *this could become a factor in human experience, the* apocalyptists *with* when *it would be realized; it is shown in this part that the second question is answered implicitly in the reply which the Hebrew prophets gave to the first.* (3) Jesus' contribution to the " gospel of the kingdom " *along the three lines:* (a) *of his teaching that it had already come,* (b) *of his indicating himself to be the agent of its establishment on earth, and* (c) *of his presenting the Lord's Supper as the symbol of the heavenly banquet.* (4) The present task of establishing the Kingdom. *This task is one inherited by the Church Universal from its Lord. It is what Paul termed* oikodomē *(building) . Prophetic realism, true to its name, has a message at this point for today and tomorrow.*

18. *The Basic Prophetic Concept—The Sovereignty of God*

I
N THE LAST SECTION we observed that God has revealed himself in three functional ways — as Creator, as Teacher, and
as Redeemer. There is, however, still a fourth category which
we must use to describe him — that of Sovereign. This is not
on a par with the others, else Rabbi Frehof must have brought
it into the picture as an element around which the Jewish worship services may be said to revolve. The concept of "sovereignty" rather underlies the other aspects and is that one out
of which they spring.

God is Lord, and *it is because he is Lord* that he creates,
teaches, saves. Deity and sovereignty in the end are the same
thing, so far, at all events, as these terms apply to the true and
living God. To be God means to have all power, all wisdom, all
truth, all goodness, all love, all justice, at one's disposal. And to
be Sovereign means to possess the right to employ these things
as one wills. For one is not sovereign at all who is not sovereign
in all. It is inconceivable that God should be all-powerful —
able to do what he wills — and yet not all-good, and so prepared to use his power only in good ways and to serve good ends.
It is equally inconceivable that he should be all-good and yet
not all-powerful, and so capable of accomplishing his holy will
in all respects.

Such is the view of the prophetic Scriptures. And it is for this

reason that these are able to answer with a degree of assurance
the query, Is it " good news " to be told that God is King? and,
Can there be a " gospel of the kingdom "? The answer is yes
when one is told that God is the kind of God whom the Scriptures describe. There could be no gospel of the Kingdom otherwise. But God is " the God of Abraham, of Isaac, and of Jacob ";
he is the God " who brought you out of the land of Egypt, out
of the house of bondage "; he is " the God and Father of our
Lord Jesus Christ." He is, moreover, the God of Cullmann's
" revelation-redemption line," the God of the *kairoi* — the
God, that is, who has taken occasion throughout history to redeem his people at this and that point, both individually and
collectively. He is the God who has sent his prophets one after
another to recall his people in repentance to himself and who in
the end sent forth his unique Son saying, " They will respect
my Son." It is *good tidings*, indeed, to know that this sort of
God is Sovereign over men's lives. Such is the declaration of
Second Isaiah in the passage that has become the inspiration for
one of the great arias of Handel's *Messiah* and that heads this
section:

' How beautiful upon the mountains are the feet of
    the Herald — the Publisher of Peace,
    the Gospel Herald — the Proclaimer of Salvation,
Who says to Zion, " Thy God has begun His Reign " ' (Isa. 52:7).

As has already been remarked, this passage from Second Isaiah
is the one that signalizes the highest development of the term
(Hebrew, *bisser;* Greek, *evangelizesthai*) meaning " to proclaim
good tidings " in the Old Testament Scriptures. For the very
pinnacle of this verb's development comes when it is associated
with the thought of the dominion or Lordship of God himself!
The practical equivalent of the passage just quoted occurs also
at Isa. 40:9 f., where the herald announces: " Behold, your God!
Behold, the Lord Jehovah will come as a mighty one, and his
arm will rule for him."

A number of the New Testament passages cited in Part II of
this book say the same thing in a variety of ways. There is first

the complete phrase " the gospel of the kingdom [of God]," an expression peculiar to Matthew (chs. 4:23; 9:35; 24:14). *Again, the verb that is usually translated " to preach the gospel "* (*evangelizesthai*), is followed by the phrase, " The kingdom of God " to express the content of the proclamation in Luke 4:43; 8:1; and Acts 8:12. Similarly, the verb meaning simply " to proclaim " or ' to herald ' (*kērussein*), is followed by the same phrase or its equivalent (" The kingdom of heaven ") in Matt. 10:7; Mark 1:14 f.; Luke 8:1; 9:2; Acts 20:25; 28:31. To these are to be added a number of passages in which other verbs meaning " to proclaim," " to preach," " to witness to," " to announce," or " to declare " are found with the phrase, " The kingdom [of God]," as their object. There are also several passages in which the noun meaning " mystery " (*mystērion* — Matt. 13:11), or that signifying account (*logos* — Matt. 13:19), is substituted for " gospel " in the expression.[1]

A comparison of the parallel passages in the Gospels makes it appear at least doubtful whether Jesus is ever clearly proved to have used the phrase, " The gospel of the kingdom of God." Probably Dalman is right in concluding that " it was within the Christian community " that the use of " gospel " or " to preach the gospel," in conjunction with the phrase, " The kingdom of God," "first attained the position of a formula." [2] But that Jesus spoke of the proclamation of " the kingdom of God " as an integral part of the gospel message, in some such fashion in the Aramaic as to suggest the Greek formula to the Church would appear to be demanded by the evidence cited above. And in any case Schmidt's conclusion from a study of these passages seems warranted, namely, that " the whole of the proclamation of Jesus Christ and his apostles concerns the Kingdom of God."

[1] Cf. K. L. Schmidt in Kittel's *Wörterbuch*, I, p. 584, lines 30 f.; also Gustaf Dalman, *The Words of Jesus* (1902), pp. 104 f.
[2] Cf. *ibid.*, p. 102.

HISTORY AND MEANING OF THE PHRASE,
" THE KINGDOM OF GOD " [3]

The prophetic teaching that God is King is far older than the
Gospels. A group of psalms teaches this fact as a *present* reality (Ps. 47; 93; 96; 97; 99; etc.) [4] Other Old Testament passages
may also be cited as suggesting the general idea, though its realization is thrown into the *future* (Ex. 15:18; I Sam. 12:12; Ps.
145:11 ff.; Isa. 24:23, etc.). Isaiah in his call-vision " saw the
Lord sitting upon a throne, high and lifted up " (Isa. 6:1).
Moreover, the idea is an ancient one in Canaanite and Semitic
circles rather generally, where the name of God is variously
spelled *Milcom* (I Kings 11:5, 33; II Kings 23:13), *Molech*
(Lev. 18:21; II Kings 23:10; Jer. 32:35), and *Melkart*, all of
these being variants from the single stem *mlk*, which means " to
rule." [5]

In both the Hebrew (*malkuth*) and the Greek (*basileia*),
the words translated " kingdom " are in the first instance abstract nouns. Accordingly, the proper rendering when these are
connected with the name of God is " the sovereignty (or Lordship) of God." The translation, " The kingdom of God," is unfortunate, as it suggests the thought of a domain or tract of territory. [6] The phrase as a whole in both languages stands for the
fact that God is over his world and demands that his creatures
shall do his bidding.

The passages in which the conception occurs have a twofold
reference — first, to God's *de facto* Lordship over all his creatures, both animate and inanimate (I Chron. 29:11; Ps. 47:2,
7 f.; 93:1 ff.; 145:10–13; I Tim. 1:17); and secondly, to his
de jure reign over the lives of men (Ps. 22:28; 96:10; cf. Matt.
5:35), and particularly over his chosen people (Isa. 52:7). All
the Kingdom of God passages in the New Testament belong to

[3] No better book on the history of the phrase is to be found than John
Bright's *The Kingdom of God* (1953). Unfortunately, this book appeared
too late for use in the present sketch, but I should like to express my general accord with Dr. Bright's thesis and conclusions.

[4] Cf. Von Rad in Kittel's *Wörterbuch*, I, p. 567, lines 18 f.

[5] Cf. T. W. Manson, *op. cit.*, pp. 143 f.

[6] Cf. Burrows, *op. cit.*, p. 65; also Von Rad, *op. cit.*, pp. 569, 579 f.

this second class (Mark 1:15; Luke 6:20; I Cor. 4:20; Col. 4:11).

Though God is Sovereign over all his world including man, yet at the moment his will is being done only to a limited extent throughout both animate and inanimate creation. For, while it is true that "the heavens are telling the glory of God" (Ps. 19:1), yet the futility already discussed to which God has subjected his world under man's sinful direction is not a part of his ultimate will for it (Rom. 8:19 ff.).

But of all God's creatures man alone is in active revolt against God's will as sovereign over his life, a revolt that has graphic recognition in the allegorical account of the Garden of Eden incident (Gen., ch. 3).[7] The prophetic Scriptures acknowledge the existence of this continuous rebellion on man's part, for example, in the injunction of the Shema, which reads, "Hear, O Israel: The Lord our God is one Lord; and you shall love the Lord your God with all your heart, and with all your soul, and with all your might" (Deut. 6:4 f.). And from postexilic Judaism to the present time, to recite the Shema morning and evening has been termed "to receive the kingdom (or sovereignty) of God" anew over one's life.[8] This twice daily sacramental recitation of the Shema has served within Judaism to convert God's rightful (de jure) sovereignty into an actual (de facto) experience in individual cases.

One of the deepest insights of the Mishnah occurs in this connection at M. Berakot 2:2, where it is declared that "a man may first take upon him the yoke of the kingdom of heaven and afterward take upon him the yoke of the commandments." The statement refers to the fact that in the recitation of the Shema the part quoted above is said first, and only thereafter is there mention of specific commands enjoined by God.[9] The inference is that God does not give particular instructions about

[7] The title of Emil Brunner's *Man in Revolt* (1947), as well as its content, is intended to give thoroughgoing recognition to this fact.

[8] The Hebrew here (*laqᵉbhal malkuth ha shāmayim*) is clearly the equivalent of the Greek at Mark 10:15 (*dechesthai tēn basileian tou theou*). Cf. T. W. Manson, *op. cit.*, p. 135, n. 1.

[9] The Shema is composed of Deut. 6:4–9; 11:13–21; and Num. 15:37–41. Reference to these passages and their order will make clear the point under discussion above.

the way of life to any man who has not first surrendered himself wholly to God's will. This is essentially the same thought as
that expressed in John 7:17 — " If any man's will is to do his
will, he shall know whether the teaching is from God." Knowledge for the way of life in any given situation comes with the
surrendered will. For God will not waste his time giving particular instructions to men who do not propose to follow them
out in any case! The acknowledgment of God's sovereignty —
the very foundation rock of the Augustinian theology — is, accordingly, a basic plank of the gospel platform throughout the
prophetic Scriptures.

19. *The Realization of God's Sovereignty —*
How? When?

I N THE preceding chapter reference was made to the fact that
God's rightful Lordship over all his creatures has not been
a *de facto* reality, particularly among men. This unrighteous
situation has given rise to two problems which have had much
attention on the part of all who are found in the Hebrew-
Christian tradition. The first of these relates to *how* God's
sovereignty may become a realized fact on the plane of history
and it has been the chief concern of those devoted to the point
of view of Scripture's prophetic realism. The second problem,
respecting *when* that sovereignty may be thought to be attained,
has been by and large the major interest of the apocalyptists.
In the present chapter we shall deal with these two problems
seriatim.

As regards the first of these problems — that relating to *the
method or manner of God's will being done among men* — the
prophets of the Hebrew tradition had two solutions:

(*a*) From the time of Amos onward they assayed the difficult
task of transmuting the nationalistic basis of God's dealings
with his people into an individual experience. The average

Israelite, and even a reformer like Josiah, desired to reclaim the whole of the nation as a unit for God's Kingdom. (Cf. II Kings, ch. 23.) The motive was no doubt a laudable one from the standpoint of patriotic loyalty to one's own people — *God's chosen people,* indeed — to whom the covenant was thought to have pertained from Abraham's time (Gen. 17:13).

The thought behind such endeavor was that God loved this people in a special way, else he would not have chosen it for his own. This idea was nourished within postexilic Judaism from the time of the Maccabees at least. In M. Aboth 3:15 two proofs are given of God's special love for the Israelites — viz., the fact of their being informed that they were "children of God" and that "to them was given the precious instrument" (i.e., the law). This nationalistic basis of God's dealing with men and consequently of his rule in their midst has become the characteristic view of continuing Judaism down to the present time. It was widely expressed in the apocalyptic literature, and through Paul's Judaizing enemies it sought to force itself into the very life and thought of the Christian Church.[1] As Paul was at pains to point out, if this "particularistic" teaching had prevailed in the Christian community, it would have resulted in a theological shift of such magnitude that the entire structure of Scripture's teaching about the gospel would have been altered.

It was Amos who gave such particularism its potential death-blow by pointing out: first, that Yahweh was no more interested in Israel than in any other people of the earth *for their own sake and as a people* (Amos 9:7); secondly, that he had chosen Israel as a special people, indeed, but that this was with a view to peculiar responsibility, not to special privilege (ch. 3:2); thirdly, that in consequence Israel need not look forward to the coming "day of the Lord" with joyful anticipation as though it would of necessity mean its vindication. On the contrary, said the prophet, that day would prove to be exactly what the phrase indicated — namely, the Lord's day and not Israel's (ch. 5:18). The implication was clear that, if Israel wished to find happiness in that day, it should resign itself to the doing of God's

[1] Cf. e.g., IV Esdras 13:34, 38, 49.

sovereign will, get onto his side in all matters of righteous dealing, assume the responsibility devolving on it as the result of *its peculiar vocation* implicit in God's "choice" of it from among the nations of mankind (ch. 2:4–8).[2]

Hope of salvation from God's impending judgment, according to Amos, lay not in the fact that there was a chosen people or that one belonged to it. Rather, such salvation would result from individual commitment to God's will. "Seek good, and not evil, that you may live; and so the Lord, the God of hosts, will be with you, as you say. . . . It may be that the Lord, the God of hosts, will be gracious to the remnant of Joseph" (ch. 5:14 f.). It was clear from this point forward, but became if anything increasingly so as a result of much re-emphasizing by the prophets, that such an *individual hope through individual commitment to God's will had universal implications.* If a man was saved, not because he belonged to a particular people, but rather because of his own attitude toward God, then obviously this would hold true of a man of any race or nation! Thus, the *individualizing,* or as T. W. Manson has said, "the deepening and spiritualizing of the conception of Jehovah's sovereignty," on the one hand, and on the other "the universalizing of its scope go hand in hand."[3]

(*b*) Again, the prophetic solution of the problem of *how* God's Lordship over men might become a reality in experience included the *gathering of those who had made the individual commitment above described into a new community.* One man does not make a kingdom, though one man can cause the sovereignty of God to become realized through his acceptance of it. But when many men individually accept that Lordship, the kingdom in the sense of the community is formed.

For this group Amos was the first on record to suggest a name — that of the "remnant" (cf. Amos 5:15 just quoted). The conception was not developed by him in any detail. This remained for later prophets like Isaiah, Micah, Jeremiah, Zecha-

---

[2] Cf. R. H. Pfeiffer, *An Introduction to the Old Testament* (1941), for further elaboration of this thesis, p. 580.

[3] Cf. T. W. Manson, *op. cit.,* p. 147.

riah, and others to do.[4] In the end it became clear that this doctrine required the establishment of a new covenant with the newly constituted people of God, inasmuch as the older one had been abrogated by a disobedient people. It was the good office of Jeremiah and Ezekiel to suggest as much (Jer. 31:31–34; Ezek. 37:26).

In the light of the above it becomes permissible to speak of the sovereignty of God as realized in both the individual commitment and the group experience. The group is constituted of those who have first made the individual consecration or dedication of life and purpose. The prophetic hint that such would be the case is first found in the account of Elijah's contest with the prophets of Baal on Mt. Carmel (I Kings 18:21). The prophet as God's messenger is far more successful on this occasion than he at first imagines as he looks back over the incident (ch. 19:14). For there are still " seven thousand in Israel . . . that have not bowed to Baal " (v. 18). This seven thousand becomes the nuclear remnant thenceforth, as appears from Paul's use of the incident at a later date (Rom. 11:4).[5]

Other descriptive epithets applied to the remnant in the prophetic tradition are — the " lame," the " driven away," the " cast off " in Micah (ch. 4:6 f.; cf. Zeph. 3:19) ; and the " lost sheep," the " driven away," the " broken," and the " sick " in Ezekiel (ch. 34:16). Though the word " remnant " does not occur in The Psalms, one may be certain that the same conception is in their writers' minds when they speak of the " righteous," the " saints," even of " I " in the representative sense (Ps. 1:5; 34:15; 30:4; 34:9; 11:1; 23:1; 25:1). Probably, too, the fact that in Second Isaiah the Suffering Servant idea appears to fluctuate between the individual and corporate aspects should be taken to indicate that in the writer's mind it was the remnant that he was describing — that is, at once the one and the many wholly devoted to the service of God and the redemption of mankind (cf. Ps. 42:1–9; 44:1–5).

Our Lord does not use the word " remnant " so far as the

---

4 Cf. Isa. 10:20 ff.; Micah 2:12; 5:3–8; Jer. 44:12 ff.; Zech. 8:6.
5 Cf. Skinner, *op. cit.*, on I Kings 19:18.

records inform us, but he does apply Micah's terminology of the "lame" to those who accept the invitation to the heavenly banquet (Luke 14:13, 21). Following his lead, the Christian Church came to think of itself in terms of the "low and despised" (I Cor. 1:28), even the "offscouring" of the human race (ch. 4:13), and so as the embodiment of the "remnant" concept or of the new people chosen of God to serve his purpose of redemption (Rom. 11:5; I Peter 2:9).[6]

As for the second problem of interest to those in the Hebrew-Christian tradition relative to the Kingdom of God, that, namely, pertaining to *when* it might be expected to be realized — this has always been the chief point of inquiry of the apocalyptist. T. W. Manson has suggested that this problem finds its answer implicitly in that given by prophetic realism to the *manner* of the Kingdom's coming. "The Kingdom of God in its essence," he writes, "is the reign of God, a personal relation between God and the individual: and there is no point in asking whether it is present or future, just as there is no point in asking whether the Fatherhood of God is present or future. It is something independent of temporal and spatial relations."[7] That is to say, when any individual experiences God's sovereignty over his life through his recognition of God's right to rule and submission to his will, at that very moment God's Kingdom becomes a present reality for such a one on the plane of history.

The apocalyptist possesses a natural flair for the dramatic and the spectacular. For him, to employ Karl Barth's expressive phrase, the Kingdom always comes *vertically* rather than horizontally and, as it were, like a flash of lightning. God accomplishes its advent, he holds, and never man with all his striving. Through the conjunction of these two motivations on the apocalyptist's part — his interest in the dramatic and his absorption in the divine working — he has found it impossible ever to be satisfied with such evidence of the Kingdom's presence as

---

[6] Cf. also Mark 14:24; Matt. 26:28; Luke 22:20; Heb. 8:6 ff.; 10:16.
[7] Cf. *op. cit.*, p. 135.

has been available. He looks with a certain scorn on the spiritual dynamic resulting in individual conversions. It is the fanfare of trumpets, the explosion of the forces of nature, the Son of Man coming on the clouds of heaven which he awaits.

And he cannot believe that God's most truly *vertical* working is through the agency of men whom he himself calls forth and directs upon the mission of establishing his Kingdom on earth. Indeed, the word " establishing " must not be employed in this connection. The Kingdom is not built, says the apocalyptist, for it is God's rule and is never embodied in any sort of human society on earth — not even in the Christian Church. Bultmann is typical at this point — though he does not wish to be considered an apocalyptist — as he interprets Jesus' message to be, " The coming of God's reign is a miraculous event, which will be brought about by God alone without the help of man " [8]; and again, " All that man can do in the face of the reign of God now breaking in is this: Keep ready or get ready for it." [9]

This travesty of the Scriptural teaching with its practical bearing on such problems as *evangelism* and the Church's program of *oikodomē* as both outlined (Eph., ch. 4, for example) and practiced by the apostle Paul — the building up of the Christian fellowship, its gathering into ecumenical oneness, its ethical impact upon a sorely needy world — resolves itself into a question of semantics. But it is one fraught with the gravest consequences. Particularly is this true of the modern apocalyptist of both the Continental and American neo-orthodox and premillenarian varieties. One imagines that the ancient Jewish and Christian apocalyptists were far more clearly aware of what they meant by their terminology than these, their modern expositors. For it is at least arguable that the ancient exemplars of the school were endeavoring to say in the language of dramatic imagery — of metaphor, parable, riddle, allegory, and symbolism in which both Semitic and Greek minds delighted — what the prophets of Israel had been saying in the more prosaic terms of straightforward prose. There are areas of spirit-

[8] Cf. *Theology*, p. 4.   [9] *Ibid.*, p. 9.

ual interest in which such metaphorical language is more serviceable than literal speech, *but it ought to be understood for what it is.*

It would seem that it ought to be self-evident that *God's reign has become a realized fact when men acknowledge his sovereignty,* that *it is God who does the establishing of his Kingdom however much he does this through men,* and that *his Kingdom is actually in process of being built up* as men are brought to acknowledge his reign whether in heaven or on earth. When the apocalyptist denies these three statements which are fundamental to Scripture's prophetic realism it appears that he is engaging in a species of logomachy without spiritual or ethical significance. The apocalyptist's question, accordingly, about *when* the Kingdom comes is already answered by the prophet. It comes when any man acknowledges God as sole Sovereign over his life. It comes when many men do the same. It comes with the formation of the ethically conditioned remnant out of those who acknowledge their allegiance to God's reign. It comes — yesterday, today, and forever — the while God gathers to himself those who submit to his sovereignty over their lives. And so for the prophetic realistic theology of the Scriptures the problem of the *time* of the coming of the reign of God is seen to take care of itself once that of the *manner* of the same is solved.

And it matters greatly for the Church's evangelistic and missionary enterprises that matters should be as the prophetic realism conceives them to be. For the evangelist and missionary may be far more aflame for their respective tasks than would otherwise be the case — not, to be sure, in the way of a cheap emotionalism, but in that of a strong confidence and deep, abiding thankfulness — if they may realize that they are the active agents in establishing God's reign among men, that in the expressive American vernacular " this is it," that God is now reigning over the people whom he calls forth by his Spirit acting through his prophetic agents!

20. *Jesus' Contribution to the Gospel of the Kingdom*

OUR LORD belongs in the camp of Scripture's prophetic realism relative to the " gospel of the kingdom of God." This, one is aware, is a somewhat bold statement to make in view of the present dominance of the apocalyptic interpretation of his teachings. Accordingly, in this chapter we are consciously taking a position which since Schweitzer's day has found less favor among New Testament scholars, particularly in America, than formerly.[1] There are not wanting strong voices, however, raised in protest against that dominant interpretation to which reference is made. With varying degrees of emphasis and commitment to the thesis of Jesus' prophetic position, T. W. Manson, William Manson, Oscar Cullmann, Maurice Goguel, C. H. Dodd, Vincent Taylor, A. M. Hunter, Henri Clavier, W. G. Kümmel, and to a certain extent Rudolf Bultmann, among others, may be cited as opponents of the extreme interpretation of our Lord's teachings in an apocalyptic sense.[2]

The problem is rendered doubly difficult of solution in view of the undoubted fact that the Church that wrote the Gospels itself held to the apocalyptic view. The a priori possibility has, therefore, to be reckoned with that it failed at certain points accurately to transcribe our Lord's teachings on the subject. We perforce view his eschatological teachings through the apocalyptic spectacles of the Church that wrote the Gospels, as Gougel has pointed out.[3] This possibility, to be sure, has no more value in itself than any similar a priori judgment, and re-

---

[1] Cf. an article in *Theology Today*, for July, 1954, entitled " From Schweitzer to Bultmann," by the present writer.

[2] Maurice Goguel was one of the first to distinguish between the eschatology of the prophets and apocalypticism. Cf. his *Jesus* (Second French Edition, 1950, p. 471).

[3] Cf. M. Goguel, *La Naissance du Christianisme* (1946). His words are, " Christianity early returned, moreover, to the Jewish apocalyptic conception which Jesus had discarded," p. 297; cf. n. 2 on that page also.

quires to be examined in the light of all the facts with a view
to final retention or rejection.

" REALIZED ESCHATOLOGY "

C. H. Dodd has espoused the view that the Church tampered
with or unconsciously perverted Jesus' teaching in the matter
of eschatology, and has made himself known as the exponent
of what he terms " realized eschatology." [4] By this he means that
Jesus accepted — as far as it went — the prophetic eschatological hope of a coming Messiah or other vicegerent of God who
should be the means of bringing in his Kingdom at the end of
history. However, Dodd holds that in Jesus' teaching there is
a sort of residual eschatology which awaits the end of the age
when history shall be no more and time shall pass into eternity.
" Realized eschatology," then, on his own interpretation of his
position, concerns the period from the incarnation to the end
of the age only. This period he thinks of as realized eschatology
because through Jesus Christ the prophetic eschatological hope
found its realization on the plane of history.

Out of fairness to C. H. Dodd, if for no other reason, it is
important to observe that he does believe in the residual eschatology to which reference has just been made. And since this
point has been denied we shall give space to a quotation from
his essay on " Eschatology and History," which constitutes the
appendix to his work on *The Apostolic Preaching* (1937).
Dodd writes: " While, however, the New Testament affirms
with full seriousness that the great divine event has happened,
there remains a residue of eschatology which is not exhausted
in the ' realized eschatology ' of the gospel, namely, the element
of sheer finality. While history still goes on, a view of the world
which, like the prophetic and Christian view, insists that history
is a unity, must necessarily represent it as having an end as well
as a beginning. . . ." (p. 161) .[5]

---

[4] Cf. C. H. Dodd, *The Parables of the Kingdom* (Third Edition, 1936),
pp. 132 ff.

[5] In a forthcoming book on The Revelation of John, the present writer
hopes to establish the thesis that John there does not attempt to look be-

In working out his thesis Professor Dodd has consistently pressed the point that the Church has tampered with Jesus' eschatological teachings and made the latter to conform to its own thought pattern. His book on *The Parables of the Kingdom* was written — as its entire content gives evidence — with a view to establishing his position through an analysis of all the available testimony of the Synoptic Gospels. Moreover, in his *Commentary on the Johannine Epistles* (1946) Dodd has committed himself to the intriguing view that "the profound reinterpretation of eschatology which is one of the distinguishing marks of the thought of the Fourth Gospel . . . appears to do fuller justice to the teaching of Jesus Christ than the naïve thinking of the primitive Church"! [6]

We are not prepared to admit that in all respects Professor Dodd's exegesis is sound, nor that his sweeping conclusion to the effect that the parables of "crisis" and of "judgment" invariably have reference to experiences of the Church within history is justified. But in our judgment his book does establish its major thesis that Jesus thought of the Kingdom as having come in and through himself at his first *parousia* and that, therefore, we are now living in the eschatological times. This is the essence of "realized eschatology" and it carries with it a necessary corollary to the effect that Jesus knew himself to be the Messiah who inaugurated God's reign on earth.

THE KINGDOM HAS COME THROUGH JESUS CHRIST

From this preamble and definition of "realized eschatology" we turn now to a consideration of our Lord's contribution to Scripture's teaching on the "gospel of the kingdom." This embraces three major topics:

(1) The first concerns the fact that through himself, his person, his teachings, and his labors the Kingdom has already come on earth. This marks a point of disagreement between the apoc-

---

yond the historical plane into eternity save in the prophetic imagination of the Church, which he portrays in Act VII of his book.

[6] Cf. also C. H. Dodd, *The Interpretation of the Fourth Gospel* (1953), pp. 379 ff.

alyptists and the prophetic theology. Bultmann has already been
quoted to the effect that Jesus " does not mean that God's reign
is already here," but only that " it is dawning." [7] Its " signs "
are present, it is true — these are " himself, his presence, his
deeds, his message! " [8] This, it need scarcely be remarked, is a
dominant position with the apocalyptists — Jesus at his first
coming does not establish the Kingdom of God on earth, nor
does it arrive through his person and work. That must await the
end of history, or at best it will come with the millennium, the
thousand-year reign of the Son of Man.

Prophetic realism is equally clear that the Kingdom did come
on earth with Jesus' appearance among men. Ethelbert Stauffer,
who stands generally among the apocalyptists, may at this point
be quoted in opposition to Bultmann's view. He writes: " Jesus
claimed for himself the title of ' Son of Man.' . . . He an-
nounced the beginning of God's reign (Matt. 4:17; 11:12). He
put together these two concepts and proclaimed: ' In, with, and
under the coming of the Son of Man comes also God's reign.
For see, the kingdom of God is in your midst ' (Luke 17:21).
It is already there, in his Person, in his work." [9] All this Stauffer
says in his chapter on " God's Reign and the Demonic Powers,"
wherein he indicates how Jesus as God's representative over-
comes such powers within time.

Dodd's " realized eschatology " described above is intended to
suggest much the same series of ideas as Stauffer's thesis. With
the incarnation, that is to say, in Jesus' person, the Kingdom of
God came on earth.[10] T. W. Manson's view that the Kingdom
came at Caesarea Philippi with the confession of Peter is a
further elaboration of the same general conception. Before that
event, says Manson, Jesus preached, " The kingdom is coming;

[7] Cf. *op. cit.,* pp. 6 f.

[8] *Ibid.,* p. 7.

[9] Cf. E. Stauffer, *Die Theologie des Neuen Testaments* (4te Aufl.,
1948), p. 103.

[10] For Dodd, Jesus Christ is as with Origen *autobasileia* — that is, the
Kingdom in his own person! Cf. Stauffer for the phrase, *op. cit.,* p. 266,
n. 394.

prepare for it," but afterward, " The kingdom is here; come in." [11] With this writer, accordingly, the coming of the Kingdom of God on earth obviously depends on acceptance of God's Lordship through accepting his Messiah, much as in more ancient times it had depended on the acceptance of Yahweh's reign through the recitation of the Shema. But essentially Manson is in agreement with the others of the prophetic realistic tradition who hold that the Kingdom in some manner came in Jesus.

The demonstration of the prophetic position depends upon a careful exegesis of a number of passages from our Lord's teaching. We shall mention here only those whose meaning is reasonably certain. Thus, in Mark 10:15 — " Whoever does not receive the kingdom of God like a child shall not enter it " — it is agreed that the Greek is a translation of the current Aramaic (and Hebrew) employed with reference to the symbolism involved in the recitation of the Shema. To " receive the kingdom of heaven " meant that the Lordship of God had there and then been realized in the life of the devout Jew who recited this creed morning and evening. The like expression on Jesus' lips can only have been intended to convey a similar meaning and will have signified to his disciples that God's Kingdom was in some sense present and ready for appropriation. As the saying occurs in the context of Jesus' rebuke of his disciples, who would have sent away the little children, and of his connecting their coming with the fact that " to such belongs the kingdom of God " (v. 14) , the conclusion seems inevitable that to receive Jesus is to receive the Kingdom because the Kingdom is present in him.

The same appears to be taught in the Q passage in Luke 11:20; Matt. 12:28: " But if it is by the finger of God that I cast out demons, then the kingdom of God has come upon you." The endeavor has been made, unsuccessfully one believes, to discredit the translation of the last verb and closing phrase as just rendered in this sentence (in the Greek, *ephthasen eph'*

[11] Cf. Manson, *op. cit.,* pp. 126, 130, etc.

hymās) .[12] It would seem that the nature of Jesus' argument relative to the exorcising of the demons demands that he be saying, that the " finger of God " thus manifested in and through him means that the Kingdom has now come among men. The contrary view should perhaps be labeled " special pleading " in support of a theory.

Probably the same is to be said also of the Q passage in Luke 16:16; Matt. 11:12, an admittedly difficult saying on other grounds: " ' The law and the prophets were until John; since then the good news of the kingdom of God is preached, and every one enters it violently.' " But however one understands this *violence* — upon which Matthew enlarges slightly more than Luke, whom we have quoted — it seems that the violence referred to comes after the Baptist and so in the time of Jesus. This will be, it would seem, because now the Kingdom is present and capable of being entered, whereas it was not so previously.

Still a third Q saying reads, " Nor will they say, ' Lo, here it is! ' or ' There! ' for behold, the kingdom of God is in the midst of you " (Luke 17:21). The saying is absent from Matthew, possibly for the reason put forward by T. W. Manson, namely, that " it lends itself to an interpretation of the Kingdom of God that would not be acceptable to the first Evangelist with his stress on the catastrophic aspect of the apocalyptic hope." [13] One cannot accept the alternative translation here — first proposed by Luther, I believe: " The kingdom of God is within you (*inwendig in euch*) ," instead of the usual, " The kingdom of God is in the midst of you (*mitten unter euch.*) ." For, as has often been pointed out, most recently perhaps by Stauffer, Jesus would not have said that the Kingdom was " within " the Pharisees, his enemies, with whom he was conversing at the moment! [14]

---

[12] For the arguments pro and con here, cf. G. Dalman, *op. cit.*, p. 107; also T. W. Manson, *op. cit.*, p. 124; and Bultmann, *op. cit.*, p. 7.

[13] Cf. *op. cit.*, p. 123.

[14] Cf. E. Stauffer, *op. cit.*, p. 266, n. 394. He refers also to the translation of the Sinaitic Syriac (*bainoth-khum*) as good evidence of the second century understanding of the passage in the sense of " in your midst."

Bultmann's recently proposed translation, " And none can say, ' Lo, here or there! ' For lo, God's reign is (all at once) in your midst! ", illustrates quite forcefully the difference between prophetic and apocalyptic views on a point such as this. The question of the Pharisees in the context had been relative to " when the kingdom of God was coming " (v. 20). Jesus' reply on the prophetic understanding of the passage is that it is not a matter of *when* at all. The Kingdom is already present. The problem is one of spiritual discernment to see this. Bultmann, on the other hand, gives the answer of Jesus the future reference in line with the apocalyptic teaching by inserting the phrase, " All at once," for which it is difficult to discover any real ground other than the necessities of a theory.[15]

In addition to the passages just discussed, it should be noted that those that speak of " entering the kingdom " (Mark 10:15; 10:23–25; 12:34; Matt. 5:20; 7:21; 21:31; 23:14), " seeing the kingdom come with power " (Mark 9:1), " sitting down in the kingdom of God " (Luke 13:29; Matt. 8:11), and " being blessed in having the kingdom in one's possession " (Luke 6:20; Matt. 5:3, 10), are at least as intelligible when interpreted in terms of the Kingdom's presence in the world as in the apocalyptic future sense. Such passages can scarcely be employed to prove either position, as they lend themselves to both.

[15] T. W. Manson, in *The Sayings of Jesus* (1949), appears to lean in the direction of Bultmann's interpretation of this passage on the ground that Jesus' reply will then appear to agree "with his genuine teaching about the final consummation as given in the Q passage which follows immediately in Luke (Luke 17:23–30)," p. 304. While I agree with Manson about the following passage and in general about the unexpectedness of the Parousia and its coming without " signs," it seems to me more likely that Q had these two passages in juxtaposition because they stressed two opposite (though both correct) facets of the Kingdom concept, namely, its *present* and *future* phases. Perhaps the " Lo, here! . . . Lo, there! " theme found in both *pericopai* also stimulated the author of Q in bringing them together as he has done. Or, alternatively, our Lord may have made up this couplet himself; there is good precedent for thinking so in some of the parable couplets (e.g., Luke 13:18–21; Matt. 13:31–33, from Q; Matt. 13:44–46, from M). I have discussed the other passages above listed in *The Religion of Maturity*, pp. 76, 187, 288, 291–293.

JESUS' PERSONAL CONTRIBUTION
TO THE KINGDOM'S COMING

(2) Jesus' second original addition to the prophetic teaching on the " gospel of the kingdom " has already been hinted at in the above discussion. This concerns the nature of his own contribution to the Kingdom's coming on earth. As has been remarked above, the Scriptures appear to teach quite plainly that it comes in Jesus' own Person, in his teachings, and in his work — or, perhaps better, with Manson, it comes as men, acknowledging Jesus as God's Viceroy, accept the Kingdom through accepting him. At this point again the apocalyptists and prophetic realism are at odds in the interpretation of the passages involved. For it is one of the anomalies of modern New Testament critical studies that those who are loudest in claiming that the Church's witness to Jesus' thought about himself, as shown in the sources of the Synoptic Gospels, is not to be trusted, are in the main members of the apocalyptic school, who insist that his apocalyptic position is established by the same Gospels written by an apocalyptic Church!

The apocalyptist generally is unable to believe that God's immanential working in his world proceeds through the medium of human personality. God must work " directly " and " vertically " or " immediately," not through man's mediation. Consequently, the apocalyptist is conditioned by his own presuppositions against believing that even Jesus could have been conscious of being the medium through whom the Kingdom comes in the world. Bultmann and some of his colleagues in the dialectic school would deny belonging to the apocalyptic school. But both he and they accept the differentia by which apocalypticism unmixed with prophetic teaching is to be known, namely, that the Kingdom of God does not come on earth and within history.[16] No amount of asserting that one does not accept the " fantasy " of the apocalyptic position, therefore, will serve to divorce one from its fundamental attitudes or conclusions.[17]

[16] Cf. *The Religion of Maturity*, pp. 222 f.
[17] The word " fantasy " is Bultmann's, cf. *op. cit.*, p. 6.

And in establishing those conclusions Bultmann and his disciples have resorted to the most radical technique at present employed in the field of Biblical criticism.

Only by employing such a radical methodology could one hope to establish a reconstruction of the facts such as the following taken from Bultmann's *Theology*. He admits that the idea that Jesus thought of himself as the Messiah or Son of Man " does agree with the Evangelists' point of view." However, he hastens to qualify this admission with the declaration that " the question is whether they themselves have not superimposed upon the traditional material their own belief in the Messiahship of Jesus " (p. 26) .

He then proceeds to show that " *Jesus' life and work* measured by traditional messianic ideas *was not messianic* " — a view in which Bultmann is undoubtedly right (p. 27) . This demonstration is followed by an argument intended, however, to disprove the idea that Jesus made a " reinterpretation and spiritualization of the Messiah-concept " (p. 28) , or even that he " was conscious of being the one *destined to be the future Messiah* " (p. 29) . As for the former of these ideas, it is true, says Bultmann, that " the Jewish concept Messiah-Son-of-Man is reinterpreted — or better, singularly enriched — in so far as the idea of a suffering, dying, rising Messiah or Son of Man was unknown in Judaism. But this reinterpretation of the concept was done, not by Jesus himself, but by the Church *ex eventu* " (p. 31) . Accordingly, he accepts Wrede's theory of a " Messiah-secret " as invented by the Church to show why, though it believed Jesus to be the Messiah, he never said so. The secret " was to remain hidden until the resurrection," according to the theory (p. 32) . But this secret is found written into only " the editorial sentences of the Evangelists." So it cannot be held to go back to Jesus (p. 32) .

Bultmann's view is given here as representative of the dominant apocalyptic position held among New Testament scholars at the present day, particularly in America. His thought is not so extensively followed among British scholars, nor even among the Continentals. From the standpoint of the apocalyptic position as a whole, Bultmann's views are as extreme in one direction as C. H. Dodd's in another. And there can be no doubt that his radical methodology in the field of form criticism is the best ally which the apocalyptic position can muster at the moment. These two scholars and their colleagues arrive at almost diametrically opposed views regarding Jesus' consciousness of mission and about his teachings on the nature and coming of the Kingdom of God. Both cannot be right. Are both perchance wrong?

Granted that Bultmann is correct in saying that the " editorial sentences of the Evangelist " are suspect (p. 32). It does not follow, however, that in the end they must prove wrong in the data they present. Further, not alone Bultmann's " editorial sentences " are suspect, but everything else in the Gospels from the standpoint of modern literary-historical research is equally so. It should be obvious, one imagines, that not alone the few words and sentences that Bultmann eliminates as " editorial sentences," but the entire Gospels are what one might term " editorial documents." The entire Gospels and their sources which passed through the hands of their authors or editors, and not a few sentences merely suspected to have been added by them, are subject to critical appraisal.

As is well known, Bultmann himself was one of the first to feel the force of this argument. There was a time, consequently, when he could write, " We can no longer know the character of Jesus, his life, or his personality . . . there is not one of his words which we can regard as purely authentic," and again, " In my opinion we can sum up what can be known of the life and personality of Jesus as simply nothing." [18] And yet, as Goguel has pointed out, Bultmann " has found it possible to draw up an outline of the thought and teaching of Jesus "! Commenting on these facts, Goguel remarks that " such inconsistency seems incompatible with such vigorous intellects as these " (Goguel couples Schweitzer with Bultmann for purposes of this criticism) ; " hence," he goes on, " we are led to inquire whether the radical skepticism against which they instinctively react may

[18] Cf. M. Goguel, *The Life of Jesus* (English Edition, 1933), p. 59.

not be a conclusion drawn from the development of some, but not all, the factors that constitute the problem as a whole." [19]

An example of Goguel's point that Bultmann's " skepticism " results from choosing some and rejecting other factors according to his own preconceived notions occurs in the matter of Jesus' awareness of his God-appointed mission. Bultmann holds that the few passages in Mark containing " the predictions of the passion (Mark 8:31; 9:31; 10:33 f.; cf. ch. 10:45; 14:21, 41) . . . are all *vaticinia ex eventu.*" [20] On the other hand he claims that " it is not to be doubted that the predictions of the Parousia are older than those of the passion and resurrection," on the ground that " Q knows only the former and not yet the latter." [21] He points out also that, in " the predictions of the Parousia " in the Synoptic Gospels, " the death and resurrection of the Son of Man " are not predicted.[22] From this evidence Bultmann concludes that the Parousia passages are " probably original words of Jesus," while those relating to death and resurrection " are probably later products of the Hellenistic Church " (p. 30).

In other words, Bultmann is prepared to follow Mark as a reliable source when he fits in with his own eschatological views, but he discards him when he witnesses to Jesus' awareness of a mission that will lead him to the cross, here preferring Q, which has no such witness. We shall return to these conclusions and to Bultmann's evidence after first having made some preparation for consideration of them. Meanwhile, it is to be remarked that his is surely an unsound methodology, one so selective, indeed, in its application to the data in hand that nearly anything could be proved by it, depending on the whim of the operator and his skill in handling his materials.

A sounder methodology would appear to involve the attempt to discover the over-all pattern of the mind of our Lord as this

[19] *Ibid.,* p. 61. Goguel has recently reprinted this criticism in the second French edition of his *Jesus* (1950), pp. 31, 33.
[20] I.e., " Predictions after the event "! Cf. R. Bultmann, *op. cit.,* p. 29.
[21] *Ibid.,* p. 30.
[22] *Ibid.,* p. 29; cf. Mark 8:38; 13:26 f.; 14:62; Matt. 24:27, 37, 39, 44—all being passages cited here by Bultmann himself.

is shown, not alone in his words, but also in his works. Perhaps, more especially in his works, in fact. Such a method would assume that the Evangelists — admittedly the editors of the entire Gospels and their sources — are making an honest effort to give us a correct picture of what Jesus said and did. It would assume also that, whereas an "editorial sentence" may, of course, represent the mind of the Evangelist as he pondered on Jesus' words and works, it is not therefore necessarily *secondary* to the transcription which he has given us of his source materials, as the latter materials also have passed through his editing hands.

The proper check against any one Evangelist's idiosyncracies would seem to be the canon of criticism that the witness of two or more writers is better than one, and the same canon holds for their sources. At the same time, once these peculiarities of the individual writers are known through a study of each in turn, their several values should be reckoned in the total assessment accordingly. One does not arrive at truth simply by "counting noses." Particularly, when a writer appears to be reporting as a saying of Jesus that which runs counter to his own predilections — or at any rate, may seem to do so at a given point or in the development of his views — such saying should be given special scrutiny as being doubly likely to be accurate, though a writer is not necessarily wrongly reporting when what he reports appears to be agreeable to his own views!

Finally, if by these means the "key" to Jesus' teaching and labors may once be found, it is reasonable to suppose that — as with other great figures in the history of thought and action — there will appear to emerge a certain pattern of consistency in his ministry and its aftermath. Nor will this pattern likely seem as simple as in the case of lesser men. There is a type of consistency that is "the logic of fools," but there is also a type that because of its depth of insight gives us a picture of a mind possessed of vast, even universal, comprehensiveness. No merit attaches per se to the simple pattern of the liberal rabbi Jesus of an older generation, nor to the equally naïve apocalyptic Jesus of the present. Jesus Christ by all accounts must have been an exceedingly complex person. The pattern of consistency which we seek for his speech and actions must prove equally so, and a kind of a priori taboo ought to attach to any endeavor to explain him that obviously ignores this fact.

When we approach the subject of our inquiry after this fashion, we discover that each of the *sources* of the Synoptic Gospels, as well as the Evangelist of each Gospel in turn, has much the same story to tell us of Jesus' *words* about himself and to a degree also of his *works* which appear generally to support that story. Each source, as also each Evangelist, of course, employs his own words, as he also makes an independent judgment regarding what incidents and teachings to select in the telling of this story — a fact which in itself goes far toward suggesting the generally disinterested character of the testimony.

This is not the place to set down a detailed reconstruction of the sources of the Synoptic Gospels (Mark, Q, M, and L). Nor shall we give space to an analysis of the contents of our Gospels as they now stand. The reader is referred to the usual *Introductions* for this sort of data.[23] In spite of much critical opinion to the contrary (including Bultmann's), what strikes one forcibly in these analyses of the contents of both Gospels and their sources is *their general freedom from interpretative elements.* As E. F. Scott has recently remarked, " Mark recounts a number of facts just as they happened, without any attempt to show how they were related or what made them significant." [24]

The same is true of all the Synoptic sources and to an extent, at least, of the Evangelists who employed them. Why did Jesus never enter the synagogue after his exclusion from it at Nazareth? Both Mark and L bear witness to the fact *merely by omitting to mention that he ever again enters the Jewish house of worship and instruction.* They do not even actually state that he never enters again, to say nothing of drawing no conclusions from the fact! What relation has this fact and the exclusion itself

[23] A convenient work for the general reader is A. M. Hunter's *The Work and Words of Jesus* (1950) ; on pages 131 to 192 he has given a complete synopsis of the Synoptic Gospel sources.

[24] Cf. E. F. Scott, *The Crisis in the Life of Jesus* (1952), p. 3. Scott has much more to the same effect and in general accord with the above argument.

to our Lord's choosing the band of "twelve"? Why, indeed, did he choose just twelve and then stop calling men to join the little band? Once again the sources and Evangelists do not say that he actually stopped such calling. But there appears to be conclusive evidence that, with one or two significant exceptions, he did so.[25] Why, for that matter, did Jesus call disciples at all? Neither the prophets, including the Baptist, nor the Pharisaic rabbis are recorded to have followed such a practice. Is this little band of the "twelve" by any chance the nuclear *remnant* of the prophets? And does Jesus consider himself to be the Messianic creator of the same?

Again, what is the significance of the *covenant* in the "upper room"? Is this the constituting act of the remnant, whereby it receives its official status?

What did the *voice* at the baptism and transfiguration of Jesus mean for him and for his disciples? Why did Jesus tell his disciples not to publish abroad his Messiahship? Did he consider himself to be the Messiah? Did he think of himself in terms of the Suffering Servant of Second Isaiah?

When Jesus speaks of the "Son of Man," does he refer to himself or to the community of God's people or to both in different contexts? If the last suggestion be correct, does he conceive of both as suffering and glorified together or does the suffering apply to himself and the glory to the community?

What is the relation between the scene in the "upper room" and that at the cross and resurrection? One would like to know the answers to these and the like questions, but the Evangelists and their sources do not supply such answers. By and large they simply allow the facts to speak for themselves so far as they are capable of doing so.

As Scott has remarked in the book quoted, "We are told of many things done by Jesus but are left asking why he did them and what was their bearing on one another and on his mission as a whole."[26] This author suggests that what we require "is some tangible clue to guide us through" the welter of events,

---

[25] Cf. the author's *The Intention of Jesus* (1943), pp. 209 ff.
[26] Cf. *op. cit.*, pp. 4 ff.

such as is sought by the physical scientist through an " intensive study of particular objects." He adverts to the fact that the scientist takes " a tool or vessel, a mound, or a faded inscription " as his clue, and through " this evidence " is enabled to feel " his way toward the real conditions of a forgotten age." He then remarks that " almost any incident in the life of Jesus, when fully examined, will in some degree serve," like the historian's tool or vessel, as a clear index of our Lord's attitude toward his mission and work.

This methodology is the same as that proposed by Oscar Cullmann in his *Christ and Time* (1950). Only Cullmann spoke of the required " clue " as " the essential Christian kernel " of the New Testament revelation (p. 12). For purposes of study Scott has taken the cleansing of the Temple as furnishing as likely material as any incident in our Lord's ministry for discovering the clue which he seeks. With the same thought in mind the present writer chose the baptism of Jesus for minute examination in *The Intention of Jesus* (1943). It is a matter of no little satisfaction that, adopting essentially the same methodology but with a different choice of incidents on the whole, scholars should find their results to tally so nearly as proves to be the case. It can only mean that the intricate pattern of consistency of which we have spoken is to be discovered woven into the warp and woof of our Lord's activity and teaching.

We shall not endeavor here to repeat the arguments advanced in the three works to which reference has just been made. Those who are interested in pursuing the subject further should consult them with a view to discovering how the over-all purpose of Jesus is laid bare once the " clue " or " kernel " is found which, so to speak, furnishes the " key " to unlock the door of his mind.

Suffice it to say that these three works are one in disclosing the " historical Jesus " to bear no similarity to the reconstructions of Wilhelm Wrede with his " Messianic secret " and of Rudolf Bultmann with his mere announcer of the eschatological times. Rather, they are unanimous in holding that the Jesus-of-history exhibits a very definite purpose to carry through a program which only one knowing himself to be God's Viceroy (Messiah, Son of Man, Suffering Servant, and the like) would or could have undertaken. For the Gospels and their sources appear to present us with one whose teaching and works of mercy can only be those of a person knowing himself to be the agent of God for establishing his Kingdom on earth.

These Gospels and their sources do not say that Jesus Christ believed himself to be either Messiah or Suffering Servant. But they indicate that from first to last he was motivated by the single intention of accomplishing what these terms stand for when taken in their highest spiritual and ethical sense. And what else would we have expected from such a one as God's true Servant? It is not in blatant arrogance and vulgar bombast that God's messengers have ever revealed themselves. Jesus did not go about speaking of himself as the Messiah, nor did he wish his disciples to do so, at any rate not during the days of his earthly ministry. Rather, he insisted that his works and words should speak for themselves and that men must make up their minds about him entirely on their own (Luke 7:18–23 from Q).

All the sources, however, witness that he did call himself the sort of " Son of man " who had " no place to lay his head " (Luke 9:58 from Q). He also connected this descriptive phrase (Son of Man) with his Passion in Mark and L, though not in Q or M. Probably T. W. Manson is right in assigning the reasons for this phenomenon, when he writes: " In the case of Q this is not altogether surprising; for . . . Q contained no Passion narrative. Again, in M it may be that an intense interest in the Parousia has tended to throw into the background the thought of the Passion, the latter being regarded as merely the prelude to the former." [27] The interest of the Early Church in Acts, chs. 1 to 12, is fair evidence for Manson's contention regarding M. And if this be so, it would seem that the burden of proof is thrown on anyone wishing to discount the testimony of Mark and L at this point in favor of the silence of Q regarding the Passion of the Son of Man.

But this is exactly what Bultmann would have us do. For

[27] Cf. T. W. Manson, *The Teaching of Jesus*, p. 227.

Bultmann's understanding of Jesus' self-awareness and motivation is in large part built on Q's lack of prophecies regarding the death and resurrection of the Son of Man. Inasmuch as Mark contains such prophecies and Q does not, Bultmann terms them " *vaticinia ex eventu* " and suggests that Q had no knowledge of them! But Bultmann's theory overlooks the certain fact that Q also contained no record of these happenings as events, and not alone as *prophecies,* a fact to which Manson's statement above quoted calls our attention. Q certainly knew of Jesus' death and resurrection *after they occurred.* Why, then, does this source not mention them? Are we to conclude that it had two reasons for not doing so — one for not mentioning them as prophecies, another for overlooking to report them as happenings? This begins to look complicated. It is simpler, one would imagine, to assume that Q never mentions our Lord's death and resurrection, either as prophecy or as historic event, *for one reason* that would serve to explain both omissions at once. This would be that motivation of Q's compiler with which scholars have long been acquainted, namely, that he wished by bringing together sayings of Jesus pertaining to both the religious and ethical aspects of the Kingdom to exhibit its character generally and so to encourage his readers to build their life houses upon its bedrock.

This alternative explanation of Q's silence in the matter of the Son of Man's death and resurrection, be it noted, finds confirmation in the further phenomenon that Q, along with all the other Synoptic sources, does attach the concept of " exaltation " to this figure. This they do in their prophecies of the Parousia,[28] as Bultmann himself observes. The significance of this fact appears in H. H. Rowley's observation that it is in connection with the future coming in glory that " the collective understanding of the phrase is attended with the least difficulty." [29] That is to say, it is exactly in connection with the exaltation

[28] Cf. T. W. Manson, *op. cit.,* p. 225, as well as Bultmann, *op. cit.,* pp. 29 ff.

[29] Cf. H. H. Rowley, *The Relevance of Apocalyptic* (Second Edition, 1947) , p. 121. Bultmann would agree with Rowley's contention; cf. *op. cit.,* p. 9.

idea that Jesus seems to be referring to the Church when he
employs the term " Son of Man! " The *prevalence* of such exaltation passages in all the Synoptic sources — though not the
bare fact that there are such at all — is to be attributed, one imagines, to the apocalyptic interest of the Church and its own
anticipation of experience in what the *eschaton* has to offer it.
This interest in the *collective* Son of Man's future, then, will
accord nicely with the general concern of Q's compiler for the
Church's welfare as above indicated.

It is, accordingly, in the " humiliation " passages which concern the Son of Man, beginning with that in Q at Luke 9:58;
Matt. 8:20 and running through Mark and both " special
sources " (M and L), that we find the distinctive thought of
Jesus about himself. That Jesus knew beforehand that he must
suffer and die was due to his knowledge of man's sin, of the
treatment meted out to God's prophets before him throughout
the length of Israel's history, of the nature of his own person
and mission, and of the fact that the spiritual and ethical values
represented by the Kingdom of God could be achieved only by
complete surrender to God's will in a sinful world. There is,
therefore, nothing miraculous about Jesus Christ's prophecies
concerning his death and resurrection; the *miracle* is our Lord
himself. His knowledge is quite normal to one such as he. Bultmann's alternative apocalyptic Jesus lacks even the specious
merit of fanaticism to explain why the Jewish Sanhedrin would
consider it imperative to turn him over to the Roman authori-
ties to be done to death! There appears to be no more reason
why the naïve Herald of the Kingdom's coming — the inven-
tion of present-day apocalypticism — should have had to go to
the cross, than the heretical rabbi of the " old liberal school "! [30]

[30] If space permitted, one would like to criticize at length Bultmann's
view that the " earliest Church " believed in Jesus as Messiah because of its
" Easter faith " in his resurrection (cf. *op. cit.,* pp. 42 ff.). In view of his
firm belief that this is so, it is disconcerting to learn that " how the Easter
faith arose . . . has been obscured in the tradition by legend and is not of
basic importance " (p. 45). One would imagine it all-important to his
theory! But why should the resurrection, even if it could be proved as a
fact, have led the disciples to conclude that Jesus was the promised Mes-

THE LAST SUPPER AND THE KINGDOM OF GOD

(3) The third contribution Jesus made on the subject of the
" gospel of the kingdom " concerns the Last Supper which he as
their host gave to his disciples during Passion Week. Probably
some connection is intended between this feast and the feeding
of the multitudes referred to in the Gospel sources (Mark
6:30–44; 8:1–10). No such connection is suggested, however,
by any of the Evangelists. As we have seen to be true of Jesus'
other works, these too are allowed largely to speak for themselves.

The connection — if such there be — is probably to be made
through the parable of the Kingdom Banquet, which was already famous long before Jesus' use of it (cf. Isa. 49:9–12;
55:1 ff.; 59:19; Ps. 23:5; 107:3, 9; Mal. 1:11 f.). In this parable
God was the Host and the good times in the Kingdom were para-
bolically suggested by the fact that around his table were gathered all his people enjoying the repast. This last was symbolical
of the salvation which God had to offer them. The parable was
greatly elaborated in the extracanonical literature and our Lord
himself used it on more than one occasion apparently (Q —
Luke 13:28 f.; 14:16–24).[31]

Against this background the Last Supper which our Lord
gave to his disciples as his guests is seen to have deep significance, and particularly so when taken in conjunction with his
words on the occasion: " Take; this is my body," and, " This
is my blood of the covenant, which is poured out for many "
(Mark 14:22–25). At the very least those present must have seen
that this was the banquet of the Kingdom of God which they
were privileged to enjoy by way of symbol or sacrament and so
to speak proleptically, that Jesus was the one who had authority
to inaugurate the same, and that the symbols of bread and wine

---

siah? If he had said nothing of either his Messiahship or his resurrection —
as, of course, Bultmann believes — it is difficult to discover wherein lay for
the disciples any connection between these two concepts!

[31] For extensive reference to the extracanonical writings on this point,
cf. Moore's *Judaism*, vol. ii, pp. 364 ff.

were the pledge of the new covenant as the Passover lamb and
its blood had been of the old. All the accounts of the incident
are one at this point.[32] John's further suggestion (John 15:13–
15) that Jesus here was gathering his disciples about himself as
a band of " friends " (Hebrew and Aramaic *hāberīm,* whence
habūrāh — fraternity) makes explicit what appears to be the
implication of the other Gospels.

The Last Supper, then, stands as our Lord's last voluntary act
relative to the establishment of God's Kingdom on earth. Hitherto he has taught and labored, gathered the little band together
and sent them out like himself to preach and heal — activities
of the Kingdom whereby its presence is felt in all that is said
and done. Now, the crisis has arrived and he is to be taken from
them. He welds them together, therefore, into a fellowship
organized about elements suggestive of his own sacrificial death.
More he cannot do; he must rather await the inevitable, as to
the last he follows out the Father's will for him. This *habūrāh*
formed the nucleus of the Christian Church, and the banquet
has ever since been the symbol of their fellowship in their Lord,
the symbol too, of the Kingdom fellowship which through his
living Spirit's presence is ever on the increase.

21. *The Present Task of Establishing the Kingdom*

A POCALYPTICISM, with its view of the Kingdom coming
vertically from heaven in the sense of requiring no effort
on man's part, cannot speak of the latter's share in the task of
establishing the Kingdom on earth. Indeed, except where apocalyptic thought has been deeply tinged with the prophetic
teaching, no mention is ever made of the Kingdom's coming on
earth at all. For this reason the idea of a millennium is in reality a prophetic one as far as it goes.

[32] Cf. I Cor. 10:16 f.; 11:23–26; Mark 14:22–25; Luke 22:14–23 (L);
cf. John's allegory of the Vine and the Branches in John 15:1–15.

The prophetic realism which is based on the Scriptures, by contrast, has no hesitation in employing a phrase like " the establishing of the Kingdom." And this, for the reason that for the Scriptures the Church of Christ is the scene of the Kingdom banquet. The Church is the Kingdom's visible societal embodiment. As the Church fellowship is built up (*oikodomē*) the scope of the divine sovereignty is more and more extended in its actual operation. The Church of Christ is all Kingdom territory, so to speak. As it grows and expands its fellowship, the reign of God becomes *de facto* increasingly realized among men. It is mere pedantry, therefore, to balk at the use of the words " building " and " establishing " relative to the Kingdom's coming on earth, if indeed such an attitude does not represent a sheer misunderstanding of what the Kingdom is.

Moreover, the Church is the " body of Christ," to use Paul's expressive phrase. It is the " extension of the incarnation " spiritually and dynamically throughout history. *Spiritually* the Church is this, in the sense that it is to the Church that the Spirit is given in this eschatological epoch. This was represented symbolically at Pentecost by the appearance of the " tongues as of fire, distributed and resting on each one of them " (Acts, 2:3) . It was out of this common experience that the Church developed its doctrine of the Spirit's oneness and his fellowship equally with the various members (I Cor., ch. 12; Eph. 2:19–21; 4:15 f.) . Spirit and Church, that is to say, go together in a unique ethical union, for " there is one body and one Spirit " (Eph. 4:4) .

Dynamically, too, the Church is the " extension of the incarnation " in the sense that, when united with the Spirit, the latter instills into the Church those powers of life and energy which make it the fit instrument of Christ and the means whereby he accomplishes his will in the world. When Jesus Christ walked among men he had a body, a fit and effective instrument for the fulfillment of his every purpose. That body no longer exists in the world of human affairs. For the efficient carrying through of his redemptive task, therefore, he requires another body. It is this redemptive function that the Church performs throughout history. It is his hands, his feet, his eyes, his voice, to do his bidding (I Cor., ch. 12).

From the earliest times the Church has realized that it sustained this relation to its Lord and that accordingly its function while on earth is exactly the same as his. This is shown in several passages in the Synoptic sources. Thus, when questioned by the Baptist's disciples about his identity with the Coming One, Jesus replied that they would do well to observe what was going on around them. He then described his task as comprising two activities. First, said he, " the blind receive their sight, the lame walk, lepers are cleansed, and the deaf hear, the dead are raised up " (Luke 7:22) — the *philanthropic activity* of the herald of Isa. 61:1 ff. (cf. ch. 35:5 f.) ; while secondly, " the poor have good news preached to them " — the *evangelism* of the same Isaianic herald. And, added Jesus, John must make up his own mind about him on the basis of such evidence (Luke 7:23).

When we turn to the earliest accounts of the sending forth of Jesus' disciples, we find that his charge to them as to their duties runs along identical lines with the above. This is sufficiently clear from the Lucan form of the Q account, where Jesus enjoins his disciples, " Heal the sick " — *philanthropy;* and adds, " Say to them, ' The kingdom of God has come near to you ' " (Luke 10:9) — *evangelism.*[1] This command is made by Matthew even closer to approximate the form of Jesus' disclosure of his own labors to the Baptist's disciples (Matt. 10:7 f.). Essentially the same wording is found also in Mark (ch. 6:12 f.), and in the alternative account in Luke (ch. 9:1 f.).

It is clear, too, from its activities as reported in the early chapters of The Acts that the Early Church understood its mission to be along these two lines. Paul also describes the work of the Christian community as the " body of Christ " after the same general pattern (I Cor. 12:29 f.). Accordingly, it is con-

---

[1] For a recent denial of the historicity of the Baptist's inquiry of Jesus as assumed in this discussion, cf. Carl H. Kraeling's *John the Baptist* (1951), pp. 127 ff.

sciously after this fashion that the Church carries on through the eschatological age as the efficient instrument of God's word and work for the redemption of mankind.

Accordingly from age to age the Church's task fundamentally remains constant. This is so for the reason that, like its Lord, it is engaged in performing a redemptive service for mankind that is all-comprehensive in its effective approach to his needs. Nothing, it would seem, is lacking in the two-sided program which it fulfills. Still there remains a prophetic function which the Church must perform from time to time. This is to view the contemporary scene in the light of God's redemptive purpose for mankind and to shift its emphasis accordingly to one or the other aspect of its task. The Hebrew prophets were accustomed at times to glance back over God's dealings with men in the not-too-distant past with a view to acquiring the necessary perspective to view the needs of their own day. With the insight gained by this backward glance, they then looked at their own day and its morrow, and prophesied of God's will for his people in their own generation.

As one who accepts Scripture's prophetic realism, it becomes the writer's duty to do the same for the present day and generation. And as he undertakes this task in the present chapter, it is with a deep sense of fellowship with those who are like-minded and who have contributed to the prophetic insights of the present community of believers in our common Lord. For our purpose, it will be convenient to scan briefly — after the manner of the prophets — the three subperiods into which modern Church history may be divided.

(1) The Period of Extension (Orthodoxy) : c. 1750 to 1900

This subperiod begins with a wholesome reaction against that movement of the human spirit known in Germany as the *Aufklärung* and in France and Britain as deism. The so-called " Age of Reason," with its skepticism of the supernatural and of a genuine divine revelation, had laid its cold hand even upon the Christian Church, as upon all of man's life. But to-

ward the end of the eighteenth century the breath of God's
Spirit began to blow across his Church, with the resultant
quickening of tempo in its spiritual and ethical living in the
lands affected by the naturalism implicit in the movement mentioned. In Germany and adjoining lands this quickening eventuated in Pietism and Moravianism; in Britain and America,
in Wesleyanism and the " Great Awakening," by whose influence all Protestantism was deeply stirred.

It is not easy at times to assess the reasons for the forms that
are assumed by movements of the human spirit. As one compares the effect of the Reformation with that of the Great Awakening, a surprising difference emerges. " There are varieties of
gifts, but the same Spirit " — not only is this true as between
Christians as individuals; it is also true as one age is compared
with another in the line of redemptive history. Undoubtedly
the same Spirit inspired both periods just mentioned, but with
what diverse results! In the Reformation the product was almost
exclusively theology; in the Great Awakening, warm religion
and evangelical ardor and outreach. It was during the latter
period and not during the Reformation of the sixteenth century that men were sent out into the far corners of the earth
with the passion of the evangel. It was now that all the great
missionary societies were formed — the Society for the Propa-
gation of the Gospel and the Church Missionary Society (both
Anglican organizations), the American Board of Commission-
ers for Foreign Missions; the Boards of Foreign Missions of the
Church of Scotland, the American Baptists, American Methodists, American Presbyterians, and others. It may be said with
truth, one imagines, that the World Council of Churches is likewise a product of this same movement guided by the Spirit of
the living God.

The keynote of the movement was *evangelism,* one of the two
sides of the program suggested by the passages that we have
just studied. Its aim was the extension of the gospel to the remotest parts of the earth. Bishop Reginald Heber's hymn, written during the earliest days of the movement, epitomizes its
spirit to a degree:

" Can we, whose souls are lighted
With wisdom from on high,
Can we to men benighted
The lamp of life deny?
Salvation! O salvation!
The joyful sound proclaim,
Till each remotest nation
Has learned Messiah's Name."

Not long after the close of the period John R. Mott's well-known book *The Evangelization of the World in This Generation* sounded that note of urgency which had been felt throughout the century and a half of its extent. Under the guidance of the Spirit who inspired the movement this task of world-wide evangelism was nearly accomplished. The names of two men whom the writer was privileged to know personally may be allowed to stand as symbols of the fact that the goal set was almost attained. Sultan Mohammed Paul, an Afghan prince and member of one of the ruling houses of that land, came down into India as a young man and was converted to the Christian faith. He never thereafter returned to his native land but became an evangelist and professor of Persian and Arabic in the land of his new-found faith. Saddhu Sundar Singh, a convert from Sikhism, spent his summers evangelizing in the Forbidden Kingdom of Tibet, because, like Afghanistan, it was closed to missionary effort. Tibet and Afghanistan — with these two exceptions, the period of *extension* found the gospel carried to the earth's remotest parts.

(2) *The Period of Permeation (Liberalism) : 1900 to 1932*

The beginning of the second subperiod of modern Church history signalized the presence of another movement of the human spirit. John Dewey has styled the psychology of the later decades of the nineteenth century " an impossible individualistic psychology," for the reason that it conceived it possible to study man's emotional and intellectual powers, indeed man's whole inner life, without considering more than man the individual. Like the chemist and the physiologist, so the psychologist thought he could tell all about a man, so to speak, just as he "stood in his shoes." As though an individual were merely so much *psyche* carved out of the psychical universe, even as he is so much *physis* carved out of a physical one!

But with the coming of sociology and social psychology, there came the attendant realization that man *as a social animal* must be taken seriously in order to be understood at all. The older individualistic psychology of Dewey's anathema then became a thing of the past. It was now seen that "an individual in isolation" simply does not exist. Mutual privilege and responsibility are phrases that cover an enormous area in the life of everyone on the plane of history in all times and places.

The individual's life is composed by and large of a network of group experiences so complicated that to find him in that nexus and to isolate him from his groups is almost as delicate a task as the endeavor to find the proverbial "needle in the haystack." Born and reared in a family, the child soon passes out into another group life, the school, where he discovers in what looks very simple from a distance classes dividing the school into segments, and within the classes natural cliques — so natural, indeed, that their members scarcely realize their separateness from the group as a whole. Thence, the individual passes out into the business world, another group life of dependence and contribution, and into the body politic (observe the corporate nature of the very phrase), where the existence of legal standards means that his life is hedged about with demands, but also that he may expect certain privileges to be derived from the group life.

All this was the rediscovery of the sciences mentioned in the early decades of the present century. But the leadership of the Church, both at home and abroad, was not slow to grasp the implications of the new ideas for the cause of the Christian movement. It soon became evident that, if the individual was to be saved at all, then he must be saved in his groups. For these constituted *life* to him. In consequence, "a saved man in a saved society" became the motto of those decades and a new emphasis was placed upon *philanthropic activity,* the second feature of our Lord's appointed program for both himself and his Church. This gave rise to the so-called " social gospel " of the liberalism of the period.

It rapidly became apparent under the impact of these new ideas that when, as a result of the evangelism of the older epoch, an individual had been baptized, he had in reality not yet been wholly " saved." For baptism, it was seen, was little less than a major operation. It had, so to speak, carved the individual out of his total environment and set him forth naked before God and man — out of his family, his intellectual, his social-economic, even his political, as well as his moral and religious groups. Such a major operation required a deal of convalescing and thereafter the building up of life after a new pattern, through keying the individual into a series of new experiences along all these group lines.

The Church, accordingly, took as its new watchword *permeation,* and its new endeavor was to leaven all man's groups with the leaven of the gospel message. The term " Kingdom of God " was simultaneously given the widest possible definition with a view to including the large area affected by such permeation. The task was the *building of the Kingdom,* understood in this sense of leavening man's group experiences, that after conversion and baptism — or even without it, as some held! — the individual might find a chastened and purified series of social units into which he could enter with a view to realizing the richness of the abundant life.

Again, a great hymn expressed the spirit of this new day. This was the hymn of Washington Gladden, himself a firm believer in and preacher of the social gospel:

> " O Master, let me walk with Thee
> In lowly paths of service free;
> Tell me Thy secret; help me bear
> The strain of toil, the fret of care."

As before, this movement of the Spirit within the Church brought forth a large measure of achievement. For in the first few decades of the present century, as perhaps never before in

the history of the Church, the Christian gospel permeated the
life of the non-Christian world and leavened the thought and
activity of that world in many ways. The *Indian Social Reformer* of Bombay, India, a weekly magazine printed in English
and for a quarter century edited by Mr. K. Natarajan, an orthodox Hindu, may be permitted to stand as a symbol of the degree
to which such permeation was achieved. No one who has read
this periodical for some years can fail to have noted that in its
every issue — in editorial or article — have occurred quotations from the Bible and particularly from the teachings of
Jesus. Such quotations have almost invariably been made by
way of commendation to be taken as criteria for social living
and have been found in articles written by Hindus, Moslems,
Sikhs, Parsis, and the devotees of other faiths.

(3) The Period of Intension (Neo-Evangelicalism) :
1932 to the Present

We are now in a new subperiod of modern Church history.
This began about 1932, though the various movements in the
churches dedicated to the contagion of the New Life did not
get under way until some years later — about 1944 (American
Methodists), 1948 (American Presbyterians), and the like.
However, it usually takes the Church half a generation to re-
spond to the activity of the Holy Spirit! It was so with the problem of the universality of the gospel message in the earliest days
of the Christian movement. And the time-span between the
Spirit-stimulus and the Church's response was even longer in the
pre-Reformation era.

It is a wonderful thing to *sit in* at the inception of a new
movement under the direction of God's Spirit. Those who did
in the decades on either side of the above-mentioned date
(1932) will recall the " blood, toil, tears, and sweat " attendant
on the death of an old ecclesiastical cultural pattern which had
long pertained on the mission fields, and the birth of a new
one. What is happening at the moment in the Oriental political
scene is the aftermath and, indeed, a sad parody of that which

occurred in the Church in the same locale between 1920 and 1936. Communism from the standpoint of "dialectical materialism" is vainly endeavoring to satisfy the spiritual hunger of peoples looking earnestly for the "liberty of the sons of God" because they have seen the light of Jesus Christ in the gospel.

Essentially this revolt has signalized the passing of an old feudal culture unworthy of the life and aspirations of mankind. In Church circles it meant primarily that the old privileged group of foreign missionaries, representing Western "vested interests" with their financial and cultural prestige, had to give way before the rise of a group of nationals representing the dynamic Church of Christ in one of its most revolutionary phases. The so-called "mission" with great difficulty learned to *decrease* that the Church fellowship made up of all peoples and tongues and races without distinction might *increase*.

The International Missionary Council which held its meeting at Madras, India, in 1938 took as its theme for study "The Church of Christ." This meant, as one of its leaders remarked, the "rediscovery of the Church in our generation." Theretofore it had been the "Kingdom of God," as we have just seen, and a loosely defined "Kingdom" at that, which had been the theme of greatest interest within Christian circles.

It started with the growing sense of men of prophetic insight everywhere — Orientals and Occidentals alike — that the generation-old emphasis upon permeation had now become obsolete. I mention the date 1932 as significant for the reason that it was in that year that the report entitled *Rethinking Missions* was published under the auspices of "The Commission of Appraisal" of foreign mission work of all the participating denominations, the general chairman being Prof. William Ernest Hocking. That book represented the last strong effort to further the "social gospel," the doctrine of permeation, and the spread of the "Kingdom of God" without placing the Church of Christ squarely at the center.

It made the quite shocking suggestion that "it ought to be the

primary business of an interpreter of the Christian religion in
the future to permeate the personal life of the individual and
the fabric of human society with creative ideals and energies
which will renew and revitalize . . . rather than to build a
church as an institution to stand out as an entity in itself apart
from the larger whole of society " (pp. 108 f.) . There were not
wanting phrases here and there in the report that helped to
mitigate the bald suggestion contained in this sentence. But on
the whole the report represented the inadequately defined
" Kingdom " emphasis rather than the Church-as-a-living-fellow-
ship point of view. But it was the *permeation* suggested in the
report that had been going on for a generation already! And the
event proved to be quite otherwise than the prophecy had fore-
cast!

It was out of the rediscovery of the exceeding sinfulness of
the old order and its group lives that the Church of Christ had
its rebirth. The title of Reinhold Niebuhr's book *Moral Man
and Immoral Society* gave expression to the nature of the discovery. Man's extant groups were found to be so exceedingly
sinful as to be unworthy of his making an attempt to live the
life of the gospel in them, nor could the hope be entertained
that they could be salvaged. The Kingdom teachings could only
cause frustration to converts attempting to live the Christ-life
within the cultural patterns of the old paganism. Far less could
those who were not even converts, and therefore without allegiance to Jesus Christ as the sole Lord of life, be expected to
live the life of the Kingdom in such an environment. Once
again it was seen how useless it is to attempt to patch an old
garment or to pour " new wine into old wineskins "!

And as men looked about them for the social group in which
the life of the Kingdom could be adequately lived, they found
it already present in the then-despised fellowship of the Church.
The *keynote* of the new movement of the Spirit, therefore, is
intension as contrasted with the extension of the older period.
Henceforth the Spirit appears to be calling the Church fellowship to the endeavor to discover by experimentation, by actual
living in local situations, by trial and error, by demonstration

of the power of united effort on given projects, and in a thousand other ways — *but always in the local situation and hence intensively* — what the Christian Church may mean for man's corporate as well as his individual living.

It is at this point as well that the function of corporate worship appears, namely, to illuminate the mind, to stir the heart, to motivate the will, so that the layman may put together the gospel message and his own particular skill or talent and, as he goes forth from the Church's worship service into the world of affairs, may seek there to do the task immediately before him and so to make over man's corporate living, but *always as a member of the Church of Christ and as one who draws his strength for living from its Spirit and fellowship.*

All this is not to say, of course, that the day of evangelism and permeation is over. The Church and the world will always require to be evangelized, even as all of men's group lives will require to be permeated anew with the leaven of the gospel, but it is necessary to recognize the fact that the Church of Jesus Christ is now everywhere, or nearly so — even behind the Iron Curtain — and that it is everywhere in force. As a result that Church's major task in the day immediately ahead would appear to be one of *boring in,* of concentration on the contribution that it as the living embodiment of the gospel may make in the local situation, of discovering the nature of its spiritual and ethical donation to the life of the community of mankind, at first locally and then universally.

It was the late Archbishop William Temple, I believe, who said some years ago: " We speak glibly of the primitive Church. *We are the primitive Church! "* In the sense just indicated this is clearly true. We have just begun to discover what in God's providence the period of intension can mean for the life of the Church fellowship and through it for the world at large. We have much to learn, much to forgive and forget, much of which to repent, much for which to strive.

The hymn that epitomizes this new movement of the human spirit under the direction of God's Holy Spirit is that of William Pierson Merrill:

" Rise up, O men of God!
The Church for you doth wait,
Her strength unequal to her task;
Rise up, and make her great! "

Used by permission of *The Presbyterian Tribune*

THE CONTENT OF SCRIPTURE'S PROPHETIC REALISM

D. The Gospel of Our Salvation

" In him you also,
who have heard the word of truth,
the gospel of your salvation,
and have believed in him,
were sealed with the
promised Holy Spirit."
— EPHESIANS 1:13.

The Content of Scripture's Prophetic Realism

D. The Gospel of Our Salvation
SYNOPSIS

*T*HERE IS *a real sense in which the whole content of the gospel is contained in the phrase that heads this last section. From the beginning God has purposed to save mankind, as the course of history and particularly of redemptive history bears witness. If man's " chief end " is to " glorify God," God's chief purpose is to glorify man that the latter may become his fit companion.*

In presenting this theme, we inquire into: (1) the prophetic doctrine of man — man-as-sinner: *we discover here that since the Fall man is immersed in the slough of* corporate sin *and that his major problem concerns how to extricate himself from the same;* (2) the prophetic doctrine of direction: *man the* individual *has to assume responsibility for turning away from the slough into which he has been born — this is what is meant by " repentance "; it follows upon the knowledge of and faith in God and its product is the acquiring of direction or motivation in one's life;* (3) the prophetic doctrine of the redemptive community, *in whose goodly company one finds oneself when one has left behind the slough of corporate sin; this is the Church fellowship — in it the individual shares with the group in God's self-vindication (justification) and in the ethical resurrection termed " sanctification ";* and (4) the prophetic doctrine of the last things, *about which the prophetic Scriptures say little, presumably because they know little; that little amounts to saying that the theater burns down and the actors go home — home to God, for whose fellowship they have been preparing while in communion with the Spirit of his Son on earth!*

22. *The Prophetic Doctrine of Man — Man-as-Sinner*

THE LAST of the gospel phrases with which we shall deal in this book is the subject of this section. In the form quoted it occurs only in the passage from Ephesians found on the section title page. There it is equated with the phrase " the word of truth," or as one might translate, the message of the divine faithfulness. This equation is quite apropos inasmuch as throughout the prophetic Scriptures the salvation of man depends upon the faithfulness of God, particularly on his faithfulness in fulfilling his promises. We have already observed that Jeremiah makes this word for truth or faithfulness (*'emeth*, in the Hebrew) the signet of God, spelling out from it the acrostic — " living God . . . everlasting King " (Jer. 10:10). It is likely, therefore, that Paul in the Ephesians passage in equating the two phrases means to say that in the message ' the living God, the everlasting King, is faithful ' lies the ground of our salvation: this, indeed, is the gospel, the good news.

Two other New Testament phrases containing the word *evangelion* are quite close to the above in meaning. These are " the gospel of the grace of God " (Acts 20:24) , and " the gospel of peace " (Eph. 6:15) . In the latter Paul is quoting from Isa. 52:7, wherein " peace " is clearly stated to mean " salvation," as often in the Hebrew. The verb *evangelizesthai* (to preach the gospel) is taken over from the Septuagint in quoting from the same Isaiah passage in Acts 10:36: " You know the word which he sent to Israel, preaching good news of peace by Jesus Christ (he is Lord of all) ," and also in Eph. 2:13–17, where, however, it is Isa. 57:19 that is being quoted, or perhaps better a combination of both Isaiah passages ("He came and preached peace to you who were far off and peace to those who were near ") . Acts 13:26 has nearly the same phraseology: " To us has been sent the message of this salvation."

In addition, there are in the New Testament a variety of expressions that interpret the subject of this section. Thus, " The gospel: it is the power of God for salvation to every one who has faith " (Rom. 1:16) ; " The gospel, which you received, . . . by which you are saved " (I Cor. 15:1 f.) ; " the Gentiles are fellow heirs, members of the same body, and partakers of the promise in Christ Jesus through the gospel " (Eph. 3:6) . The word *kērygma,* which we have already seen to be the practical equivalent of gospel, literally, " the thing preached," should also be noted in the present connection, for it tells the same story as *evangelion.* In I Cor. 1:21 we read, ' God was pleased through the foolishness of the *kērygma* to save believers' (cf. chs. 2:4 f. and 15:14) . Peter's " spiritual milk " by which men " grow up to salvation " is this same gospel (I Peter 2:2; cf. ch. 1:10) .

These passages taken together give us the essentials of a doctrine of salvation. It might be stated somewhat as follows. The *content of the gospel* — so these passages inform us — is in the last analysis *the manner of the working of the salvation which God offers to man.* In that working we see the fulfillment of God's purpose in history. For from the beginning that purpose has been man's salvation. And in His carrying through that purpose to its intentioned goal *God's faithfulness* is thrown into bold relief. It is the rock of this character of faithfulness in God upon which the gospel of our salvation finds its sure *foundation* (Eph. 1:13) . Again, the *impelling force* behind this saving activity of God is his grace (Acts 20:24; Rom. 1:16) , the set or determination of his person in favor of man's good in spite of everything — in spite even of man himself and his sin. Then, there is the *new stand* taken by the individual who is evangelized and his entrance into the body consecrated to God's service

(I Cor. 15:1; Eph. 3:6). And finally, the *goal* of the divine purpose is the accomplishment of peace between himself and man (Acts 10:36).

In this statement of the " gospel of our salvation " there is obviously an interplay between God's purpose and man's response which calls for some development as we proceed. Meanwhile, it should be noted at the start that the entire doctrine may be stated in terms of the *interplay* referred to. Thus, the Westminster Shorter Catechism begins with the thought that " *man's chief end* is to glorify God, and to enjoy him forever." But it is equally true that *God's central purpose* in all his creative activity has been to glorify man and to make him worthy of fellowship with Himself. Such is at once God's purpose in history and the aim of the gospel.

In glorifying man, however, God glorifies himself. For it is only and precisely as man is His own " image and likeness " that God glorifies him. In the end, then, man's glory never becomes his own but remains God's and only God's. Just as the light of the moon is borrowed light and of no significance in itself, so man in the light of God is glorified by a light which can never become his. God made man thus to bask in His glory. What we shall have now to say in detail is merely an elaboration of these fundamental ideas.

THE PROPHETIC DOCTRINE OF THE FALL

The prophetic Scriptures teach that man was made " in the image and likeness of God." Man was in consequence *perfect* in the sense of being devoid of sin, even as God is perfect or holy and so separate from sin. Man has too — for this is certainly the meaning of the narrative in Gen., ch. 3 — the capacity for moral growth (vs. 4 f.). Herein is said to lie his temptation: " Your eyes shall be opened, and ye shall be as God, knowing good and evil." It is futile to deny this capacity for growth and equally to affirm that man was made perfect in the sense of morally mature. It is the former potentiality that distinguishes man from the animals and the latter equally that separates him from God.

Man is worthy of dominion over the brute creation precisely because of his capacity for moral character (ch. 1:28), but also he is made as one dependent upon God at every stage of his development. This capacity for moral character which separates man from the lower creatures means that he has a certain freedom of choice — he may choose to obey or to disobey God. "Thus," as Brunner remarks, "the essential mark of man is this: freedom in this dependence" [1] (cf. Gen. 2:17). Man's temptation to sin, then, consists in wishing to displace God with his own *self*. He would "be as God, knowing good and evil" (ch. 3:5), on his own, that is to say, and without dependence on God. Man would become his own "god." [2]

The prophetic doctrine of the *Fall* means simply that man has succumbed to this temptation. Donald Baillie describes this in the words: "In the story of Eden the serpent says to the woman: 'Ye shall be as gods.' This is the temptation to which mankind has succumbed: we have put ourselves, each one individually, in the center of our universe, where God ought to be. And when persons do that, it separates them both from God and from each other. That is what is wrong with mankind. That is original sin." [3]

The Scriptures do not make much of the original rebellion — one passage in each of the Testaments (Gen., ch. 3, and Rom., ch. 5:12 ff.), with occasional possible allusions elsewhere (I Cor. 15:21 f.; James 1:14 f.). But there is much on the subsequent sin resulting from the Fall. Baillie quotes Luther on the point to the effect that the result of the Fall is that man "is *incurvatus in se,*' bent inward upon himself,' instead of looking away from himself toward God and his fellows in love." [4]

Man in his totality, man as a whole, has become a moral "introvert"! He concerns himself constantly and wholly with his own standards, his own whims, his own little world of values.

---

[1] Cf. Emil Brunner, *The Divine Imperative* (1937), p. 153.

[2] Cf. R. Bultmann as cited in Kittel's *Wörterbuch,* I, p. 312, n. 153: "Sin . . . is man's desire to assert his 'self,' to exalt his claim to 'selfhood,' to be as God"; cf. also Quell, *ibid.,* p. 283, lines 30 ff.

[3] Cf. Donald Baillie, *God Was in Christ,* p. 204.

[4] *Ibid.,* p. 204.

Baillie has illustrated the point with a most engaging myth in which he speaks of mankind as like children playing a game in a circle, " linked together with lovingly joined hands, facing toward the Light in the center, which is God " — that is the way God would have us play the game. Instead, however, we men turn our backs on the Light at the center and on each other, each endeavoring to become the center on his own. The result is of necessity " blind confusion, and not even any true knowledge of God or of our neighbors." [5]

THE ORIGIN OF THE STORY OF THE FALL

For our purposes here the story of the Fall presents three problems for solution: first, its origin (both in Genesis and in Paul) ; secondly, how it is to be classified from a literary and religious standpoint; and thirdly, its essential teaching regarding the nature of sin.

(1) As for *the origin of the story of the Fall*, this is generally traced to ancient mythological materials, while Paul's use of it in Rom. 5:12–21 is attributed to Hellenistic or Jewish sources which have worked over these older stories.[6] Bultmann thinks, for example, that " in describing the curse that lies upon Adamitic mankind, Paul is unquestionably under the influence of the Gnostic myth." [7] In this writer's opinion, this is only one of many illustrations of the employment of the *Gnostic motifs* in the " *Kērygma* of the Hellenistic Church." [8] Others, on the other hand, like Sanday and Headlam, C. H. Dodd, and N. P. Williams would refer Paul's teaching on the subject of the Fall of mankind in Adam to IV Esdras and the Apocalypse of Baruch, or to other similar apocalyptic sources wherein again Hellenistic influence is strongly to the fore.[9] Thus, N. P. Williams holds

[5] *Ibid.*, p. 205.

[6] Cf. Gottfried Quell, in Kittel's *Wörterbuch*, I, p. 282, lines 12 ff. and notes for references to the sources.

[7] Cf. R. Bultmann, *Theology*, p. 251.

[8] Cf. *ibid.*, pp. 164–183, for a detailed statement of his thesis.

[9] Cf. C. H. Dodd, *Commentary on Romans* (1932) , *in loc.;* Sanday and Headlam, *A Critical and Exegetical Commentary on the Epistle to the Romans* (Second Edition, 1896) , *in loc.;* N. P. Williams, *The Ideas of the Fall and of Original Sin* (1927) , pp. 118–122.

that the doctrine came to primitive Christianity and so to Paul
by way of Galilean Jewish tradition, which had embraced more
of the apocalyptic point of view than the Judaism of Judea and
the capital had done.[10] He believes that Jesus also gave " such a
measure of approbation as is involved in the fact of delicate
toleration " to this doctrinal teaching.[11]

We are in general agreement with Williams' views as just expressed relative to Jesus' loose attachment to Galilean apocalyptic teaching. Its terminology was in the air, so to speak, just as
" atomic fission," " neuroses," and " metabolism " are the common patter of our day. But Jesus never set out to teach his
disciples or the multitudes the doctrines of the current apocalypticism. He never sat down, as it were, and said, " Go to now:
I will indoctrinate you into the mysteries of apocalyptic lore —
the truth about the devil and his myriads, the two kingdoms of
light and darkness, the cosmology of earth, heaven, and hell,
and the like." Rather, using the well-known terms, he taught
and preached by their means the " gospel of the kingdom," even
as he could have done the same in another age in a quite different vocabulary.

I would be inclined to extend Williams' argument to cover
Paul's use of the apocalyptic phraseology as well. Indeed, it
would appear less likely that Paul, a Tarsian and disciple of
Gamaliel at Jerusalem, would take the apocalyptic teaching regarding the Fall, for example, at its face value than would Jesus.

As regards the whole matter of " origins," the suggestion of
Millar Burrows is to be taken to heart and applied here as elsewhere. " Ideas," he remarks, " like men, must be judged on
their own merits, not by their pedigrees. Sometimes their worth
is in proportion to the distance they have traveled from their
origins." [12] I should add that the tone and quality of a religion
— and hence, also our assurance that it has behind it genuine
contact with the living God — will be reflected in what that religion does with an idea after it gets hold of it. If it transforms
it, raising it to a plane of spiritual and moral excellence which
it did not previously enjoy, then the credit for the same should

[10] *Ibid.*   [11] *Ibid.,* p. 120.   [12] Cf. Millar Burrows, *op. cit.,* p. 62.

go to the religion incorporating it and transmitting to it of the religion's own inner worth. This is what, in my judgment, Paul's use of the story of the Fall has done for it. Paul's manner of employing that story was determined by the gospel motivation which was central to all his thinking; hence, he made this old well-known material shine with a new light and serve a new and exalted end.

THE LITERARY FORM OF THE STORY

(2) Turning now to the second of the problems raised by the account of the Fall — that pertaining to *its literary and religious nature,* particularly as it is recounted by Paul in Rom., ch. 5 — several alternative suggestions have been made. Some interpreters hold that Paul took the story as historic fact and as referring to an individual named " Adam." Others believe he accepted it in the sense of *myth* — that is, as a dramatization for religious purposes of a spiritual reality defying ordinary literal methods of statement. Others still suggest that, following the apocalyptic pattern, Paul projected the myth into the suprahistorical world. He thought of Adam in this case as a superhistorical person (*urgeschichtliche Mensch*), paralleling such angelic figures as Gabriel, Lucifer, and Michael.

C. H. Dodd, who holds that we should not too readily assume that Paul accepted the story as literal historic fact, remarks that " the subtler minds of his age (like Philo of Alexandria, and the Egyptian Greek who wrote the Hermetic tract *Poimandres*) treated it as a symbolic allegory, and Paul's too was a subtle mind. . . . It is enough for him and for us to recognize that the wrongdoing of an individual is not an isolated phenomenon, but part of a corporate, racial wrongness which infects human society as we know it, and affects the individual through heredity and environment." [13] Brunner and Donald Baillie appear to waver between the mythological and *urgeschichtliche Mensch* theories, probably seeing no great difference between them.[14]

[13] Cf. *op. cit.,* on Rom. 5:12–21, p. 80.
[14] Cf. Emil Brunner, *Man in Revolt* (1947) , pp. 139 ff., 155, and Donald Baillie, *op. cit.,* p. 204.

From the standpoint of the prophetic theology, however, there is a vast difference between the two points of view just mentioned. For on the usual *mythical view* — whatever the story may be thought to stand for as far as symbolic or literal fact is concerned — at all events its action is represented as transpiring on the historical level and on creation's stage. In this view, accordingly, the story is not to be thought of as far removed from the actuality of history. Prophetic realism can employ " myth " in this sense, even as it can find a place for parable, allegory, and the other literary forms. But it is quite otherwise with the theory of *a superhistorical person* so dear to the mind of the Barthians. For here we confront a type of mythology that is characteristic of apocalyptic thought exclusively, or nearly so, and one that has nothing in common with the simplicity of the *this-worldly* prophetic teaching.

In such apocalyptic mythology the great moral and spiritual movements that determine the destinies of men are transferred from the plane of history — where men may share in determining their own fate — and therefore of actuality, to the eternal order, and on that plane are fought out the great battles of good and evil, of life and death, of light and darkness.[15] Such teaching has been most congenial to Gnostic speculation, to Zoroastrianism, to Jewish apocalypticism, and to the cabala of the Middle Ages, as well as to astrologers and theosophists in all ages. It has given rise time and again to views of a deistic, deterministic, magical, and irrational nature whose issue can be nothing but despair.

There is no evidence that either the author (the prophet designated as " J " by Old Testament scholars) of Gen., ch. 3, or the apostle Paul entertained such apocalyptic views. It is far

[15] To take the " superhistorical man " theory as implying that *every man is his own Adam* would, of course, bring the struggle onto the historical plane. But this interpretation again is neither Pauline nor in line with the prophetic teaching of the Scriptures. Paul's argument in Rom. 5:12 ff. requires that there exist a relationship of moral responsibility between the *one* and the *many*, as regards both Adam and Christ. And further in the prophetic teaching this is demanded by the concept of " corporate personality." That *every man is his own Adam* is good Pelagian individualism.

more likely that Driver is correct in suggesting that the former has taken materials common to many mythologies of primitive man and, using the " figurative or allegorical dress " in which he found them, has transformed their actual content into " a variety of ethical and theological truths " conforming to his own " deep thoughts upon man and God." [16]

The same may be said for Paul without doubt. For as Bishop Nygren and others have been at pains to point out, *Paul's major interest in the passage (Gen., ch. 3) is not Adam at all for his own sake.* " For Adam did not signify to Paul something independent of Christ. It is Paul's intention to discuss Adam only as the antitype of Christ." [17] Adam is, so to speak, only brought in as an aside in the Pauline passage in Rom. 5:12–21 as a foil to Christ. This is because Paul hopes that, starting with the known and believed about Adam which he may assume on the part of his Jewish Christian readers, he may argue to the unknown and perhaps not-yet-believed about Christ.

Jesus Christ, however, here as always with Paul is the type or original and Adam is the antitype or copy. This is so even though Paul can go to the length of speaking of Christ as the " Second Adam " in I Cor. 15:45 ff. For Paul, *the Adam concept was under the control of the Christ concept* which he entertained and never the reverse. In consequence, it is inadmissible to commit Paul to all that the Adam " myth " may have meant to the apocalyptists whether Jewish or Christian. Paul simply used the story of the Fall as far as it suited his purpose. And this, be it noted, was in connection with the elaboration of the doctrine of justification by grace through faith. He saw in what happened as between Adam and the race of mankind the reverse of what was true of the relationship between Jesus Christ and man in the matter of justification (Rom. 5:18 f.). Mankind had been plunged into corporate sin and was as a result under God's judgment of condemnation — all through Adam's rebellion against His will. Man had equally been given the opportunity

---

[16] Cf. S. R. Driver, *The Book of Genesis* (Fifteenth Edition, 1948), p. 54.

[17] Cf. Anders Nygren, *Commentary on Romans* (1949), p. 211.

of sharing in a new corporate righteousness through Jesus Christ's acceptance of that will (I Cor. 15:22).

THE TEACHING REGARDING THE FALL

(3) The third problem arising from the story of the Fall in Gen., ch. 3, and in Rom. 5:12–21 concerns *the teaching involved particularly as to the nature of sin.* There appears to be more general agreement at this point than with reference to the other two problems just discussed. In the first place, it is agreed that the sin of which both accounts speak is in the nature of rebellion against the will of God. Again, most would no doubt agree with Brunner against the " older Barth " that the entrance of sin into human experience — and it is this of which both accounts speak, and not of the origin of sin in a metaphysical sense, if there be such a thing — did not render man *Unmensch,* that is to say, did not reduce him to a level below that of his status of man and so to that of the animals. " The ' natural man,' that is, man outside the realm of faith, does not cease to be man because of the existence of sin." [18] If Brunner is right in his recent interpretation of Barth's latest writing, Barth himself is no longer on this point the old Barth of the *Ich Sage Nein* days, when he held that the Fall robbed Adam and so man of the *imago Dei* which distinguishes man from the lower animals.[19]

But there is still a third factor in the teaching of the story — a factor implicit surely in the Genesis account and providing Paul's motivation for using it at all in Romans. This is the thought that *death in the ultimate sense of a breach of fellowship between God and man has resulted from Adam's transgression.* This appears very clearly in the Genesis story in the fact that Adam is banished from the Garden of Eden — the garden of intimate, firsthand communion with God (ch. 3:22–24). Paul calls this banishment " death " in accordance with the suggestion of God himself in the Genesis narrative. " In the

[18] Cf. Emil Brunner, *The Divine Imperative* (1937), p. 155.

[19] Cf. Brunner's article on " The New Barth " in the *Scottish Journal of Theology,* vol. iv, No. 2, June, 1951, pp. 123–135.

day that you eat " of the forbidden fruit, says God in that narrative, " you shall die " (ch. 2:17). Obviously, therefore, for the narrator of the incident banishment is to be equated with death in the high spiritual sense entertained by him.

Bultmann has, I think, put Paul's argument at this point in proper perspective. He writes: " It must be noted that the real theme of Rom. 5:12 ff. is not the origin of sin but the origin of death; more accurately, even the origin of death is the theme only as the negative side of the positive theme, the origin of life, for the meaning of the passage in its context is this: The certainty of the Christian hope set forth in ch. 5:1–11 has its foundation in the fact that Christ has obtained life for mankind instituted by him, and obtained it with the same certainty with which Adam brought death upon Adamitic mankind (so also in I Cor. 15:21 f.)." [20]

Understood in this sense, there is no essential difference between Genesis and Paul at this point. Paul takes up the story where Genesis leaves off, accepts the thought that *death* is banishment from God's presence — a rift in fellowship with God on man's part — and declares in the Romans passage that this whole delicate situation is reversed by Jesus Christ: " As in Adam all die, so also in Christ shall all be made alive " (I Cor. 15:22). The plan of salvation is to be stated, if done after the manner of the prophetic Scriptures, in terms not of restoration of the *imago Dei* to man — for that has never been effaced — but rather as the means whereby fellowship is restored between God and man. It is just exactly because the image of God remains intact in man — however marred it may have become through sin — it is just because man is still man with that capacity of communing with God which the animals do not enjoy that man's salvation is possible of achievement. This is the a priori condition of salvation which is assumed throughout Scripture.

[20] Cf. R. Bultmann, *op. cit.,* p. 252.

THE NATURE OF SIN

It is necessary, finally, to say a word about the nature of sin as conceived in both of these accounts. Augustine is responsible for speaking of the sin which is man's lot through Adam as "original sin" and for the suggestion that "all men have sinned in Adam" who was their representative before God. This he does on the assumption that in Rom. 5:12 the phrase *eph' hō pantes hēmarton* should be translated, "In whom all sinned." It is now clear that such a translation is inadmissible. Either we must translate with Origen, "In that all sinned," or with Bishop Nygren — and I believe this to be preferable — "It was under these circumstances, under these auspices, that all sinned." [21] Nygren's translation preserves unbroken Paul's well-knit argument of "the one and the many" as relates to both Adam and Christ, and men. Origen's translation lends itself to a purely Pelagian understanding of the verse which was surely not Paul's intent — nor, for that matter, Origen's!

But to discard Augustine's translation of this phrase does not permit us to overlook the validity of his major argument with regard to the meaning of the passage. By "original sin" Augustine meant that for Paul, as for Genesis, Adam was in a real sense the leader or representative of the race of mankind and that when he sinned all mankind sinned with him and suffered in consequence. Moreover, he meant also to infer that Paul says as much merely to serve as a foil for his intended deduction that in similar fashion Jesus Christ is the Leader or Representative of the new humanity. Since Jesus Christ has performed "one act of righteousness" — as Adam, one act of transgression — it will lead to "justification of life" for all men (vs. 17–21). That Augustine is right in thus interpreting the thought of Paul there can, one imagines, be no question.

For one thing, it has long been noted that Paul employs the singular word for sin (*hamartia*) throughout Rom., chs. 5 to 7, in a strange, almost personified sense (*personhafte Erscheinung*). Accordingly, the individual man is represented as sin's

[21] Cf. Anders Nygren, *op. cit.*, p. 214.

slave (Rom. 6:16, 20) .[22] Individual men have become sin's slaves because of Adam's transgression (*parabasis, paraptōma*) — because Adam by disobeying God opened the door and allowed this giant with its confederate, death, to enter into human relations and experience. Obviously for such sin — not to be confused with individual " sins " — we require a special vocabulary. Augustine, therefore, proposed the term " original sin " to serve this purpose. The phrase, however, is unfortunate for the reason that it seems to say — what Augustine himself never intended, we may be sure — that man as man is a sinner and that God so made him! This is both un-Pauline and contrary to the prophetic teaching in Genesis and everywhere else throughout Scripture.

A better word would be *corporate sin*. For it is fairly well agreed that it is the prophetic concept of " corporate personality " that lies behind Paul's teaching here, as regards both Adam and also Christ. The conception of corporate personality explains much in the prophetic Scriptures, as we have already seen. The stock example is that of Achan who " broke taboo (Josh., ch. 7) ," and as a result his entire family, his servants, and even his cattle, " fell under the curse." [23]

The Second Commandment of the Decalogue gives expression to the same idea when it speaks of Yahweh as ' visiting the iniquity of the fathers upon the children, upon the third and fourth generation of them that hate me, and showing lovingkindness unto *a thousand generations* [literally, thousands] of them that love me and keep my commandments ' (Ex. 20:5 f.; Deut. 5:9 f.) . It is probable that the italicized words in this sentence represent the prophetic thought of the author, as they accord better than the translation in brackets with the corporate personality idea evidently intended in the Commandment. The thought of " a thousand generations," on the one hand, and of only three or four, on the other, is suggestive also of the great

[22] So Gustav Stählin in Kittel's *Wörterbuch*, I, p. 298, lines 21 f., 27–31.

[23] Cf. Emil Brunner, *Der Römerbrief* (1948) , *in loc.;* Nygren, *op. cit.,* pp. 213 ff.; R. Bultmann, *op. cit.,* p. 251; C. H. Dodd, *Commentary on Romans, in loc.;* Walter Grundmann in Kittel's *Wörterbuch*, I, p. 313, lines 15–20.

magnanimity of God's loving-kindness — an idea that probably was in the prophetic writer's mind at the moment.

This concept of corporate personality is too well known to require further elaboration here. The fact too that Hebrew has no distinctive word for mankind — Adam being used for both the individual and the race — should no doubt be taken as reflecting the prophetic thought at this point. Individual and race are bound together, so to speak, in a mutuality of privilege and responsibility in the Hebrew prophetic thought scarcely to be duplicated elsewhere save in our modern social psychology which so largely agrees with it.

Accordingly, for both Genesis and Paul it is in the corporate Adam — that is, as members of the human race — that we "die." We do so because by man (again, Adam), the door to corporate sin was opened by his transgression of the command of God.[24] Adam in this double sense is to be thought a historical figure — that is to say, either literally or mythically so — as accords with the prophetic psychology which both Genesis and Paul accepted, and not a superhistorical person, a mythological figure of the apocalyptic type. Christ, then, also in the Romans passage will be both an individual and corporate figure (namely, the Christian Church). Of this, more below.

Meanwhile, it should be noted that this idea of "corporate responsibility" is one recognized by us as pertaining in all walks of life. The individual by joining the group shares responsibility for its faults even as he joins with all his fellows in enjoying the privileges of the group life. When one moves from one community to another and makes common lot with the new group sharing a common life, he takes upon himself a responsibility for what the community has become through the years which he cannot avoid. He may or may not like what he finds in the new environment. Nonetheless, the state or even the nation will

---

[24] H. H. Rowley, in *The Relevance of Apocalyptic* (Second Edition, 1947), has a fascinating note in which he explains the concept of *Beliar* on this same basis of "corporate personality" (p. 162, n. 1)! I agree and would extend the idea to that of "Satan" or the "devil" in all parts of Scripture, as the latter figure in my judgment represents a personification of man's "corporate sin" as a whole.

hold him responsible with all his fellow citizens for what the communal life now is — whether he had a share in making it so or not!

It is through one's merely joining the group life that such responsibility and privilege is seen to attach to one. And there is a general sense on mankind's part, one believes, that it is fitting that a sort of *retroactive character* attaches to such responsibility and privilege. This is easily seen in the case of the privilege referred to. No one questions the right of the new citizen to partake of all the intellectual, physical, scientific, recreational, and general cultural advantages enjoyed by the community with which he has cast his lot. It ought to be equally evident that he makes himself at the same time responsible for what through the years the community has become.

It is in this sense that the individual shares the guilt of the corporate sin of the human race. He does so as a responsible member of that race, as a unit in the society known as the *genus homo sapiens*. Nothing can possibly release him from his responsibility to do something about man's corporate sin. What he must do it is our intention to discuss in the next chapter.

23. *The Prophetic Doctrine of Direction — Repentant and Forgiven Man*

IN THE LIGHT of the discussion in the last chapter, it should be apparent at what point and how the prophetic doctrine of salvation must make its start. All men are involved in the morass of sin — societal or corporate sin. For men, then, salvation begins when each individual determines to take a stand *as an individual* against this evil thing. Each must arise, stand upon his own feet, acknowledge his individual responsibility to withstand the common drift, and so return to God and his will. *Individually men must seek to acquire a new direction for their lives.*

It is this acquisition of new direction that the Scriptures consistently term " repentance." One of its clearest illustrations is
that given in our Lord's parable of the Prodigal Son. When he
has " come to himself," this boy remarks, " I will arise and go
to my father " (Luke 15:18). In the Hebrew the verb for " repent " is *shūbh* and it has this identical meaning of " to turn "
or " to return." And though the metaphor is slightly different
in the Greek *metanoein* (literally, " to change the mind "), yet
here the meaning is essentially the same. Both verbs stand for *a
rightabout-face* of the human spirit which involves acquiring
of a new direction for the life of the individual. It is the imperative mood of *shūbh* that the prophets use without exception
when calling back God's wayward people to follow in his ways.
Unfortunately for English readers, the word is often translated
" turn " or " return " and then again " repent " without any
warrant for the change. That the prophet is throughout calling
for repentance, accordingly, is at times obscured.[1]

The same thought is also otherwise expressed by the Hebrew
prophets. This is true, for example, of the doctrine of the
two ways, which is at least as old as Jeremiah, who reports
Yahweh as saying, " Behold, I set before you the way of
life and the way of death " (Jer. 21:8).[2] The thought is
that man must choose for himself either the one way or the
other. At times throughout Israel's history such a challenge is
thrown out to the people as a whole, as one prophet or another
calls them to choose between Yahweh and the gods of the sur-
rounding peoples. At the first giving of the law on Sinai the
ratification of the *covenant* by the people signifies essentially
their making such a choice as a group (Ex. 19:8; 24:3; Deut.
5:27). The same may be said for its ratification in Moab (Deut.,
chs. 29 and 30), in Canaan under Joshua (Josh. 24:16 ff., 24),
and in Josiah's time after the discovery of the " Book of the
Covenant " (II Chron. 34:29 ff.).

---

[1] Cf. Joel 2:12 f.; Jer. 3:1, 12, 22; Ezek. 14:6. I have collected all the
passages concerned in my book on *The Intention of Jesus,* p. 231.

[2] Cf. further Jer. 5:4; 10:2; Deut. 30:15 ff.; Ps. 1:1 ff.; 16:11; Prov. 10:17;
15:24; Matt. 7:14; John 17:3.

But the thought that *the individual* must take his stand alone, covenant with his God, and turn to His will and His ways is the more prominent feature of the prophetic Scriptures. The prophetic " remnant " is composed of those who, after the example of the " seven thousand " in Elijah's day, have not " bowed unto Baal " (I Kings 19:18), but have individually responded to the prophet's plea: " How long will you go limping with two different opinions? If the Lord is God, follow him; but if Baal, then follow him " (ch. 18:21). Typical in this connection is Amos' plea for this sort of individual repentance. " Seek good, and not evil, that you may live. . . . Hate evil, and love good, and establish justice in the gate; it may be that the Lord, the God of hosts, will be gracious to the remnant of Joseph " (Amos 5:14 f.; Joel 2:12 ff.).

It was in this same prophetic spirit that the Baptist carried on his ministry of " a baptism of repentance for the forgiveness of sins " (Mark 1:4). And in this respect there is no new note even in the teaching of Jesus at the beginning of his ministry. He follows, indeed, in the prophetic tradition exactly at the point where the Baptist had begun.[3] For example, " mourning " had long since been a sign, or symbol, of repentance in Judaism — since at least Joel's day and that of Second Isaiah. It is likely, accordingly, that in the second Beatitude — " Blessed are those who mourn, for they shall be comforted " (Matt. 5:4) — our Lord has reference to mourning in this sense and that by " comforting " he means to refer to the divine forgiveness. Both words ("mourn" and "comfort") are quoted by him from Isa. 57:18, where the " mourners " are those who turn from the *corporate attitude* of forgetfulness of Yahweh and acquire the new direction which means salvation in the Father's house (cf. also Joel 2:12 ff.).

The prophets never exhibit any doubt about God's forgiving the repentant sinner. ' Thou, Lord, art good, and ready to forgive ' (Ps. 86:5); " there is forgiveness with thee, that thou mayest be feared " (Ps. 130:4); " I will forgive their iniquity, and their sin will I remember no more " (Jer. 31:34). Such is

[3] Cf. R. Bultmann, *op. cit.*, p. 21.

the prophetic teaching first and last. God forgives the repentant sinner because he is a forgiving God. Such is, indeed, the theme of Hosea's entire prophecy. And, as we have already seen in connection with the doctrine of the atonement, the New Testament makes no advance on the prophetic realism at this point. It is, in fact, this forgiving God who is seen " in Christ reconciling the world unto himself " (II Cor. 5:19) . The cross is the culmination of the evidence that God is that kind of God, One who forgives to the uttermost.

Man's Faith a " Sine Qua Non " of Forgiveness

Two other items call for comment at this point, namely: (*a*) the nature of his preceding attitude (s) conditioning the individual for the act of repentance, and (*b*) the effectiveness of repentance as regards the destruction of sin in the life of the individual. As for the former of these, the *attitude* in the individual that calls forth repentance on his part is one of *faith in God*. This in turn results from a certain knowledge about God's willingness to forgive. " Whoever would draw near to God must believe that he exists and that he rewards those who seek him " (Heb. 11:6) . Jeremiah had taught this by announcing that Yahweh proclaimed to his people, " Return, O faithless sons, I will heal your faithlessness." And then by reporting that the people came to Him saying, " Behold, we come to thee; for thou art the Lord our God " (Jer. 3:22) . Isaiah's teaching about the remnant follows the same lines (Isa. 10:20–23) .

A considerable amount of teaching on the part of a forgiving God was necessary to pave the way for this attitude of faith on the part of his people. The entire history involved in the redemption-revelation line of Cullmann's thesis from the deliverance from the bondage in Egypt right through the period of the monarchy constituted God's teaching technique, as it were. There was also the preparation of the individual spirit through contact with the divine Spirit. The prophetic Scriptures draw a veil over the intimacy of such indoctrination by the Spirit to a degree. Paul hints at it, however, in Rom. 10:14 ff.: " But how are men to call upon him in whom they have not believed? And how are they to believe in him of whom they have never heard? . . . So faith comes from what is heard, and what is heard comes by the preaching of Christ."

Faith in a forgiving God, then, is a *sine qua non* of repentance and the forgiveness resulting therefrom. It is the experience of the evangelist, the psychiatrist, and the social worker alike that many people cannot accept forgiveness because they cannot believe in such a forgiving God! This is because they project their own attitudes of bitterness, spite, and unwillingness to forgive into their idea of God, making their " god " in their own unworthy image and likeness. " Forgive," therefore said Jesus, " and you will be forgiven " (Luke 6:37), or perhaps better as the saying is found at Mark 11:25, " Forgive . . . so that your Father also who is in heaven may forgive you your trespasses." God is ready to forgive, but man is not always " forgivable " in the sense of being ready to receive his forgiveness.

THE RECURRENCE OF SIN IN THE CHRISTIAN'S EXPERIENCE

As regards the problem of the recurrence of sin in the life of the forgiven sinner after the new direction has been acquired — it is to be said at once that there is nothing in the prophetic Scriptures to suggest that one is freed from recurring temptation and sin. Quite the contrary, the sinner who is on the way to his Father's house appears to become more sensitive to sin in his life the farther along the way he proceeds. There is nothing morbid about this discovery, as has at times been claimed. This experience is paralleled in every field of human endeavor. The more one learns in any realm of scientific research and the more expert one becomes in a given discipline or art, the more one realizes the vast world beyond and senses one's own finite ability and knowledge. This needs no proof. It is the common heritage of those who have matured in any phase of human living. There is no reason to suppose it should be otherwise in the realms of religion and ethics.

Such, one believes, is the teaching of the vexing passage in

Rom. 7:14–25. I incline to the belief that Bishop Anders Nygren has at long last solved this perennial problem by pointing out the simple fact that Paul nowhere in the passage speaks of *two wills* as battling against each other, as has hitherto been assumed. Rather, as Nygren indicates, the struggle is between what Paul terms the " flesh " (the lower nature) and the " mind " or " inner man " (the higher nature), the *will* all the while being properly motivated as the apostle clearly states. " For I do not do the good I want, but the evil I do not want is what I do " (v. 19). This struggle of the flesh versus the mind or will, then, suggests Nygren, is " the tension which exists, in the Christian life, between will and action, between intention and performance," between motivation or direction and achievement.[4]

Bishop Nygren's exposition of this difficult passage brings its teaching immediately into line with the experience of every Christian man who finds that his good intentions outstrip his actual achievements. Moreover, it squares that teaching with the prophetic Scriptures as a whole. Throughout these Scriptures it is clear that *the acquisition of direction is possible for God's children.* Otherwise the prophetic call for the individual to make a decision to follow in the way of obedience and commitment to God's will would be futile. Every new phase of the movement of the Spirit of God among his people, such as that exemplified by John the Baptist on the banks of the Jordan, places those who are aware of it in the *hour of decision for or against the call of God.*

Such a " crisis," once recognized by the individual, obviously is not to be ignored without doing despite to the Spirit of God whose work it represents. There can be no doubt that this is at least one reason why Jesus himself came down from the hills of Galilee to ally himself with this new prophetic movement (Mark 1:9). We recognize this same fact when, in our young people's conferences conducted by the Church today, we confront our youth with the challenge of the " gospel of the kingdom " in the hope that out of such conferences there will come

---

[4] Cf. Anders Nygren, *op. cit.,* p. 293.

decision on the part of the individual and the resultant acquisition of direction for the life.

At the same time, however, one is then and long afterward constantly reminded by one's failures that one has not yet " arrived," nor been " perfected." One, therefore, presses on toward " the goal for the prize of the upward call of God in Christ Jesus " (Phil. 3:7–16). *Direction,* not perfection, has been achieved and it is direction that is maintained. Paul realistically reserves two Greek words for sin — *parabasis* and *paraptōma* (going beside the road and falling off the road, or trespasses and transgressions) — for the type of sins that beset the steps of the man headed in the right direction (Rom. 4:15; 5:14; II Cor. 5:19; Col. 2:13). These are quite other than *hamartia* — that slough of corporate sin from which the individual has emerged through faith and repentance. The remarkable thing is that by the power of God's Spirit the " son of God " is brought back onto the way after each digression therefrom (Rom. 8:1–11). Such is the " perseverance of the saints " — of those, that is to say, who have achieved direction and are on the way to the Father's house.

The diagram below will serve to illustrate the thought of this and the preceding chapters:

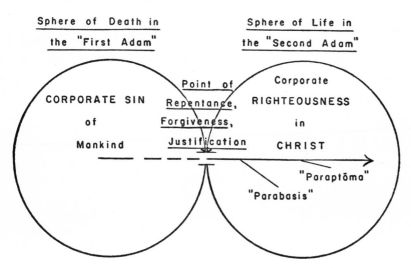

The above diagram is intended to make two points clear. The first of these concerns the nature of the Christian's digressions from the " straight and narrow way." At this point Arminians and Calvinists have been at odds since the Reformation. The traditional Methodist idea of " backsliding " — as understood by his Calvinistic brethren, at all events — has involved the thought that when the Christian sins he backslides all the way to the point of repentance and conversion, and he has in consequence to " start from scratch " all over again, as it were. This thought is intolerable to one who follows carefully Paul's argument in the passages above cited. When the Christian digresses from the way, instead of going back to the point of decision or crisis, he falls into the arms of Christ. This is because, having left the slough of corporate sin experienced by all mankind, he is now " in Christ." Accordingly, the Spirit of this living Christ puts him right back onto the way again!

The second point illustrated by the diagram is the fact that the justification to be discussed at some length in the next chapter is a historic act of God which is intended to give recognition to the individual's severance from the corporate sin of the race. The Christian acquires direction, as we have just seen through exercising faith in Jesus Christ and turning away from mankind's sin to the righteousness which is to be found only in Christ. His passing from the old sphere to the new one is an instantaneous process and in that instant the individual is pronounced forgiven by God and vindicated (or justified) for the step that has taken him into living fellowship with his Saviour.

24. *The Prophetic Doctrine of the Redemptive Community*

I N THE old Adam, the sociological unit consisting of mankind as a whole, there is a fellowship in *death*. In the new Adam, the sociological unit known as " Christ," the " remnant," the

" Church," there is a fellowship in *life*. In the former Adam there is a sharing in the corporate sin of the group, in the latter Adam there is a sharing in the corporate righteousness of the group (Rom. 5:15–21). This is *doctrine*. It is also an *exhortation* to everyone concerned to realize the latter fact in experience, to bring it out of the limbo of the " unconscious " or the " subconscious " and to make it a living reality (Rom. 6:11 ff.). But it is more than either doctrine or exhortation: it is also a matter of genuine *experience* and has been such for many who are or have been " in Christ " through the centuries past.

" Nature abhors a vacuum." The same is true in the spiritual order. When, accordingly, God saves an individual through his grace which has sent the " Hound of Heaven " (his Holy Spirit) out to search for him perhaps for years — to use the expressive phrase of Francis Thompson's poem, a poem written by one who had experienced that of which we are here speaking — he does not thrust that individual, so to speak, into a moral vacuum. For there are none such in God's spiritual order. The order of events here is, rather, out of the old Adam, into the new Adam; out of the group of sinful humanity, into the fellowship of the new humanity *in Christ*.

Only at the single moment of decision does the individual stand alone before God and man — at the moment of instantaneous transition from one sphere into the other. For when a man hears God's " call " to the new life and answers it, he finds that through the same " narrow door," along the same straightened way by which he is entering into life, many others are doing the same. And it is not long before he meets his fellow pilgrims along the way. So true is this in actual experience that if one does not meet with such fellow pilgrims, it may be taken as a sure sign that he is himself not on the way! This is one of the themes of Bunyan's *Pilgrim's Progress* which is seen still to have validity. That book was by and large overindividualistic, but not entirely so, for *Christian* did meet up with *Faithful* on the way. There are many Faithfuls, as there are many Christians, if one will but look out for them!

The continuity within Scripture's prophetic realism is no

more strikingly exhibited anywhere than at the point of identification of Jesus Christ and his Church with the prophetic *redemptive remnant*. The thought flows on unimpeded from the Old to the New Testament Scriptures with the single new factor that the Leader or Redeemer of the group is now Jesus Christ. This of necessity at once identifies the remnant as the group — the Church — which is formed about him.[1] We have already indicated how this group is constituted of those who have made the individual commitment to God's Lordship over their lives and what it means both *spiritually* and *dynamically* that the historic Christian Church is the *remnant*. It remains for us here to point out what the experience of membership in the redemptive community implies in the case of the individual.

THE FAMILY OF GOD

In the first place, it means for him that he has now been " adopted " — to employ Paul's term (Rom. 8:15 f.; Eph. 1:5; Gal. 4:5) — into the " family " or " household " of God (Eph. 2:19). Or, as John prefers, the individual has been *reborn* (John 3:3; cf. James 1:18; I Peter 1:23; I John 3:9). This is, of course, metaphorical language intended to express the fact to which reference has just been made, namely, that when the individual has committed himself to God through the expression of his faith in God's working by His Son, he immediately enters the new group of the people who have made a like commitment. These are they who have become separated from the *old Adam* and its corporate sin.

This is distinctively a " household of faith " (Gal. 6:10). That is to say, it is characterized by what all families should possess — *trust in one another on the part of all the members*. It was faith

---

[1] Cf. for Jesus as the Leader, Acts 2:36; Eph. 2:15–18; Col. 2:18–23; Heb. 2:9–18, and for the Church as the new people of God, I Peter 2:9; Gal. 6:16; Rom. 9:6; Eph. 2:12; Heb. 3:6. To the view here expressed the term " Hero-Christology " has recently been applied; cf. W. L. Knox, *Harvard Theological Review,* Oct., 1948, article on " The Divine Hero Christology in the New Testament "; also William Manson's *The Epistle to the Hebrews* (1951), pp. 103 f.; and F. W. Dillistone's *Jesus Christ and His Cross* (1952), ch. 3.

in God and in his Son in the first place that brought the several members together in this unique union. And that faith not only continues to be reposed on Father and Son, but its contagion spreads and attaches to all members of the family circle. This means, of course, that *love* also characterizes the group, the warm love of family affection at its best and deepest (Rom. 5:5; Gal. 5:6, 13, 22; Eph. 1:15; Col. 1:14; I Peter 2:17), self-sacrificing love like that of God in Christ.

C. H. Dodd has rendered valuable service in pointing out that three phrases commonly employed by the apostle Paul — " in Christ," " in the Spirit," and " in the Church " — are intended to elucidate as many elements in this unique experience of the Christian in the " family of God." Of this trilogy, the " Church " is the redemptive remnant, the " Spirit " the power through which new life is infused into the former (Rom. 8:2), the " Christ " the Redeemer in and through whom the Church is redeemed (Rom. 3:24; 6:3; Gal. 3:26 f.). For the actual historic experience in which the believer thus participates, Dodd has coined the term " Christ-mysticism." As he remarks: " The ' Christ-mysticism ' of Paul is not exactly analogous to what is usually called mysticism. The typical mystic has an intensely individual experience of ineffable union with God (*solus cum Solo*), conceived as the One or the All. Paul's sense of union with Christ is conditioned by the experience of life in a society controlled by His Spirit, as well as constituted historically by His act." [2]

The atomizing individualism of much of modern thought is thus displaced by the prophetic concept of *corporate personality*. The Church is the " body of Christ " in the sense that it is the active instrument of Christ's present will in the world and controlled by his indwelling Spirit (I Cor. 12:12 f.). Every individual shares in the Spirit as he shares in the body. From the Spirit he draws the power to use all his talents for the good of the whole and for its upbuilding (*oikodomē*). " The whole body, joined and knit together by every joint with which it is supplied, when each part is working properly, makes bodily

[2] Cf. C. H. Dodd, *op. cit.,* on Rom. 6:5, pp. 87 f.

growth and upbuilds itself in love " (Eph. 4:16).

This is in line with the prophetic teaching of Scripture throughout. As Anderson Scott says (quoting Hort): " ' The prophet, the people to whom he speaks, and the dimly seen Head and King of the people all pass insensibly into one another in the language of prophecy.' In some of the psalms ' the distinction between the King and his people seems often a vanishing one.' It will probably remain always uncertain whether ' the figure of the Suffering Servant in the fifty-third of Isaiah is intended by the writer as an individual or as a personification of the righteous and suffering remnant of Israel.' And in particular the designation ' Christ,' or ' Anointed,' was applied almost without distinction to the people or to the individual who represented them. Thus in Habbakkuk (ch. 3:13), ' Thou wentest forth for the salvation of thy people, to save thy Christ.' " [3]

The individual Christian, then, does not stand alone when he plants his feet in the way and achieves the *direction* of which we have spoken. Rather he finds himself surrounded by " brethren " in this new " family of God," Jesus Christ being the great " elder brother " (Rom. 8:29) and the " head " of the family in its historic manifestation (Eph. 4:15), and he applies himself vigorously toward making the contribution to which his talents point as these are empowered by the Spirit who dwells in the family (I Cor. 12:4–13). This he does, moreover, without either superiority (v. 21) or inferiority complex (vs. 16 ff.), by reason of the differing of his talents from those displayed by other members of the " household of faith."

It scarcely requires to be added that the *prophetic universalism* attaches itself to this New Testament doctrine of the Church. There are in it no racial, class, or other separating or disruptive divisions (Gal. 3:28).[4] By the same token the individual Christian, employing all his powers as indicated above, learns that he belongs, not to a " *saved* remnant," but in ac-

[3] Cf. Anderson Scott, *op. cit.,* pp. 155 f.

[4] Cf. T. W. Manson, *op. cit.,* p. 148. Manson has shown that one of the contributions made by the Hebrew prophets was the achievement of a genuine universalism transcending the " national and limited monarchy recognized by the nation as a unit."

cord with the best prophetic thought to a "*saving* remnant." [5]
The essential disinterestedness of this prophetic Christian attitude is patent. It bears no similarity to the *particularism* and
self-centered individualism of that historic apocalypticism which
has done great harm in disrupting the unity of the Christian
Church.[6]

THE JUSTIFICATION OF THE CHURCH

Again, for the individual to be a member of the fellowship
that is " in Christ " means that *he shares in the justification
or vindication that it experiences.* This doctrine too, is pro-
phetically conceived and expounded in the New Testament.
T. W. Manson has shown that, of the popular ideas held within
Israel which it was the historic mission of the Hebrew prophets
to correct, one concerned the problem of whose vindication
might be expected to transpire on the coming " Day of the
Lord." " It is evident that for the people of Israel the Day of
the Lord is not his day but theirs, the day of their triumph and
their prosperity. The Day of the Lord is Israel's trump card.
Amos announces that, on the contrary, it will be in truth Jehovah's Day, the day of the revelation and complete vindication
of his character as a God of absolute righteousness. It will,
therefore, be a day of judgment on all evildoers, Israel included." [7]

Paul, the expositor of the doctrine of justification for the
Church of the New Testament, accepts this prophetic teaching
and gives it further development. Certainly this precisely is his
meaning in the classical passage in Rom. 3:26. Here he is speaking of the ' manifesting (or communicating) of God's righteousness ' through His ' freely justifying those who are in Christ
Jesus.' And he remarks that the entire procedure was ' with a
view to the showing forth of His righteousness at the present

[5] The phrases are again Manson's, *ibid.,* p. 181. In his recent book on
The Church's Ministry (1948), he remarks, " Church history is the biog-
raphy of Christ continued, the record of the life of the body of Christ,"
p. 84.
[6] Cf. *The Religion of Maturity,* pp. 162, 228 f.
[7] Cf. his *Teaching,* p. 248.

opportunity, for Himself to be righteous and for the justification of him who is of that faith that reposes on Jesus.' In other
words, it is fundamental to Paul's doctrine of justification that
in the first instance it is God who justifies himself and not man.
It is his own righteous reign that is vindicated. It is his righteousness that is manifested (vs. 21 ff.) . This vindication of himself God accomplishes through the setting forth of his own Son
as the " means of expiation " (*hilastērion*) , or the " meeting
place " between God and man (v. 25) . The Church as a whole,
then, shares God's vindication at this meeting place in Jesus
Christ in so far as it comes to this place of tryst with him, and
only to that degree. For fundamentally it is his and not its
justification that is in question.

In like manner, it is only as the individual comes " in Christ,"
and so " in the fellowship " of the body of Christ, to this same
tryst with God that he shares in the justification proclaimed.
*The individual accepts it on faith that God, in justifying himself
and his righteous rule of men, justifies him in the Church and
in Christ.* (V. 22.) The individual, in fact, is justified just because he does accept it on faith that this is so. He is not, then,
justified alone or apart either from Christ or the fellowship of
the Church, nor is he justified apart from the justification which
God accomplishes of his own sovereign rule over men. He is
justified precisely because " his life is hid with Christ in God "
through faith union with both and through sharing in the benefits that come to the fellowship of the " people of God " whom
he is concerned to save.

It is, therefore, quite absurd to argue, as the Roman Catholic
Church does, that the doctrine of justification by grace through
faith is an immoral doctrine inasmuch as in it God is said to
treat sinners as though they were righteous which they are not.
Such criticism may be a fair sample of Roman legalism, but
it is poor prophetic theology, for it overlooks entirely the nature of the doctrine as above expounded. That doctrine does
not pronounce sinners *as sinners* to be righteous. Rather it pro-
nounces God to be righteous (v.26), and as justifying or vin-
dicating sinners who have come within the orbit of the divine

saving energy through accepting Jesus Christ and being in living fellowship with him in his body, the Church. It is because they had faith to take God at his word as he appealed to them in his Son that their justification along with his takes place. Christians " in Christ " are justified or vindicated *precisely because that is where they are.* They are not justified otherwise or elsewhere, and they are justified *there* because that is exactly where God told them to be and called them to be, because they took him to be a faithful God who fulfills his promises and so accepted Jesus Christ in faith, becoming thereby a part of the fellowship that is " in him." Jesus Christ, in a word, is God's justification of his righteous rule of mankind and those who are *in Christ* obviously share in God's self-vindication through him.

It is to be noted that the doctrine of justification carries with it the necessary implication that the man who is " in Christ " is justified on the historical plane. Such vindication does not await eternity for its accomplishment. This is a point that works notably in favor of Professor Dodd's " realized eschatology." For the justification awaited by the Hebrew prophet was one to be expected on the " Day of the Lord " and at the end of the then-present age. That day of vindication came with the appearance and work of Jesus Christ on the historical plane. This is Paul's teaching in such a passage as that at which we have been looking (Rom. 3:21–26). The prophet's present age, with its " Day of the Lord " at the end, then, is something upon which we look back as a realized experience in the life of the historic Christian Church. We are, accordingly, living in the resultant eschatological time, as Dodd contends.

Ethical Resurrection

Finally, for the individual to be " in Christ " and in the Church fellowship means that he shares the ethical resurrection that is the experience of those who are " in Christ." We are dealing here with what is generally termed the doctrine of sanctification. And there is a certain parallelism between justification and sanctification that has often been overlooked.

*Both concern only those who are living in fellowship with the
"blessed community."* We have just been adverting to the
significance of this fact as regards justification. It is just as
significant for sanctification. The recluse ideal, with its with-
drawal from the "world" and contamination with one's fellows lest this tend to "worldliness," works neither in the teaching of the prophetic Scriptures nor in experience. It is in a
spirit of *togetherness* that believers grow into 'mature manhood, according to the stature of Christ's perfection' (Eph.
4:13). For in that spirit and fellowship each contributes his
bit to the good of the whole (vs. 17 f.).

The disciple of Jesus Christ discovers in this fellowship a
certain aid in his manifold weaknesses. For the Christian is
by no means yet entirely delivered from those weaknesses of
the *old Adam* as he pursues his life in Christ (Rom. 7:15–24).
He commits the acts of transgression and trespass of which we
have spoken already. But he finds among his "brethren" in
Christ a spirit of forgiveness that the world cannot share. This
is because on the one hand the world does not really discern
sin and sinfulness in the perspective of God's judgment upon
it as the Christian does, and on the other hand it knows nothing
by experience of God's forgiveness; hence, it also does not forgive.

Too, in spite of all his faults and failings — which he rec-
ognizes when he has his moments of "realism" — the Christian
man is conscious of *a new power* working within him. He is no
longer under the specious lordship of the "flesh" or of sin,
but rather has come under the power of the Spirit and His
righteousness (Rom. 6:18 f.; 8:2 ff.). The Christian now has
to worry only over the paradoxical difference between his motivation and achievement, his "good intentions" and accomplishment, as Bishop Nygren has understood Paul to mean at
Rom. 7:7–25 — and rightly so in my judgment.

No two Christians' lives would show the same graph ethically,
of course. Men are individuals — even Christian men — and
God's Spirit deals with them as such. There is, accordingly,
no such thing as a "standard Christian pattern of living." It

is only a legalistic religion that imagines any such pattern to be possible or, for that matter, desirable. Generally speaking, however, it may be said that through the Spirit who produces life in Christ Jesus there is an unmistakably upward curve in the case of every Christian's ethical life (Rom. 8:2). This again is not alone doctrine; it is also experience. Moreover, it is a fact that the writer believes is too little recognized as true, even within Christian circles, and more especially by the currently dominant apocalypticism of our day.

Provincialism means lack of proper perspective for forming adequate judgments. And there is currently far too much provincialism in the Christian Church. Such provincialism breeds cynicism and there is much cynicism at the moment in theological circles — cynicism for which there is in the long view no adequate and justified reason. We gave an example in the early pages of this book of the type that brands the Christian community with the charge of " anti-Semitism." A good antidote for Christian cynicism or provincialism would be to project such Christians into a reading course in the history of the civilizations (or lack of civilization) of the past, on the one hand, and, on the other, to force them for a time to live in the midst of an admittedly pagan environment. For most of such pessimism is due to the fact that even Christian theologians — the " ivory tower " variety, at any rate — do not begin to " know how the other half live."

What we are just writing will be branded by such Christians as " unrealistic," " divorced from the facts of life," and the like. We are impelled with an inner conviction of great arrogance — the sort that led the apostle Paul to suggest that the Corinthian Christians become as " humble " as he was or he would come to them with a club and make them so! (I Cor. 4:14–21.) And this Christian arrogance compels the remark that it is the theological pessimists of our day who are unrealistic, and not those of us who adhere to the prophetic realism. To give at this point but one illustration of our meaning: it needs hardly be said that America is not a Christian nation — this is a platitude to which we all subscribe. But it does need saying, and it needs saying badly, that there is much more real Christianity in America than is usually credited. By and large our culture, with its " four freedoms," is founded upon certain principles for which the prophetic realism of the Scriptures can readily be shown to be the true sponsor and creative force. And there are far too many people in this land who are, so to speak, " sponging off " the Christian faith of the founding fathers and not giving that faith the credit it deserves for what America is today. This is by no means to equate Christian teaching or the Christian ethic with " what we do in America " or with our way of life. But it is to assign credit where it is due, " lest we forget," and, forgetting, drift back into the Dark Ages that again loom on our horizons.

The *ethic* that emerges in the teaching of the ongoing Church is an ethic of the Spirit that bears no remote resemblance to the sort of morbid legalism (or even of sadism) that has from time to time been promulgated under the name of " Christian." It is by no means a bouquet of negative " virtues " such as that taught in post-Reformation circles and even in Puritan " piety." Certainly it bears no slightest resemblance to the asceticism of Roman or any other sort of " catholic " monkery or celibacy. It is rather the sort of *moral extroversion* found in the teachings of Amos, Jesus, Paul, James, and the like.

This Christian ethic is in a real sense *a community ethic*. It presupposes the moral Headship of Jesus Christ in the community that practices it and the acknowledgment of him as the only Lord of life. It emphasizes the social aspect of the individual's life and his societal duties: to others in the brotherhood — the Church; to those outside the Church — his neighbors; to all human institutions including the State (Rom., chs. 12 to 15; I Peter 2:17, etc.). The community ethic is the product of the work of the Spirit, whose fruitage includes the social graces known as " love, joy, peace, longsuffering, kindness, goodness, faithfulness, meekness, self-control " (Gal. 5:22 f.) .

The Christian ethic longs for the Christian's growth in character without being morbidly introspective, or worrying overmuch when he " backslides." It looks for positive goodness in all his relationships. It expects his actions to reflect the innate goodness which the Spirit is producing within *his* spirit. It does not decry evil after a legalistic fashion but preaches a divine righteousness, believing that a positive gospel will drive out the evil of itself. It takes no morbidly ascetic attitude toward the matter of sex, but it anticipates that the sex life will be enjoyed under the same discipline that pertains to every other phase of a dedicated life in order that the person's contribution to the whole of Christian living may not be impeded (I Cor. 7:4 f.). It is behind all " good causes," and through the spirit of Jesus Christ it sends forth its servants into the world of human affairs to share in and lead in all these.

As the focal point of Scripture's prophetic realism is the Love of God (*Agapē*), which is seen in all his efforts through his prophets and above all in his Son to redeem men, so love is the center and circumference of the Christian ethic, its dynamic and lifeblood. As Anderson Scott has said: " It was no mere sentiment . . . no mere emotion, disposition, or feeling to which Paul appealed when he set *agapē* at the center of his ethical system. It was the same compelling and controlling force that had moved God to give his Son. It could be trusted to move men to all needed subordination and sacrifice of self. . . . It is both central and all-comprehensive. ' All the law is fulfilled in one word, even in this, Thou shalt love thy neighbor as thyself ' (Gal. 5:14). ' He that loveth another hath fulfilled the law ' (Rom. 13:8). ' Above all these things put on *agapē*, which gives cohesion to the perfect life ' (Col. 3:14) ." [8] It is such *agapē* that binds the fellowship of believers together in a pagan world and that motivates the activities within and without on the part of all members of the community.

[8] Cf. Anderson Scott, *op. cit.*, pp. 204 f.

25. *The Prophetic Doctrine of the Last Things*

THE PROPHETIC WRITERS of the Old Testament Scriptures declared that in the "beginning" God had prepared a stage (Creation) upon which the drama of history could be enacted. But if there is a beginning, there is also an end. There must come a last act of the drama of history some time or other. Then "the heavens . . . will perish . . . they will all grow old like a garment, like a mantle thou wilt roll them up, and they will be changed" (Ps. 102:25–27 as quoted in Heb. 1:10–12).

As regards the cosmic catastrophes of the end there is a certain stereotyping observable in the prophetic Scriptures. Compare the above from The Psalms and The Epistle to the Hebrews with this:

> "And I will show wonders in the heaven above
> and signs on the earth beneath,
> blood, and fire, and vapor of smoke;
> the sun shall be turned into darkness
> and the moon into blood" (Joel 2:28 ff.; Acts 2:17 ff.).

and with this:

> "I looked, and behold, there was a great earthquake; and the sun became black as sackcloth, the full moon became like blood, and the stars of the sky fell to the earth as the fig tree sheds its winter fruit when shaken by a gale; the sky vanished like a scroll that is rolled up, and every mountain and island was removed from its place" (Rev. 6:12–14).

Such is the prophetic eschatology, and the stereotyped form and content suggest that by and large it is a confession of ignorance. It amounts to saying that there will be an end to history because its stage will be no more. The theater burns down; so the actors wrap themselves in their cloaks and go home!

Home! — that is exactly where they do go. Home for the believer is where God is; home stands for fellowship with God. It is precisely for his return to the garden of fellowship with

God that man has been in training on the plane of history. To be in close communion with God one must be " holy as he is holy " (Lev. 19:2). It is in this sense that man is to reflect his image.

Had a Greek philosopher written the book of Genesis, he would have meant by the " image of God " reason, intelligence, wisdom, and the like. And he would have made Yahweh declare: " You shall be rational, for I the Lord your God am not a moron " or, " You shall love wisdom even as I, your God, seek above all else to pursue the happy mean." But the prophetic concept of personality, while assuming intelligence, wisdom, reason in God, looks beyond these to *his ethical character* which is the pivot and focus of his Person. Consequently, to reflect God's image means, for the prophet in Israel, to acquire love of righteousness for its own sake and to exercise one's will — which *is* the person — toward acquiring righteous ends. And to be sanctified results in being morally prepared to live in eternity with God.

This has come about through one's learning how to live with the Spirit of his Son on the plane of history. For " we all, with unveiled face, beholding the glory of the Lord, are changed into his likeness from one degree of glory to another; for this comes from the Lord who is the Spirit " (II Cor. 3:18). Those who learn within history to live with Jesus Christ in this sort of intimate fellowship, who are transformed more and more into his likeness, should have little difficulty in living in the Presence of his Father in the eternal order.

Such in substance is the prophetic eschatology. Much more may, of course, be said on the subject but this would be merely by way of exposition of what has just been said. Furthermore, it would take one into the field of controversy to a degree. For nothing has been so hotly contested in recent times as the subject of the *eschaton* and what lies beyond it. There is a certain validity attaching to such thought and speculation, to be sure. Particularly is this the case where bereavement supplies the motivation for anxious inquiry of pastor and Christian worker. But there is also considerable morbid interest attaching to many of the discussions about the future. Christians may learn better how to employ their time if they will look about them at the world's present dire needs. The future may well enough be left to take care of itself if men and women are brought face to face with God in Jesus Christ now — on the plane of history. This is the realism of the prophetic theology.

Because of his sharing the prophetic belief in the actuality of history, the Christian's passing from the temporal to the eternal order at death is a mere incident in his career. Indeed, he has already experienced eternal life here below. Death, therefore, holds no fears nor the future any really new excitement for him. And the same is to be said for history's final end itself. There will be an end even as there has been a beginning. But the Eternal has come onto the stage of creation far too often in the redemptive activity of the true and living God for the end of history to afford anything distinctively new or novel.

Judgment there will be — but there has already been judgment. Every man has judged himself already if he has had a chance to take a clear look at Jesus Christ (John 3:18; 12:48). Van Dyke's reputed comment on the trial of Jesus before Pilate to the effect that it was, not Jesus, but Pilate who was on trial, represents an insight that is true for all of God's dealings with men everywhere. Men judge themselves as they accept or reject the light which he has given them (Rom. 1:18 ff.).

Salvation there will be — but there has already been salvation. The seventh and last act of The Revelation of John begins at ch. 20:4 and depicts the Christian Church seated and reigning with Jesus Christ on earth. Before that Church then passes a series of seven pageants — the final judgment, the end of earth and heaven, the coming of the new Jerusalem. What this most certainly means is that to the Christian fellowship is granted the spiritual and moral insight to *see* the drama of God's purpose in history — the restoration of men who have his image and seal upon their countenances to a place of fellowship with him. This insight and this restoration, both occurring on the plane of history, *are* salvation. What else do we await?

It is this sanity and entire lack of morbid interest in " the future " that is Scripture's most commendable feature. It is " today," the present, that is real and actual and important — for " today if you will not harden your hearts," God can be met and known through the Spirit of his Son.[1]

---

[1] For a discussion of some of the critical problems involved in a study of the " Last Things," the reader is referred to *The Religion of Maturity,* particularly chapter 12.

Epilogue

This book has been an essay in the general field of Biblical theology. Its author set himself the task of discovering the *kernel* (Cullmann), or the *clue* (Scott), or the *key* which should serve to give meaning to the gospel message and so to illuminate the whole content of Scripture. This task is a comparatively modest one.

To state that gospel in the language and idiom of contemporary thought and to draw out its implications for modern life are far more difficult ventures. These are usually assigned as a chore to the systematic theologian. And yet the labors of the Biblical scholar and his theological colleague cannot be quite so rigidly separated. For the prophetic writers of the Scriptures stated the theology of prophetic realism in the terms of their own day and generation. In like fashion, in the present volume the writer could not avoid occasional reference to contemporary scientific and philosophical thought.

But there is another and more important point wherein the tasks of Biblical and systematic theologians are one. Both these are, so to speak, caught up by the divine grace in the stream of redemptive events and given a place together in the priesthood of all believers. And this requires that, along with the Christian layman, they must *act* as well as speak their respective parts.

One is reminded of the remarks of Sir Arthur Eddington many years ago apropos of the difficulty that a scientist experiences in going through a door! He realizes successively as he attempts this feat, said this author, that he must press against a force of some fifteen pounds per square inch of the surface of his body — no mean achievement in itself; that he must land his foot on a plank revolving at a terrific rate of speed around the sun — he just could miss it; that even if he succeeds in stepping on this plank, he might fall through it — there is more empty space than filled in what appears to be solid matter; and that if he did fall through, he would surely be beaten to death by the atomic energy which he should encounter on the way! And so, said Eddington, in such circumstance it is always best for the scientist to become for a moment a common man, and — whether the door be that of his home, his office, his laboratory, or even of a church — to step across the threshhold and ask no questions for the sake of conscience!

So matters stand with the theologians of which we speak. When they have said their little say about prophetic realism, they have by no means completed the task God gave them to do. For they too are " common men," and as such they must undertake the layman's priestly task of sacrifice — sacrifice of self, of life. This is the final word which any man may utter relative to the prophetic realism of the gospel. And it is by all odds his most important task.

INDEX OF NAMES AND SUBJECTS

277

INDEX OF SCRIPTURE REFERENCES